THE
POLITICS OF

Pollution

SECOND EDITION

J. CLARENCE DAVIES III
and
BARBARA S. DAVIES

PEGASUS
A division of
THE BOBBS-MERRILL COMPANY, INC.
INDIANAPOLIS

For Elizabeth and Eric

The Bobbs-Merrill Company, Inc.
4300 West 62nd Street
Indianapolis, Indiana 46268

Second Edition
First Printing 1975

Library of Congress Cataloging in Publication Data

Davies, J   Clarence.
    The politics of pollution.

    Includes bibliographical references and index.
    1. Environmental policy—United States.
I. Davies, Barbara S., 1938–   joint author.
II. Title.
HC110.E5D35 1975   353.008′232   74-20996
ISBN 0-672-53720-6
ISBN 0-672-63720-0 pbk.

Contents

PART II—THE POLICYMAKERS

PART III—THE POLICY PROCESS

Preface

POLLUTION CONTROL has become a major issue of public policy. In this book we have tried to describe how government pollution policy is made and to analyze the interests and ideas competing for dominance over pollution control.

In discussing the politics of pollution we have used an amalgam of rather orthodox political science concepts. The book is divided into three parts. The first part, "The Pollution Challenge and the Legislative Response," describes the nature of the pollution problem and the growth of interest in environmental quality. We discuss each of the major air and water pollution acts passed by Congress and the controversies surrounding them.

Part II deals with the forces which have shaped pollution policy—Congress, the Executive Branch, the courts, public opinion, interest groups, and state and local government. The role which each has played and the interaction among these different forces is analyzed.

The final section examines the major policy processes in controlling pollution—research, standard-setting, and compliance. A last chapter examines some of the broader issues raised by viewing pollution control as part of the overall thrust towards improved environmental quality.

The explosive growth of concern and interest in pollution that has occurred since 1969 has made the first edition of this book outdated. Thus, this second edition has been extensively revised. A new chapter on the courts has been added and most of the text of the other chapters has been rewritten to take account of the many changes which have taken place during the past five years.

Portions of chapters three and five of this new edition have been previously published in a work entitled *The Federal Law of the Environment*, published by the West Publishing Company, St. Paul, Minnesota. Permission to reproduce these materials has been granted by the publisher, the copyright holder.

Preparation of the manuscript was greatly aided by the typing services of two outstanding secretaries—Katherine Soaper and Jane Davis. The editorial staff at Bobbs-Merrill was most helpful at all stages of the work.

J.C.D.
B.S.D.

Part I

THE POLLUTION CHALLENGE AND
THE LEGISLATIVE RESPONSE

CHAPTER 1

What Is Pollution?

EVERYONE OPPOSES pollution, yet we find pollution everywhere. One can search the *Congressional Record* in vain for a defense of foul air or dirty water. One can similarly search in vain for a metropolitan area which does not suffer from the fumes of automobiles, from belching smokestacks, or from untreated sewage flowing into its lakes and streams. The explanation for the gap between intention and reality lies to a great extent in the realm of politics.

POLLUTION AS A POLITICAL PROBLEM

Although there are significant gaps in our scientific and technological knowledge about pollution, the technology is available now to control most of the pollutants currently considered dangerous. More economic research is needed to tell us how to clean our air and water as efficiently as possible, and technological improvements are needed to lower the cost of control measures. However, the funds to control pollution now can be made available if we want them to be. The key to unlocking the funds is for politicians at all levels of government to place a higher priority on pollution control than they do at present. If fighting pollution were considered as important as fighting a war, sufficient public money would be available to meet the problem and sufficient pressure would be placed on business and industry so that adequate investments to combat pollution would be made by the private sector.

Money is not the only element needed to achieve clean air and water. Government must set sufficiently stringent standards to achieve the level of environmental quality which people want. It must have the will and the political muscle to see that the standards are enforced. Standard-setting and compliance, while they must take into account economic and technological factors, are heavily dependent on the political pressures applied to the government and the political power available to the pollution control agencies.

Control of pollution is unavoidably the responsibility of the government. The private market, which allocates so many of the costs and benefits in the American society, is inadequate to deal with the costs and benefits of pollution. The reason for this is that pollution is what the economists refer to as an "externality." The costs of pollution are usually not paid for by the person doing the polluting, and the benefits of controlling pollution are not gained solely or even primarily by the person who installs the control measures. If, for example, a paper mill is polluting the water, the damage done by the dirty water will be felt by the users downstream, not by the paper mill. If a power plant is polluting the air, the plant does not have to pay to use the air but the costs in terms of poor health or added cleaning bills are borne by the people who live in the area around the plant. The effect of the marketplace is to encourage pollution, because air and water tend to be free goods. But we have learned in recent years that they are not so much free goods as public goods, and that the public must take steps to protect them. The only way it can do so is through political action, and the only instrument which can attempt a proper allocation of costs and benefits is the government.

Not only is the control of pollution a political problem; the very definition of pollution hinges on politics. Pollutants are those substances which interfere with the use of air, water, or soil for socially desired purposes. If we want to use a particular part of a river for swimming, the water is "polluted" when we cannot swim in it. If we want to remain healthy, the air is "polluted" when it causes disease. Pollution cannot be defined with any scientific or mathematical finality. The definition hinges on the concept of human use, and thus, while we may be able scientifically to define what level of environmental quality is necessary for particular uses, the definition of what constitutes pollution is dependent on the public's decision as to what use it wants to make of its environment. It becomes a political decision, a voicing by the community of its concept of the public interest.

This definition of pollution is not an arbitrary construct. It is the only way in which pollution can be understood, at least from the viewpoint of the policymaker. Scientists can describe the harmful effects of a particular substance, but they transcend the bounds of science when they try to prescribe what should be the level of that substance in the environment. Only by linking scientific knowledge with a concept of the public interest can one arrive at a working definition of pollution.

Underlying much popular discussion is the idea that pollution is the artificial befouling of the pure state of the environment. This is reflected in the many appeals to return our air (or water, or soil) to its "natural state." There are two problems with such a notion. First, several major forms of pollution, and many minor forms, are not artificial but are produced by nature without human interference. Sediment in water is perhaps the best example, but pollen in the air and pollution of water by salt and algal growths are other examples of natural pollution. The natural processes which give rise to these pollutants may be retarded or accelerated by human action, but the fact remains that in a "pure state of nature" one would still have some pollution.

The second problem with the popular definition is the difficulty of defining what the "pure" state of the environment is. Nowhere does there exist a formula describing "pure" air. Scientists are still attempting to define the many constituents of the earth's atmosphere, and many of the elements found in all air are considered pollutants when they exceed a particular threshold. Likewise, drinking water, under the glare of modern analytical techniques, turns out to be a highly complex liquid, with many component parts. Pure H_2O tastes "flat" to most people, because of the absence of the many other components found in all drinking sources. What is considered "pure" water for drinking purposes may be unusable for certain industrial purposes, and vice versa.

At the present time, scientific knowledge of the effects of various pollutants is inadequate. But even if it were adequate, and even given consensus on certain broad conceptions of the public interest, it would be impossible to avoid making difficult decisions as to the desirable level of environmental quality. There is widespread agreement, for example, that substances which harm human health are pollutants because the maintenance of health is in the public interest. However, even with the universal application of the best possible control devices, the health of a few persons (probably those already sick in some respect) would suffer. The only way to protect the health of everyone would be to stop most industrial production. Anyone advocating the cessation of all or some production must implicitly or explicitly calculate the benefits of production against the benefits of health for some members of the society. This is a difficult calculation to make, morally and technically, but it is unavoidable.[1]

The weighing of costs and benefits arises in all governmental programs. In the starkest terms, governments make decisions all the time which they know will result in death or injury to some persons. We know that if we spent an additional amount of money on early cancer detection, for instance, we could save more lives. We know that new highways are safer than old ones, and thus each additional dollar spent on highways will save lives. And yet we do not spend billions more on cancer detection and highways because other matters are considered equally or more important. The same is true of pollution control. Resources are limited and choices must be made, even though the choices will result in injury.

As the nation has become increasingly concerned with controlling pollution, more attention is being focused on the difficult questions of setting priorities and finding politically workable methods for accomplishing program goals. In the past these questions have usually not been considered explicitly, and programs have developed in whatever directions scarce resources, limited scientific knowledge, and the political climate would permit. The "coming of age" of pollution control programs is beginning to change the haphazard nature of program decisionmaking.

GROWTH OF INTEREST IN POLLUTION CONTROL

Underlying the post-World War II concern with all forms of pollution is the affluence of American society. The massive growth in production and in the availability of resources which has characterized the U.S. economy in the past two decades affects the problem of pollution in several ways. The increase in production has contributed to an intensification of the degree of actual pollution; the increase in the standard of living has permitted people the comparative luxury of being able to be concerned about this; and the availability of ample public and private resources has given the society sufficient funds and skilled manpower to provide the potential for dealing with the problem.

The correlation between production and pollution generated is high, although this may be counteracted by the installation of pollution control technologies or by new industrial processes which produce less waste. As the number and size of plants in the nation increase, the amount of liquid, solid, and gaseous wastes produced by the industrial sector tends to increase. The pollution produced by the nonindustrial sector also increases. (People have more cars and use them more frequently, thus contributing significantly to air pollution) The widespread use of such technological innovations as automatic washers, kitchen disposals, and agricultural pesticides and fertilizers add to the water pollution problem. The lessened need to reuse resources because of the society's affluence results in a large increase in the per capita trash and garbage load. When increased production is accompanied by an increase in population, as it has been in the United States, all of these trends are reinforced and the pollution problem becomes more and more serious at an accelerating rate. Urbanization also contributed greatly to the growth of the problem by concentrating pollution in particular locations.

If the United States were not an advanced industrial nation

with a booming economy, it is doubtful that either the public or the government could be induced to pay much attention to pollution. Concern with pollution is a luxury in the sense that a nation or an individual who is forced to be preoccupied with obtaining sufficient food, clothing, and shelter will not have the time or inclination to worry about pollution, except in those cases where it is an obvious and imminent threat to public health. Important as the pollution problem may be, it is less important than the more obvious prerequisites for survival. On the other hand, the conditions of life in an affluent society do tend to contribute to a concern with pollution. The greater amount of leisure time enjoyed by the population leads to a greater demand for recreational resources and aesthetic satisfaction, and the higher level of education enables people to comprehend better the dangers and dynamics of pollution.

The control of pollution requires considerable resources, both human and financial. It has been estimated that it will cost $280 billion between 1971 and 1980 to bring air, water, and solid waste pollution in the United States down to levels now considered acceptable by the government.[2] The availability of trained personnel has also been a limiting factor on pollution control programs in this country, even though the resources devoted to control have been small compared to the need.[3] If money or manpower to control pollution were clearly not available, it is unlikely that any government would try to focus attention on the problem. Affluence allows a society to become concerned because it holds out the possibility of sufficient resources to permit action.

Once a government has taken action on pollution, the very fact that something has been done tends to create a demand for further action. The issue is given publicity and "respectability" by governmental recognition, and the public learns that something can be done to alleviate the problem. Once an official agency has been established to control pollution, that agency becomes a focal point for bringing the issue to the attention of the general public as well as of other government officials. The members of the agency have a vested interest in drawing attention to the problem. If they are successful, private interest groups will take up the call for action, and new groups will be created for the specific purpose of doing something about pollution. This public concern will in turn strengthen the hand of the governmental agency. The concern with pollution thus becomes institutionalized and the pressure to take action becomes constant. The federal pollution control agencies have played this kind of role, and many state and local agencies have also succeeded in stimulating interest and pressure for pollution control.

One final factor contributing to the post-World War II concern with pollution has been its attractiveness as a political issue. Although many industrial groups oppose stringent control, their opposition must be indirect because one cannot gain many allies by publicly favoring dirty air or water. The cause of public health is very popular with legislators and the public, and thus the opponents of action have been on the defensive from the beginning. Also, the fact that pollution affects all citizens works in its favor. Particularly in a period when much governmental action is directed toward deprived segments of the population, a program which does something for everybody becomes highly attractive.[4]

A turning point in public interest in the environmental issue came in 1970. In January, President Nixon devoted a major part of his State of the Union Address to environmental issues declaring that, "The great question of the seventies is, shall we surrender to our surroundings, or shall we make our peace with nature and begin to make reparations for the damage we have done to our air, our land and our water?"[5] Less than three months later came "Earth Day" which produced a remarkable outpouring of grassroots citizen concern about the environment. It showed that for the first time the environmental problem had become an issue for the average citizen in all parts of the nation.

Why this upsurge of public interest occurred in 1970 and not in 1960 or 1969 or 1971 is not and probably never can be known with any degree of certainty. But it rested on a long series of previous events. Contrary to the opinion of some, the environmental issue did not spring into full-bloom in 1970 from the head of Richard Nixon or the Earth Day organizers or anyone else. Throughout the 1960s it had been an important political issue at the federal, state, and local level. The historical roots go back much farther. The proper handling of waterborne sewage has been a problem of public policy at least since the time of ancient Rome. In 1273, Edward I banned the burning of sea coal in London in order to alleviate air pollution, and in 1388 Richard II forbade river pollution.[6]

WATER POLLUTION

Water pollution today comes primarily from four sources: domestic sewage, industrial and agricultural wastes, and natural processes. It is difficult to estimate "how much" of the pollution problem arises from each of these sources because of lack of data and because there is no single measure of the degree of water pollution. The standard most often used is "biochemical oxygen demand" (BOD), the amount of waterborne oxygen consumed by wastes. However, the BOD measure does not take into consideration the toxicity of the wastes to men, fish, or other forms of life. Domestic sewage today accounts for about 30 per cent of man-made BOD, while industrial and agricultural wastes account for about 70 per cent.[7]

Domestic Sewage

Domestic sewage, although it contributes less to BOD, contains most of the bacteria and viruses which account for the disease-producing potential of water pollution. Until recent years, concern with water pollution was focused almost entirely on the health effects of polluted water. Typhoid, cholera, and other waterborne bacterial diseases were constant and serious dangers in the United States as well as all other countries. However, with the discovery of the bacteria-killing powers of chlorine and the widespread application of filtration and other purification processes, the first decades of the twentieth-century witnessed the almost total elimination of such diseases in the United States.[8]

The virtual elimination of cholera and typhoid did not eliminate national concern with water pollution. If anything, there was an inverse correlation between the threat of waterborne disease and the efforts made to control pollution. The first stream pollution investigations by the federal government began in 1910,[9] and in 1912 the U.S. Public Health Service (PHS) was authorized by statute to conduct investigations into pollution of navigable waters.[10] The first major PHS investigations were of pollution in the Great Lakes, the Potomac River, and the Ohio River.[11] Today, sixty years later, these three areas are still polluted and are high-priority objects of government enforcement efforts.

The construction of municipal waste treatment plants for the processing of domestic sewage has been the primary aim of water pollution control policy for the past sixty years. Before the enactment of the landmark legislation of the past few years, the most significant efforts in the pollution control battle were the New Deal public works programs, which spent millions of dollars on the construction of waste treatment works. As a result of the New Deal expenditures, combined with the reduction in economic output caused by the depression, the years 1930 to 1940 marked the first actual reduction in water pollution in this country.[12]

Waste treatment plants employ one of three types of purifying processes: primary, secondary, or tertiary treatment. Primary treatment involves simply screening-out the floating solids in the water and then holding the water for a period of time to let other solids settle to the bottom of a tank. This process can remove about 30-to-50 per cent of the BOD. Secondary treatment adds a biological process to primary treatment by allowing bacteria to consume some of the wastes in the water. The addition of this step eliminates 75-to-95 per cent of the BOD. Primary and secondary treatment remove some of the disease-carrying bacteria, and chlorination can be used after treatment to eliminate the remainder of such disease agents. But neither primary nor secondary treatment is very effective against the viruses and chemicals which currently represent the most important water-related health problems.

Tertiary treatment entails adding one or a series of chemical removal processes to the physical and biological treatment stages. This can remove most of the phosphorous components, thereby retarding or preventing eutrophication (see below), and can also remove a variety of other chemicals which the wastewater may contain. Tertiary treatment makes it technically possible to have a "closed system" whereby water in a community is continually recycled, the sewage being treated and placed back into the potable water system. However, there are major psychological and economic obstacles to the use of such closed systems, and also the health problems caused by viruses and small amounts of chemicals may remain.

Much remains to be learned about the transmission of virus-caused diseases, such as hepatitis, and current evidence is equivocal as to the portion of cases of viral diseases that are caused by waterborne agents. Between 1946 and 1960, for instance, out of 115,690 cases of hepatitis reported by PHS, only 417 were due to infected water.[13] The health implications of the many man-made chemicals introduced into the environment are just beginning to be explored, but there is ample evidence that consumption of pesticides, for example, is unhealthy, at least if they are consumed in sufficient quantity. The minimum quantity of pesticides or other chemicals which is sufficient to produce adverse affects to our health is a question which has not been satisfactorily answered.

In addition to a treatment plant, any plan to prevent pollution from domestic sewage must include an adequate sewer system feeding into the plant. In 1972, about 81 per cent of the population in the United States was served by sewers. Of the population with sewers, about 60 per cent had their wastes processed through a plant providing secondary or tertiary treatment; about 35 per cent were served by a plant giving only primary treatment; and the remainder dumped the wastes collected from sewers directly into the receiving waters.[14]

In many of the older communities of the nation, the existing sewer system is one of the major causes of water pollution. In these communities, the sewers which collect wastes from households and some industries are also used to collect the water from rain storms. Even a small amount of rain is usually enough to put more water in the sewer lines than can be processed by the treatment plant. When the plant becomes overloaded in this way, the amount of water that exceeds the capacity of the treatment plant is dumped directly into the receiving stream and gets no treatment at all. While much of this water is runoff from the storm, some of it is also raw sewage, since the two sources of water are combined in the sewer lines. The storm water also flushes out wastes which have accumulated in the sewer lines, thus adding significantly to the pollution load. The cost of separating all combined sewers has been estimated at $49 billion,[15] and the federal government has undertaken a major research program to develop less expensive ways of eliminating this cause of pollution. Until it is eliminated, domestic sewage will continue to be a major source of water pollution.

Industrial Wastes

Industrial wastes take many forms, but generally they account for more BOD than municipal wastes and for less of the disease-carrying bacteria and viruses. Two categories of industry—primary metals, and chemical and allied products—account for more than one half of the waste water produced by industrial sources. As shown in Table 1.1., paper mills, food-processing plants, and the petroleum and coal industries are other major pollution sources.[16]

The major health threat from industrial wastes lies in the approximately five-hundred new chemicals which are produced in this country yearly and the many older chemicals and metals used in industrial processes.[17] A number of these chemicals and metals are capable of causing cancer, birth defects, and various other illnesses if humans are exposed to them in sufficiently high concentrations. The threat from these substances was explicitly recognized in 1971 when the administration submitted to Congress a "Toxic Substances Control Act" which would require manufacturers to test new chemicals before they were commercially produced and would give the government authority to control the use and production of chemicals and metals. The bill was passed by both the House and Senate, but the 92d Congress ended before the two houses could reconcile the differences which existed in the versions passed by each.[18]

The mining industry has contributed a particularly troublesome problem to the water pollution scene: acid mine drainage.

Table 1.1. **Major Industrial Sources of Water Pollution, 1968**

Industry	Volume of Intake Water (billions of gallons)	Volume of Process Water (billions of gallons)	BOD Concentration of Process Water (ppm)	Suspended Solids Concentration of Process Water (ppm)
Primary metals	5,005	1,201	18	259
Chemicals	4,476	716	130	225
Paper	2,252	1,486	336	388
Petroleum and coal	1,435	100	52	76
Food and kindred products	811	292	87	703
Transportation equipment	313	62	NA*	NA
Machinery	189	28	NA	NA
Textile mill products	154	109	304	70
Rubber	135	24	17	30
Electrical equipment	127	47	NA	NA
Fabricated metals	68	37	NA	NA

Source: Adopted from U.S. Environmental Protection Agency, *The Economics of Clean Water* (Washington: GPO, 1972), vol. 1, pp 37–38.

* Not available

Both active and abandoned coal mines, primarily in Appalachia, pour out large amounts of water which has mixed with sulfur-bearing minerals within the mine to form sulfuric acid. This acid can destroy almost all forms of life within the streams. It is estimated that 11,000 miles of streams presently suffer from such conditions.[19] A number of techniques are available, both to prevent the acid from forming and to treat the water once it has become polluted. Most of these techniques are still in an experimental or demonstration stage, and no federal program to control acid mine drainage has yet been initiated.[20]

The fastest-growing problem of industrial pollution is what is known as "thermal pollution," the heating of streams caused by the discharge of water used for cooling purposes in industrial and power-generation plants. What has made the thermal pollution problem so pressing is the rapid growth of the electric power industry, together with the proposed construction of a large number of nuclear power plants which discharge significantly more heat into the water than conventional power plants. By the beginning of 1973, 160 reactors for nuclear plants were either in operation, under construction, or on order, and the size of nuclear plants is increasing steadily.[21] The Department of the Interior has estimated that by 1980 the electric power industry will require about one-sixth of the total available fresh-water runoff in the entire nation for cooling purposes.[22] Thermal pollution can be controlled by means of cooling towers, but such towers are quite expensive to build and operate. According to one government forecast, utility companies may have to spend a total of $2 billion for cooling towers in the next five years.[23]

The increase in the number of nuclear power plants poses a host of potential pollution problems in addition to thermal pollution. A very small amount of radioactive material escapes into both the water and the air during the normal operations of a nuclear plant. Of even more concern is the possibility of an accident which might result in massive radioactive discharges, and the problems of disposing of nuclear wastes. There is no method available for rendering nuclear wastes harmless—they are simply stored in containers. The Atomic Energy Commission has been trying to locate a site for burying the containers, but a combination of technical and political factors has so far frustrated this effort.

Several dramatic events within the past few years have focused national attention on the problem of oil pollution. The break-up of the giant oil tanker *Torrey Canyon* in 1967, the grounding of the tanker *Ocean Eagle* off Puerto Rico in 1968, and the leakage of large quantities of oil from a well off the shore of Santa Barbara, California, in early 1969, were front-page news items throughout the country. The major sources of oil pollution are ships, offshore oil wells, and a variety of onshore sources such as oil-loading facilities, storage tanks, and even gasoline stations. The routine dumping of oil used in operating vessels has long been a pollution problem, but a new and much more serious hazard is posed by the great increase in the size and number of ships used to transport oil. The average size of oil tankers increased by more than 50 per cent between 1955 and 1965, and the number of tankers increased during the same period from approximately 2,500 to 3,500.[24] An accident involving just one of the new super tankers is enough to cause serious damage over large sections of the nearest coast, as happened in the case of the *Torrey Canyon*. Another new hazard is the drilling of oil wells in the ocean floor. Such drilling is taking place at an extraordinary rate off the coasts of the United States, with more than 1,000 new wells being drilled each year.[25] Given our lack of knowledge of the geological characteristics of the areas being drilled and the inadequacy of technology to control accidental leakages, each new well has the potential of becoming a major pollution problem.

Natural Forms of Pollution

The pervasive presence and impact of industrial society in America makes it almost impossible to talk about "purely" natural phenomena. However, two major water pollution problems, sediment and eutrophication, occur as part of natural cycles and developments. Both problems have been greatly accelerated, however, by the acts of man.

The sediment problem is caused by the presence of soil particles in water and by the accumulation of such particles on the bottom of streams, reservoirs, and lakes. Sufficient quantities of such soil particles in water render it unusable for certain purposes and also make the lake or stream less able to purify itself of other pollutants. This poses a particularly acute problem in artificially created reservoirs. Many of the dams built today will be useless in thirty or forty years because of the accumulation of silt behind them.

Silt enters water naturally by runoff from rain which carries soil particles with it and by the erosion of riverbanks. Road and housing construction and agricultural practices often result in a great increase in the amount of soil which is washed into the stream, and the construction of dams and irrigation channels further complicates the ability of streams to assimilate the load of silt.[26] Control of sediment and siltation has generally relied on dredging the silt out of the river, but this is an expensive method and is ineffective in removing the soil particles actually flowing in such heavily silted streams as the Mississippi or Potomac

Rivers. The soil particles suspended in the water can be removed before the water is used by means of filtration or other treatment processes, but this does nothing to alleviate the harmful effects of silt on the river itself. Steps can be taken to minimize the flow of silt into the river by controlling the methods used for construction and agriculture, but even the best techniques will only alleviate the problem, not solve it, in most cases.

Eutrophication is another problem with no easy solution, in part because the process involved is one that occurs naturally. All lakes follow a process of aging, eventually filling up with silt and vegetation which consume increasing amounts of oxygen in the water until the oxygen is totally exhausted. Finally, the lake becomes swampy and disappears. This aging and eventual "death" of lakes is known as eutrophication. It is a process which is not yet fully understood by the scientists,[27] but we do know that it has been greatly accelerated by the actions of man. Although Lake Erie is not in imminent danger of becoming dry land, the eutrophication process there has been telescoped from several thousand years to a few decades by the man-made pollutants dumped into it.

The pollutants which contribute to the eutrophication process are plant nutrients, which feed the algae in the water until eventually the entire lake becomes a soupy green mixture because of the growth of the algae. Phosphorus is probably the most important nutrient in most lakes, although there has been considerable controversy over which nutrients control the rate of eutrophication in particular bodies of water. Many of the nutrients enter water from natural sources, but fertilizers, phosphorus-containing detergents, and municipal sewage are also very significant contributors to eutrophication. Normal secondary waste treatment removes only a small part of the nutrients from wastes. Thus, if the man-made sources of eutrophication are to be controlled, either tertiary treatment must be applied or the sources themselves must be controlled by such steps as preventing the use of phosphate detergents.

Agricultural Wastes

Agriculture contributes to the sediment and eutrophication problems as well as to a variety of other water pollution problems. Soil erosion from poor farming practices is one of the major sources of the more than four billion tons of soil washed into the Nation's waterways annually.[28] The use of fertilizers, which doubled between 1950 and 1970, has contributed to the growing seriousness of eutrophication.[29]

Agriculture and other "non-point" (not entering the water from a pipe or other single identifiable point) sources of water pollution probably account for far more of the pollution problem than is generally realized. For example, the increasing tendency to concentrate the raising of large numbers of cattle, hogs, chickens, and other animals in a small area has created a major problem. The pollution load just from cattle in feedlots is estimated to equal almost the entire sewage load from the human population in America.[30] Most of this waste receives no treatment before it finds its way into our rivers and streams.

Pesticides enter the water when rain or irrigation washes them from soil or vegetation where they have been applied for agricultural purposes, or when they escape or are released from factories manufacturing them. Several serious fishkills have been traced to pesticides in the water, and the effect of pesticides on man has been the subject of much controversy. Any pesticide sold in the United States must be registered with the Environmental Protection Agency (EPA) which can withdraw or refuse registration if the pesticide is found to substantially harm man or the environment. A new pesticide law passed in 1972 should result in significantly tighter controls over the production and use of pesticides.[31] Also, the increasing shift to biological and other non-chemical methods of pest control should markedly reduce the use of chemical pesticides.[32]

This brief discussion of some of the major water pollution problems does not cover all the known water pollutants, nor all of the problem areas; it does, however, describe the areas which have been of major concern to the policymakers. The water pollution control legislation which has been enacted in recent years has been primarily devoted to solving these problems and to providing resources for research into better methods of controlling them.

AIR POLLUTION

The first air pollution law in the United States was an 1881 ordinance adopted by the Chicago City Council. The council declared that "the emission of dense smoke from the smokestack of any boat or locomotive or from any chimney anywhere within the city shall be . . . a public nuisance." [33] Other municipalities followed Chicago's example, but there was little interest at the state or national level. Not much effort was put into enforcing the local laws, and they had little impact on the pollution problem.

All of the pre-World War II efforts to control air pollution were concerned exclusively with smoke, or what is now known technically as "particulate matter." The existence of other air pollutants was for all practical purposes unknown. This situation changed with the initiation of what might be considered the first modern air pollution control program in Los Angeles in 1947. The Los Angeles effort began because of public objection to the odors of a wartime industrial plant. It soon expanded into a general drive against the eye-irritating smog which plagued many Angelinos. Severe curbs were placed on oil refineries, which represented the major industry in the area, and on backyard incinerators. Then, in 1951, Dr. Arie Haagen-Smit of Cal. Tech. pinpointed the automobile as the major contributor to the Los Angeles air pollution problem. This discovery marked the beginning of the drive on the invisible odorless substances which are the major focus of air pollution control today. There is no longer any validity to the commonsense notion that if you can't see it, it's not pollution.

The growth of concern over pollution has been stirred by crises, both real and created. Rachel Carson's *Silent Spring*[34] had a catalytic effect in the area of pesticides, and the fallout from nuclear testing awakened concern about radioactive hazards. The air pollution problem was widely dramatized when, in October 1948, twenty deaths and almost 6,000 cases of illness were attributed to a prolonged smog in the industrial community of Donora, Pennsylvania.

The Donora incident was extensively investigated by the Public Health Service. In announcing the report of the investigation, the administrator of the Federal Security Agency, of which the Public Health Service was then a part, stated, "We can now say positively what couldn't be said before with scientific proof—that contamination of air in industrial areas can cause serious acute disabling diseases." [35]

However, twenty-five years later there is still considerable debate about the health effects of particular air pollutants. Those stricken by air pollution, such as the people in Donora, did not suffer from some particular disease associated with the pollution but rather experienced aggravation of a previous weakness, usually due to some prior illness. It has also been virtually impossible to distinguish the effect of individual pollutants, because pollution almost always involves a mixture or combination of several different pollutants. There is no dispute over the fact that air pollution is harmful—the problem lies in knowing what kind of harm is done and what specific pollutants are responsible for it.

Sources of Air Pollution

Governmental efforts to control air pollution have concentrated on six pollutants: carbon monoxide, nitrogen oxides, hydrocarbons, photochemical oxidants, sulfur dioxide, and particulates. The first four of these come primarily, but not exclusively, from automobiles. Sulfur dioxide and particulates are emitted from a variety of sources.

Table 1.2 shows the amount of these pollutants emitted in 1970 and the major sources responsible for this pollution. Photochemical oxidants are not shown, since they are produced by the mixing of nitrogen oxides, hydrocarbons, and sunlight in the atmosphere. The tons of carbon monoxide emitted exceeds that of the other four pollutants combined. Similarly, transportation, primarily the automobile, accounts for more pollution than all the other sources combined. However, this is somewhat deceptive. We worry about these pollutants primarily because of their effects, and the health and other damage caused by a ton of carbon monoxide is much less than that caused by a ton of sulfur dioxide or a ton of particulates. Table 1.3. shows the percentage of pollution accounted for by each source by weight, and then the same figure corrected for the amount of damage to health and welfare done by the pollutants emitted from that source. The latter figures provide a better picture of which sources are responsible for the most serious air pollution.

Table 1.2. **Estimated Emissions of Air Pollutants, by Weight, Nationwide, 1971**
(in million tons per year)

Source	CO	Particulates	SO₂	HC	NOₓ
Transportation	77.5	1.0	1.0	14.7	11.2
Fuel combustion in stationary sources	1.0	6.5	26.3	.3	10.2
Industrial processes	11.4	13.6	5.1	5.6	.2
Solid waste disposal	3.8	.7	.1	1.0	.2
Miscellaneous	6.5	5.2	.1	5.0	.2
Total	100.2	27.0	32.6	26.6	22.0
Percent change 1970 to 1971	− .5	+ 5.9	− 2.4	− 2.6	0

Source: Environmental Protection Agency as reported in U.S. Council on Environmental Quality, *Environmental Quality—1973*, p. 266.

Abbreviations used: CO — Carbon monoxide
                 SO₂ — Sulfur dioxide
                 HC — Hydrocarbons
                 NOₓ — Nitrogen oxides

On an adjusted basis, the emissions from transportation drop from being the most important source to being the third most important, ranking behind stationary combustion and industrial processes. However, pollution from automobiles is probably more concentrated in urban areas than are the other sources, and thus if one examines the ambient air quality in cities automobile-related pollution may still be the most important problem.[36]

The influence of meteorological factors on air pollution should also be noted. The amount of pollution which exists at a given place and time is highly dependent on wind and other climatic conditions. The phenomenon known as an "inversion" is of particular importance. An inversion takes place when cool air near the ground is trapped beneath a layer of warmer air. This prevents the air at ground level from rising and the pollutants in that air from dispersing. The pollutants cannot escape until the inversion is broken, and they continue to accumulate over the area, causing increasingly dangerous levels of pollution. Almost all the serious air pollution disasters and alerts have been associated with an inversion.

Table 1.3. **Air Pollution Emissions, 1971,
by Weight and by Weight Adjusted for Effects**

Source	Unadjusted Emissions		Adjusted Emissions	
	Weight (in millions of tons)	**% of Total**	**Weight (in millions of tons)**	**% of Total**
Transportation	105	51	40	19
Fuel combustion (stationary sources)	44	21	85	41
Industrial processes	36	17	60	29
Solid waste disposal	6	3	4	2
Miscellaneous	17	8	19	9
Total	208	100	208	100

Source: Adopted from U.S. Council on Environmental Quality, *Environmental Quality—1973*, pp. 266 and 328. The computations are based on an index developed by Lyndon R. Babcock, Jr., and Niren L. Nagda of the University of Illinois.

The inversion phenomenon is not uncommon in the United States. An inversion exists over cities on the Atlantic Coast 10 to 35 per cent of the time, and on the West Coast 35 to 40 per cent of the time.[37] Usually the inversion lasts for a few hours and then dissipates, but New York City also experiences an average of four days during each year where an inversion lasts for at least twenty-four hours.[38] It is at such times that air pollution does its maximum damage.

Our knowledge of the technological means to control air pollution varies widely depending on the type of pollutant and its source. A variety of methods exist to control particulates and some of these will control 99 per cent of the particulate matter emitted from a given source. Control of sulfur oxides is a much more difficult problem. A variety of methods for removing sulfur from the stack gases of large sources, such as power plants, are being tested, but none of the methods have proved fully reliable. Thus, the primary control technique has been to change to low-sulfur-content fuel, although there will not be enough low-sulfur fuel available to meet all of the standards which have been promulgated. Changes in fuel strike at the heart of the American energy-based economy. Thus, regulation of sulfur oxides has been one of the most politically sensitive subjects in the air pollution field.

Even more politically charged has been the battle over automobile emission controls. Starting with the 1968 models, the federal government has promulgated air pollution standards which must be met by manufacturers of new automobiles. There have been problems with deterioration of the control systems installed, and the control systems have actually increased the oxides of nitrogen emitted. In the 1970 Clean Air Act Congress wrote into law stringent new standards for new motor vehicles, and gave the manufacturers until 1975 or 1976 to meet the standards. These standards and the likelihood of their being met will be discussed in Chapter 8.

AIR AND WATER POLLUTION COMPARED

Air, unlike water, cannot be centrally collected in one place and then run through some type of plant to cleanse it of pollution. This fact influences the whole nature of governmental programs for controlling air pollution because it means that control must be done on a source-by-source basis. Thus, given the current state of technology, air pollution control is primarily a matter of enforcing regulations against individual polluters, whereas water pollution control is much more concerned with the construction of public projects.

The evidence to date indicates that we are making more progress in controlling air pollution than water pollution.[39] The factors that account for this are numerous and any simple explanation is bound to be misleading. But one important factor is the greater dependence of water pollution control on efforts by the federal, state, and local governments to construct the necessary facilities. Uncertain financing, poor planning, and a lack of commitment have slowed down these efforts. The air pollution control effort is much more dependent on private sector financing (see Figure 1.1.). It is hard to avoid the

Figure 1.1. **Distribution of Cumulative Incremental
Environmental Expenditures, 1972-1981**[1]

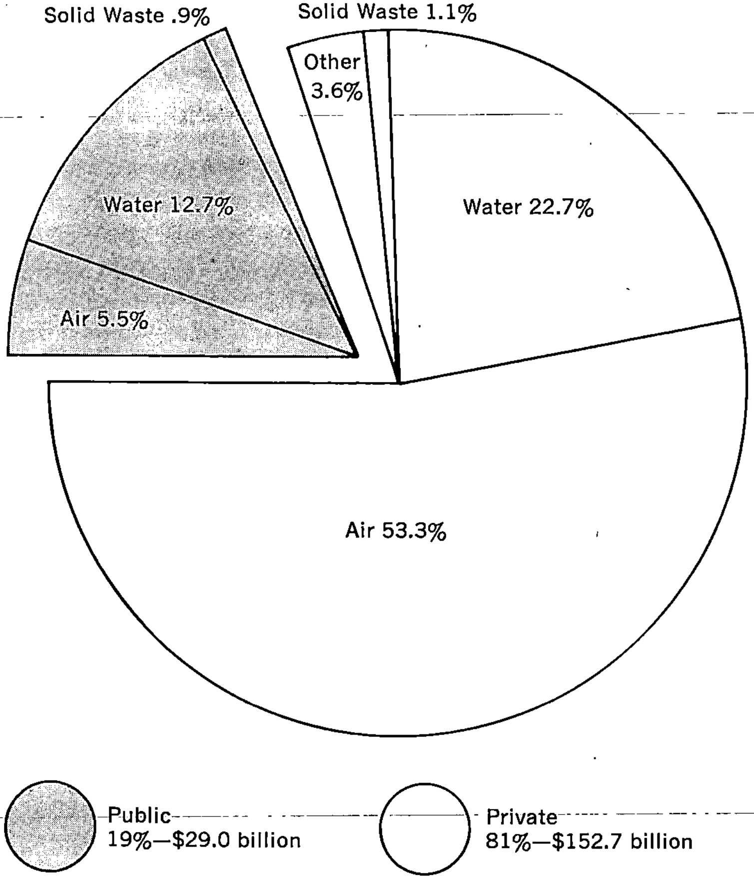

Solid Waste .9%   Solid Waste 1.1%

Other
3.6%

Water 12.7%   Water 22.7%

Air 5.5%

Air 53.3%

Public
19%—$29.0 billion

Private
81%—$152.7 billion

[1]Figures do not total due to rounding.

Source: U.S. Council on Environmental Quality, *Environmental Quality—1973*
(Washington, D.C.: Government Printing Office, 1973), p. 102.

conclusion that public regulation to force action by the private sector is a more effective method of getting the job done than action by the public sector to undertake the clean-up itself.

The linkages between air and water pollution are critical factors which must be considered in any sound pollution policy. Many pollutants such as radiation, pesticides, and many chemicals, are found in air *and* water. Establishment of adequate standards must take into account the exposure to humans which comes from all sources, and thus the air or water problem cannot be considered in isolation.

Another aspect of this same problem is the interchangeability of the media, into which many pollutants can be emitted. If sulfur oxides air pollution is controlled by using wet scrubbers, the sulfur problem may simply be shifted from being an air pollution problem to being a water or land pollution problem. This same flexibility is applicable to most pollutants. Some wastes can be recycled and some can be reduced to harmless constituents, but in many cases the control question must be, "where is the least harmful place to put the waste?"

It should be clear from this discussion that pollution is not a simple problem. Although most forms of pollution are due to the central difficulty of disposing of wastes created by the society, the particular source of the wastes, their specific effects on uses of the environment, and the medium in which they are disposed are all crucial factors in determining how a particular pollution problem is to be controlled. For practical purposes, there is not one pollution problem but many distinct pollution problems. This complexity is reflected in the pollution legislation which has been passed in recent years.

CHAPTER 2

Federal Pollution
Control Legislation

SINCE the mid-1950s, the basic framework for pollution control has been increasingly determined by federal legislation. However, most major legislative innovations require long periods of gestation and pollution control has been no exception. Twenty years elapsed between the first major push for federal water pollution control legislation and the passage of the Water Pollution Control Act in 1956. The 1948 Donora disaster brought the air pollution problem to national attention, but it took fifteen more years until passage of the first permanent control law. Neither the Congress nor the Executive moves swiftly in recognizing new problems. There must be a significant demand from powerful interest groups before important action is taken, and it takes a long time for awareness of a new problem to enter into the demands of the existing group structure.

Once the federal government has ventured into a new field, the pace of legislation is likely to accelerate. The initial hurdle of federal responsibility having been overcome, the search for more effective ways of accomplishing the task begins. Over the past eight or ten years a large number of proposals designed to improve or expand pollution control have been introduced in each session of Congress, and several major proposals have become law. Innovations in water pollution legislation have generally come first with parallel laws on air pollution following a few years later. Thus, the 1956 water pollution enforcement procedures were adapted for air pollution control in 1963. The standard-setting process contained in the 1965 Water Quality Act was included, with some modifications, in the 1967 Air Quality Act. However, the 1970 air pollution legislation and the 1972 water pollution legislation did not follow this pattern.

There is nothing inevitable about the pattern of pollution legislation. The scope and pace of federal intervention and initiative obviously depends greatly on the nature of the administration in office. The rapid growth of federal powers in the 1960s was due in no small part to the activist inclinations of Presidents Kennedy and Johnson. But it was due also to the growing awareness of the dimensions of the problem and to discontent with unsatisfactory progress being made in controlling pollution. The Nixon Administration submitted major new bills for air and water pollution control.

WATER POLLUTION LEGISLATION: 1899–1961 [1]

Until 1948, legal authority to control water pollution belonged almost exclusively to the states and localities. In almost all states jurisdiction had gradually passed from the local to the state level as it became apparent that the localities which suffered the effects of pollution were unable to control its upstream sources. By 1948, all the states had some agency responsible for water pollution control, although the legal powers of such agencies varied widely.

Before passage of the first federal legislation directed at the major sources of water pollution, two acts had been passed which dealt with aspects of the pollution problem. An 1899 law prohibited the dumping of debris in navigable waters, but it was designed to prevent impediments to navigation, not to clean up the water.[2] A 1924 Federal Oil Pollution Act prohibited oil pollution from oceangoing vessels but did not deal with the many other sources of oil pollution and was not very effective in controlling the pollution from vessels.[3]

The eager response of states and localities to the New Deal public works assistance for the construction of waste treatment plants led to efforts to make such assistance permanent and laid the groundwork for the 1948 Water Pollution Control Act.[4] Between 1935 and 1940 numerous bills were introduced in the Congress calling for federal financial assistance for treatment plant construction. Most of the bills also provided for federal support for comprehensive pollution control planning, and a number of them contained provisions for federal enforcement powers to curb pollution in interstate streams.[5]

Three of the prewar bills succeeded in passing at least one House of Congress. In 1936, Representative Vinson of Kentucky introduced a bill containing financial assistance, planning, and enforcement provisions, which passed the House, but died in the Senate.[6] Vinson reintroduced his bill the following year;[7] it was passed by both the House and Senate but was vetoed by the president in June 1938 because a section of the bill authorized the surgeon general to submit requests for waste treatment projects directly to Congress, by-passing the president and the normal budget process.[8]

Following the veto of the Vinson bill, Senator Barkley, on behalf of the administration, introduced similar legislation with the financing section rewritten to conform to normal budgetary procedures.[9] Differing versions of the Barkley bill passed the House and Senate, and the conference committee was unable to resolve the differences before the close of the 76th Congress. By this time the nation began to be totally absorbed in the war effort, and all consideration of the water pollution problem was postponed for the duration of the war.

In 1948, the first major federal water pollution control legislation was finally passed. The bill had bi-partisan backing (it was introduced in the Senate by Barkley and Taft) and administration support. The authority contained in the legislation was limited to a five-year period, but the act was extended for an additional three years in 1953.[10] In 1956, the first permanent Water Pollution Control Act became law, and in the first year of the Kennedy Administration the 1956 act was strengthened in several important respects.

For the twenty years between 1945 and 1965 controversy over water pollution legislation centered on two major areas—federal enforcement powers and financial assistance for the construction of waste treatment plants. These two subjects occupied the bulk of the debate on the 1948, 1956, and 1961 acts, just as they had been the major subjects of controversy during the New Deal period.

The extent to which the federal government must rely on state initiative or permission in enforcing pollution control has major implications for the balance of power in the federal system and for the way in which the pollution program is conducted. The states have been jealous of their prerogatives, and they have been supported by many congressmen who believe in "states rights." The state officials have often been further supported by industry groups who feel that they have more influence at the state than at the federal level.

The 1948 act established the authority of the federal government to have some role in abating interstate water pollution, although the role was a subordinate one to that of the states. The provisions for federal enforcement in the act were extremely cumbersome and proved to be so unworkable that the House Appropriations Committee denied fiscal 1956 funds to the Public Health Service for enforcement, on the grounds that the existing law was "almost unenforceable." [11]

After extended negotiations, in 1956 the Congress passed a revision of the enforcement provisions which eliminated many of the difficulties of the 1948 act. The new provisions represented a compromise between the Department of Health, Education, and Welfare (HEW) and the state health agencies. They provided for a conference among the interested parties; a public hearing if the conference did not result in action within six months; and then another six-month waiting period, after which the case could be taken to court. This became the basic pattern for federal enforcement in both air and water pollution.

The 1956 act failed, however, to remove the greatest single obstacle to federal enforcement, the necessity for getting state consent before federal court action could be initiated. In his 1961 Message on Natural Resources, President Kennedy endorsed a bill sponsored by Representative John Blatnik of Minnesota which eliminated the state consent provision, and also changed the scope of federal enforcement powers by extending the federal jurisdiction to interstate *or navigable*

Table 2.1. **Major Federal Water Pollution Control Legislation**

Date	Title*	Major Provisions		
		Enforcement	**Financial Aid****	**Other**
1948	Water Pollution Control Act (P.L. 80–845)	Weak and cumbersome, heavily dependent on states	Loans for treatment plant construction	Temporary authority
1956	Water Pollution Control Act Amendments of 1956 (P.L. 84–660)	Conference-hearing court action process for interstate waters	Grants for treatment plant construction. $50m annual authorization	Permanent authority
1961	Federal Water Pollution Control Act (P.L. 87–88)	Federal jurisdiction extended to navigable waters	Authorization of $80m in 1962, $90m in 1963, and $100m annually 1964–67	Research on municipal treatment. Seven field labs authorized
1965	Water Quality Act (P.L. 89–234)	Federal-state standard-setting. Streamlined enforcement process	Authorization of $150m in 1966 and 1967	Project grants for R&D on combined sewers
1966	Clean Water Restoration Act (P.L. 89–753)	Responsibility for Oil Pollution Act transferred to Secretary of the Interior	Authorization $450m in 1968, $700m in 1969, $1b in 1970, $1.25b in 1971. Federal % of costs rose to up to 55%.	Project grants for R&D on advanced waste treatment and on industrial wastes
1970	Water Quality Improvement Act (P.L. 91–224)	Absolute liability for oil spills. Federally licensed facilities must get State certificate		
1972	Water Pollution Control Act Amendments of 1972 (P.L. 92–500)	Federal effluent standards. Federal-State permit system	Authorization for treatment plant construction of $5b in 1973, $6b in 1974, $7b in 1975. Additional $6b for other provisions	National goal of eliminating pollution. Citizen suits.

* Despite differing titles, all legislation after 1948 actually constituted amendments to the Water Pollution Control Act.
** Abbreviations used: m = million, b = billion.

waters. The 1956 act limited enforcement authority to interstate waters, which were defined as waters which flow across, or form a part of, the boundaries between two or more states. Although these proposals met with some opposition, the Blatnik bill passed both Houses of Congress without major changes.

In addition to problems of enforcement, the federal government devoted considerable effort to trying to decide on the nature and amount of financial assistance to be provided to states and localities for the construction of waste treatment plants. In January 1946, President Truman had recommended a federal program of loans and grants for the construction of waste treatment facilities. However, the following year fear of inflation produced a stringent budget and brought about a change of administration policy. The grants section which had originally been contained in the 1948 bill was deleted, and the final legislation authorized $22.5 million annually for construction loans.

Throughout the Truman and Eisenhower administrations there was opposition to any kind of financial assistance to states and localities for treatment plants. The loan program contained in the 1948 act was never funded. The White House objected vehemently to a provision for $500 million over a ten-year period in federal waste treatment grants which was added to the 1956 legislation. A veto was considered, but President Eisenhower signed the bill into law with a statement indicating disapproval of the grants section.

Eisenhower's opposition to waste treatment grants was considerably strengthened in 1958 by the report of his Joint Federal-State Action Committee.[12] After a thorough search for federal programs which could be turned back to the states, the committee had succeeded in finding only two eligible programs —vocational education and waste treatment grants. In May 1958, Eisenhower submitted draft legislation to the Congress designed to implement the committee's recommendations. The Congress declined to take any action.

Rebuffed in his direct attempt to eliminate the waste treatment grants, the president sought to accomplish the same goal through the budgetary process. In his January 19, 1959, budget message he asked Congress to reduce, and, after 1960, to eliminate financing for the program. The Democrats, however, favored increasing the program, and they controlled the Congress by almost 2-to-1 majorities in each House. Representative Blatnik thus introduced a bill doubling the grant authorization to $100 million a year and extending the program for ten years.[13] The House voted in favor of the bill by 255 to 143, the vote being along party lines. The Republicans in the Senate were somewhat divided on the issue, and the Senate approved a slightly amended version of the bill by a vote of 61 to 27. Eisenhower, as expected, vetoed the legislation. An attempt in the House to override the veto fell 22 votes short of the necessary two-thirds majority.

Kennedy came into office sharing the dominant Democratic view that financial assistance for waste treatment plant construction was an important and necessary function of the federal government. The legislation he submitted in 1961 called for an increase in the authorization for the grant program and in the dollar limits on individual grants. There was no serious opposition to these proposals, the Republicans being evenly split on the issue and the Democrats overwhelmingly in favor. On July 20, 1961, the president signed the bill which authorized appropriations for waste treatment grants of $80 million in 1962, $90 million in 1963, and $100 million for each fiscal year between 1964 and 1967.

THE WATER QUALITY ACT OF 1965

In the early 1960s, Congress was still discontent with the pace of pollution control. It was felt that the states were not doing an adequate job, and that the Public Health Service, the federal agency responsible for administering the Water Pollution Control Act, was unwilling or unable to push them into taking more action. The discontent was given legislative form by Senator Edmund Muskie, chairman of the newly created Senate Subcommittee on Air and Water Pollution.

In 1963 Muskie introduced a set of far-reaching amendments to the Water Pollution Control Act. The proposals transferred federal administrative authority for the act from the Public

Health Service to a new Federal Water Pollution Control Administration which was to be created within HEW. Federal and state enforcement was to be based on water quality standards for interstate waters, a proposal first made by the Eisenhower Administration in 1955. The standards could be established by the secretary of HEW if the states did not, after being requested by the secretary, establish standards which met with his approval.[14]

The bill passed the Senate by a large majority in October 1963. After almost a year of hearings and negotiations, primarily on the water quality standards provisions, it was reported favorably by the House Public Works Committee. However, the House failed to take final action before the 88th Congress adjourned. In January 1965, at the start of the 89th Congress, Muskie introduced and the Senate passed a new bill containing the same provisions as the one it had passed in the previous Congress. The House passed an amended version of the bill which contained a substitute for the Senate standards provision. It required only that the states signify their intent to set water quality standards for interstate waters. If such a letter of intent were not filed, federal funds would be cut off.

The House and Senate versions of the bill went to a conference committee in April 1965. After five months of bargaining, a compromise was reached whereby each state would have one year from the date of enactment of the bill to file a letter of intent stating that it would establish water quality standards for its interstate waters before June 30, 1967. The standards would be subject to approval by the secretary of HEW. If the state failed to file a letter of intent or failed to establish standards, the secretary could establish the standards, subject to review by a hearing board. The bill as reported by the conference committee retained the provision for the creation of a Federal Water Pollution Control Administration, doubled the ceiling for individual waste treatment grants, and initiated a new demonstration program for dealing with the problem of combined storm and sanitary sewers. The conference report was approved by the House and Senate without dissent on September 21, 1965. On October 2 the legislation was signed by

President Johnson, who stated: "Today, we proclaim our refusal to be strangled by the wastes of civilization. Today, we begin to be master of our environment."

THE 1966 CLEAN WATER RESTORATION ACT

When he signed the 1965 act the president also remarked, "Additional bolder legislation will be needed in the years ahead." In fact, both the Congress and the Executive Branch had already begun work on what was to become the Clean Water Restoration Act of 1966.

During the spring and summer of 1965, Muskie's subcommittee held hearings to determine the extent of need for treatment facilities. The subcommittee concluded that $6 billion in federal funds would be needed over the next six years. In January 1966, Muskie, joined by forty-seven co-sponsors, introduced a bill authorizing a total of $6 billion for construction grants, removing the dollar ceiling on individual grants, and increasing the federal share of the costs of construction.

The Executive Branch was prompted to submit legislation to ward off Muskie's huge proposed increase in the grant authorization. Several factors influenced the content of the administration bill. Early in 1966 the newly created Federal Water Pollution Control Administration was transferred from HEW to the Department of the Interior. The latter was much less committed to working through the states than HEW had been. Furthermore, the Democratic administration was less convinced of the value of a strong state role in pollution control than was the Congress. Thus the major thrust of the 1966 act, as developed by the administration, was to move the control of water pollution toward a regional basis, despite the fact that the 1965 act had given the states a pivotal role in standard-setting and enforcement.

The administration's proposal provided for regional agencies to be established in selected river basins. The regional agencies would have their administrative expenses paid by the federal government, and $50 million was to be authorized in 1968 to finance waste treatment plant construction within basins which had established such agencies. The regional agencies were to draw up comprehensive plans for pollution control, and it was envisioned that they would have strong powers to set standards, enforce pollution control, and construct the necessary treatment plants.

The administration bill ran into determined opposition in the Congress, particularly from Senator Muskie. Muskie believed that the water quality standards provisions of the 1965 act represented a viable way of approaching the pollution problem. He had no intention of starting a new tack and weakening the states before the water quality standards approach had even begun to be put into effect. Accordingly, he produced a drastically rewritten version of the bill which retained some vestiges of the river basin approach but removed any real incentive to establish basin-wide agencies of the kind the administration had contemplated. The heart of the rewritten bill was Muskie's original grant proposal.

The Congress, always enthusiastic about public works programs and suspicious of regional approaches which might undermine the political base of senators and representatives, was far more receptive to the Muskie approach than to the administration bill. Congress was also reluctant to tamper with the state allocation formula contained in the existing act. In conference the construction grant authorization was scaled down to $3.55 billion over five years, and several other lesser changes were made; but the bill which passed the Congress in October of 1966 was primarily Muskie's handiwork. The administration, which had submitted the river basin program to avoid a large increase in the construction grant program, was quite unhappy with the final product. There was some discussion of a veto, but the president was anxious to salvage something in the way of pollution control legislation, and on November 3 he signed the 1966 Clean Water Restoration Act.

THE WATER QUALITY IMPROVEMENT ACT

Consideration of water pollution legislation between 1967 and 1970 focused primarily on particular pollution problems which had been dealt with only fleetingly or not at all in the 1965 and 1966 acts.

In December 1967, the Senate passed a bill dealing with oil pollution, acid mine drainage, and research on eutrophication. In July 1968, it passed a second bill covering waste treatment grant financing, vessel pollution, and thermal pollution. The House held hearings on most of these matters in the spring of 1968, but it did not take any immediate action.

The two thorniest problems were oil pollution and thermal pollution. The oil industry is one of the most powerful in the country, with many friends and protectors both within and outside the Congress.[15] The 1966 Clean Waters Act had amended the 1924 Oil Pollution Act, but the 1966 amendments contained a slight change of wording which crippled all enforcement against oil pollution. Representative James Wright, from the oil-producing state of Texas, introduced in the Rivers and Harbors Subcommittee a change in the definition of "discharge" requiring that the discharge of oil had to be "grossly negligent or willful" before the government could bring suit against the polluter.[16] The amendment went unnoticed and was incorporated in the law signed by the president. Enforcement then became impossible, because of the almost insuperable difficulty of proving that the operator of a ship had been "grossly negligent or willful." The need to correct the situation created by the 1966 amendments was underscored by the dramatic sinking in March 1967 of the huge *Torrey Canyon*.[17]

The section on thermal pollution contained in the Senate-passed bill was designed to meet the basic problem of no federal agency having jurisdiction to prevent thermal pollution before it occurred. This problem was most acute for nuclear power plants, where the Atomic Energy Commission licensed the plants but claimed that it did not have authority to consider thermal pollution effects in deciding whether or not to grant a license. Muskie had held extensive hearings on the subject of thermal pollution, but the language which he put into the bill had not been considered in any of the hearings. It stated, in part, that "any Federal department or agency . . . which carries out, or issues any lease, license, or permit or enters into any contract for, any activity, shall, insofar as practicable . . . cooperate with the Secretary [of Interior] . . . to insure compliance with applicable water quality standards and the purposes of this

Act." [18] This sweeping language would give the Interior Department a voice in all federal licensing and contracts. The "Section 11" provision, as it came to be called, since it amended Section 11 of the Water Pollution Control Act, became a major focus of controversy.

The House Public Works Committee bore the full brunt of reaction to Muskie's Section 11 proposal on thermal pollution. Within the committee, Representative William Cramer, the ranking Republican, was strongly opposed to the proposal. The electric utilities and the Chamber of Commerce lobbied vigorously to defeat Section 11. Within the Executive Branch, the Corps of Engineers made no secret of its fears that the proposal would seriously interfere with its function of licensing the dumping of dredging material from rivers and harbors. The Atomic Energy Commission was even more ardent in its opposition to Section 11. The Commission did not limit itself to defending the interests of the nuclear power industry, but acted as a spokesman for all of the electric utilities.

In the fall of 1968 the life of the 90th Congress was drawing to a close. Pressure was building up for the House to take action on water pollution legislation before the end of the session, which was scheduled for October 11. On October 3 the House committee reported out its version of the Senate bills. The House committee bill deleted Muskie's Section 11 provision entirely; it deleted any coverage of offshore and onshore facilities from the oil pollution section of the bill; and it reduced the amount of liability for damage caused by oil discharges from vessels. Overall, the House version represented a set of significant concessions to polluting industries.

The bill was brought to the floor of the House on October 7 under suspension of the rules, which meant that debate was limited, floor amendments could not be made, and a two-thirds vote was required for passage. After brief routine debate the bill passed, 277-to-0. The managers of the bill decided not to seek a conference with the Senate, but rather to try to get the Senate to accept the House version.

Muskie refused to be pushed into accepting the House bill. He was particularly adamant about retention of Section 11, which he viewed as the most important part of the legislation and which Cramer, the key figure in the House, viewed as the most unacceptable provision. On October 11, the Senate passed an amended version of the House bill which restored both Section 11 and coverage of offshore oil facilities.

Adjournment of the Congress had been delayed until Monday, October 14. Both Houses desperately wanted to avoid responsibility for failure to pass the water pollution legislation. The House therefore met on the fourteenth, agreed to a series of technical amendments made by the Senate on the preceding Friday, but voted to disagree to the Section 11 and offshore provisions. Normally it takes only a few minutes for a measure approved by one House of Congress to reach the other. However, the House vote was taken at 12:55 P.M. on Monday and somehow failed to reach the Senate floor before the Senate adjourned at 2:17.[19] Each House blamed the other for the failure of the 90th Congress to take any action on water pollution control.

The urgency of passing the pending water pollution legislation in the new session of Congress was underscored by a massive oil leak from a drilling rig off the shore of Santa Barbara, California. On January 28, 1969, a Union Oil Company well, located six miles offshore from Santa Barbara suffered a "blowout," and oil from the hole drilled in the ocean bottom began to spread on the water and drift toward the coast. The oil leaked at the rate of 20,000 gallons a day for several weeks, polluting beaches along twenty miles of the California shore, and the story occupied the front pages of newspapers across the nation for two or three weeks. The pressure was on Congress to take action.

During February both the Senate and House committees held hearings on the legislation, now reintroduced, which had died in the previous Congress. On March 25, the House Public Works Committee reported out a bill, HR 4148, which covered oil, vessel, thermal, and acid mine drainage pollution, and eutrophication.[20] The bill provided for penalties for oil pollution from onshore and offshore facilities, although the penalties were less severe than those contained in the Senate bill of the previous year. Thermal pollution was provided for by a rewritten version of Muskie's Section 11, based on modifications made by Muskie himself in the new bill which he submitted in the 91st Congress. This new version called for any applicant for a federal license or permit to obtain a certificate from the appropriate state agency certifying that the activity to be carried out under the license would not violate water quality standards.

On April 17, 1969, the House passed HR 4148. In May and June, Muskie's committee held further hearings on the bill. It reported out a revised version in August, which was passed with some modifications by the Senate in October. The House and Senate bills were sent to a conference committee which, after five months of negotiation, finally reported out a bill which closely paralleled the Senate-passed version. The concessions the House conferees made to the Senate side were generally attributed to the fact that a serious oil spill occurred in the home district of Representative Cramer, the senior Republican conferee for the House. Cramer had insisted on the weaker House provisions regarding liability for oil spills, but with the voters in his own district aroused he accepted the absolute liability provisions of the Senate bill.[21]

The conference bill was approved by both houses of Congress on March 25, 1970 and was signed by the president on April 3. The bill held the owners of vessels liable for oil spills up to a limit of $14 million except if the spill resulted from an act of war or some other uncontrollable circumstance. If the oil spill resulted from willful negligence or misconduct there was no limit on the liability of the owner. The law dealt with the thermal pollution problem by requiring any applicant for a federal license or permit involving the construction or operation of facilities which might pollute navigable waters to obtain a state certification that there was reasonable assurance that the facility would not violate water quality standards. The license or permit could be revoked if the standards were violated.

THE WATER POLLUTION CONTROL ACT AMENDMENTS OF 1972

In the closing months of 1969 it became increasingly clear that major revisions in the Water Pollution Control Act were called for. Public clamor about pollution control was at a high pitch. Congress was under pressure to take action. Disappointment with the pace of air pollution control was leading to a complete overhaul of the Clean Air Act, and the performance under the existing water pollution law was no better than under the air pollution law. The new Republican administration had decided that environmental quality would be one of its primary issues, and if environment was to be a major issue then one of the first orders of business would have to be water pollution control.

On February 10, 1970, Nixon sent a special message on the environment to Congress. He recommended new water pollution control legislation which would impose federally approved effluent standards on all industrial and municipal pollution sources. The Nixon proposal also called for increasing the authorization for waste treatment grants to $1 billion annually for four years and for creation of an Environmental Financing Authority to ensure that states and localities would be able to sell their bonds to finance their share of the construction of waste treatment plants.

Muskie's subcommittee held hearings on the administration bill and other water pollution control measures in the spring of 1970, but it took no action. It had its hands full with the Clean Air Amendments (see below), the Water Quality Improvement Act, and the Resource Recovery Act, and it was not until 1971 that the Congress was able to focus its attention on a major overhaul of the water pollution law.[22]

In February 1971, Muskie held general oversight hearings on the water pollution program. Beginning in March, the subcommittee began a series of hearings on the administration and other proposals. Beginning in May, the House Public Works Committee also held hearings on the numerous water pollution bills which had been proposed.

The bill which the Senate Public Works Committee finally reported out at the end of October 1971 was an extraordinary measure by any standard.[23] The committee report was 120 pages long, and the bill itself was 190 pages. The first section of the bill declared it to be national policy that "the discharge of pollutants into the navigable waters be eliminated by 1985" and that "wherever attainable, an interim goal of water quality which provides for the protection and propagation of fish, shellfish, and wildlife and provides for recreation in and on the water be achieved by 1981." [24] To achieve these goals, the committee bill called for federal effluent standards requiring the use of the best practicable control technology by industries and secondary treatment by municipalities by 1976. By 1981 industries would be required to install the best available control technology. Because the effluent standards would be established by the federal government, the states' role in setting standards would be greatly diminished. The Senate bill authorized $14 billion over four years to finance new construction of municipal waste treatment plants, and an additional $2.4 billion to reimburse states and localities for past construction costs. Enforcement was to be based on a system of permits. The bill contained a large number of other significant changes to the existing law and carried a total price tag of more than $18 billion.

The White House, alarmed by the impact of the bill on the federal budget, tried to get the full Senate to reduce the funding authorizations, to modify the sweeping goals contained in the bill's statement of national policy, and to give the states more power to set standards. The Council on Environmental Quality issued an analysis to show that satisfactory water quality could be achieved at much less cost and that the goal of eliminating all water pollution was unfeasible. But these efforts failed. On November 2, 1971, the Senate passed the Public Works Committee bill by a vote of 86-to-0.

Following Senate approval of the bill, the White House announced that it opposed the Senate version. It appealed to the House Public Works Committee, which had already held extensive hearings, to re-open its hearings so that opposition to the Senate provisions could be voiced. The administration also rallied industrial groups and some state officials to oppose the Senate bill.

The House committee did hold further hearings in December, but waited until the convening of the new Congress before reporting out its bill. Although the bill was much less to the liking of environmental groups than the Senate version, it was not totally pleasing to the White House. The environmentalists objected because the House bill made implementation of the 1981 and 1985 goals dependent on further congressional action, contained a restrictive citizen suit provision, and weakened several other provisions of the Senate bill. The administration was unhappy because the House committee had raised the price tag still further, providing an authorization of $18.4 billion for waste treatment grants alone.

On the floor of the House, the environmentalists, spearheaded by Representatives John Dingell and Henry Reuss, made a concerted effort to strengthen the committee bill. However, the Environmental Protection Agency, the Council on Environmental Quality, and a variety of industry groups supported the committee version against the environmentalists' amendments, and most of the amendments went down to defeat. On March 29, 1972, by a vote of 380-to-14, the House passed a bill which was almost identical to that reported by the Public Works Committee.

The House and Senate conferees began the work of reconciling their respective versions of the bill on May 11. Several times the negotiations seemed on the verge of collapse. But finally, on September 14, after 40 meetings, they agreed on a compromise bill. The compromise declared the 1985 and 1981 deadlines as "national goals" as provided by the House, not "policy" as voted by the Senate; adopted the higher House-passed authorization of $24.7 billion over three years; required polluting industries to install the best practicable control technology by 1977 and the best available technology by 1983 rather than by 1976 and 1981 respectively, as provided in both the House and Senate versions; gave EPA veto authority over individual permits, as in the Senate bill; gave the EPA Administrator discretion in initiating legal actions against polluters, as in the House bill, dropping Senate language making such actions mandatory; allowed citizen suits against violators of the act if the citizens had an interest which was adversely affected, a broader provision than the House but narrower than the Senate; and added new language exempting EPA regulatory actions under the act from the requirements of the National Environmental Policy Act.[25] Although clearly a compromise, the conference bill was somewhat closer to the Senate version and was clearly much tougher than the bill which had passed the House.

The conference report was approved by the House and Senate

on October 4, 1972. In both houses there was a sharp awareness of the possibility of a presidential veto. Many Congressmen who spoke during the debate pointed out that the conferees had loosened the spending requirements so that the administration would not necessarily be forced to spend all of the money authorized.

The president had until October 17 to sign the bill. Congress was also scheduled to adjourn on the 17th, elections for the new Congress being less than a month away. If Congress adjourned before midnight on the 17th, and the President did not sign the bill, it would not become law under the "pocket veto" provision of the Constitution. If Congress did not adjourn on the 17th, the bill would become law without the president's signature. The proponents of the water pollution bill decided they would not let Congress adjourn before midnight, believing that they had the votes to override the president if, at the last moment, he decided to veto the bill.

On the night of the 17th the Senate considered a conference report on a bill, backed by the administration, which would have set a $250 billion ceiling on the federal budget and given the president authority to withhold funds to meet this ceiling. Late in the evening, the Senate voted to reject the conference report. Presidential adviser John Ehrlichman, who had been sitting in the Senate gallery, thereupon delivered a presidential veto of the water pollution bill, stating to the press that the president had instructed him to deliver the veto if the spending ceiling was rejected. The president's veto message focused on what he called the "staggering, budget-wrecking $24 billion" which the bill authorized. "There is a well-worn political axiom," said Nixon, "which says that any election year spending bill, no matter how ill-advised, defies veto by the president. But I say that any spending bill this year which would lead to higher prices and higher taxes defies signature by this president. I have nailed my colors to the mast on this issue; the political winds can blow where they may." [26]

Whether because it was an election year or because of the basic support within Congress for environmental improvement, the president did not have the votes to sustain his veto. The veto message had been delivered shortly before midnight on

October 17. At 1:30 in the morning the Senate voted 52-to-12 to override the veto. Early in the afternoon of the 18th the House followed suit by an overriding vote of 247-to-23. Thus the most sweeping environmental measure ever considered by the Congress became law over the objections of the president.

Air Pollution Legislation: 1955—1965 [27]

The current concern with air pollution control in the United States began with the efforts of Los Angeles to control smog in the late 1940s and with the Donora incident of 1948. The 1949 report of the Public Health Service on the Donora episode had stressed the need for research on the nature of air pollution and its effects. Between 1950 and 1954 a number of resolutions calling for increased federal research on air pollution were introduced in Congress. In 1952 one such resolution passed the House but was killed in the Senate, and in 1954 Senators Thomas Kuchel and Homer Capehart unsuccessfully tried to add air pollution sections to the housing bill of that year.[28]

President Eisenhower, responding to a suggestion from Kuchel and Capehart, in 1954 established an interdepartmental committee to examine what action the federal government should take in the air pollution field. In the fall of 1954 the committee reported to the president that legislation should be passed creating a broad federal program of research and technical assistance. Eisenhower did not submit legislation to the Congress, but in his January 1955 health message he recommended stepped-up research on air pollution. Kuchel introduced legislation authorizing a federal program of research, training, and demonstrations. The administration did not oppose the bill and there was only minor controversy over some of the provisions in the Congress. The act was signed by the president on July 14, 1955. It authorized $5 million annually for five years to support federal research and to give assistance to states and educational institutions in training personnel and carrying out research and control.

It took a long time for the federal government to perceive the nature and dimensions of the air pollution problem: seven years elapsed between the time of Donora and the passage of the first legislation. At the time the 1955 act was being considered by Congress, HEW told the chairman of the Senate Public Works Committee that "instances of troublesome interstate air pollution are few in number." [29] An internal Bureau of the Budget memorandum pointed out that "unlike water pollution, air pollution . . . is essentially a local problem." [30] The Public Health Service and HEW were divided on the need for federal enforcement authority, and Eisenhower and the Budget Bureau were definitely opposed to such authority. These views of the problem resulted in eight more years elapsing between the 1955 act and the passage of the first permanent federal air pollution legislation.

In 1959, the 1955 act was extended for four more years.[31] In 1960 and again in 1961 the Senate passed a bill sponsored by Senator Kuchel authorizing the surgeon general to hold hearings on particular interstate air pollution problems, but in both years the House failed to take action. In 1961, in his Special Message on Natural Resources, President Kennedy stated, "We need an effective Federal air pollution control program now." [32]

In 1962 the president asked the House to pass the bill which had already cleared the Senate, and he also submitted legislation expanding the research provisions of the existing act and providing for federal grants to state and local air pollution control agencies for developing and initiating, or improving, programs. The House again deferred action because Representative Kenneth Roberts, chairman of the Subcommittee on Health and Safety, stated that he wanted to go into the proposals more thoroughly in the next session of Congress. The House proposed a simple two-year extension of the current authority. This was approved by the Senate and signed by the president, although the administration was clearly not satisfied with this outcome.[33]

During 1962, because of the White House request for new legislation and because of the impending expiration of the existing authority, a number of air pollution bills were introduced in both Houses of Congress and extensive negotiations took place within the Executive Branch on what role the federal government should play in controlling air pollution. The ques-

Table 2.2. **Major Federal Air Pollution Control Legislation**

Date	Title°	Major Provisions Enforcement	Major Provisions Other
1955	No title (P.L. 84–159)		Temporary authority for research, demonstrations, training.
1963	Clean Air Act (P.L. 88–206)	Hearings-conference-court procedure for interstate air pollution	Permanent authority. Grants to state and local control agencies.
1965	Motor Vehicle Air Pollution Control Act** (P.L. 89–272)	Federal regulation of emissions from new motor vehicles	Research on motor vehicle and sulfur oxides emissions.
1966	Clean Air Act Amendments of 1966 (P.L. 89–675)		Authorizes maintenance grants for air pollution control agencies.
1967	Air Quality Act (P.L. 90–148)	Federal-state standard-setting for air quality control regions. Streamlined enforcement process.	Registration of fuel additives. Establishment of advisory groups.
1970	Clean Air Amendments of 1970 (P.L. 91–604)	National emission standards. Stringent auto emission standards.	Citizen suits. Increased authorizations.
1974	Energy Supply and Environmental Coordination Act of 1974 (P.L. 93–319)	Allows EPA to waive emission limits and delays application of auto standards	Exempts Clean Air Act actions from impact statement requirement

* Despite differing titles, all legislation after 1963 actually constituted amendments to the Clean Air Act. However, only part of the 1974 legislation was an amendment to the Clean Air Act; the remainder dealt with matters other than air pollution.
** The Motor Vehicle Act was Title II of P.L. 89–272. Title I consisted of minor amendments to the 1963 act and Title III was the Solid Waste Act.

tion received added emphasis from the "Killer Smog" which hit London in December of 1962. In February 1963, President Kennedy recommended legislation

authorizing the Public Health Service of the Department of Health, Education, and Welfare: (a) To engage in a more intensive research program . . . (b) To provide financial stimulation to states and local air pollution control agencies through project grants . . . (c) To conduct studies on air pollution problems of interstate or nationwide significance; and (d) To take action to abate interstate air pollution, along the general lines of the existing water pollution control enforcement measures.[34]

Debate in the Congress centered on the proposal for federal enforcement powers. A bill containing the administration's provisions passed the House in July, with the Democrats voting almost unanimously in favor and a majority of Republicans opposed. In November the Senate passed an amended version of the House bill, and on December 10 both Houses approved a version of the bill produced by a conference committee. On December 17, 1963, President Johnson signed the Clean Air Act into law. The final bill squared with the recommendations which Kennedy had made at the beginning of the year. The enforcement provisions followed the pattern of the water pollution abatement procedure. At the request of a state, HEW could hold a public hearing on pollution within that state, then a conference, and finally federal court proceedings if satisfactory action was not taken by the polluters. If the pollution originated in one state but affected persons in another, then HEW could act on its own initiative without state permission. The bill authorized $95 million over a three-year period for the air pollution program.

With the passage of the Clean Air Act, attention shifted to the problem of air pollution from automobiles. Since the 1951 discovery that automobiles were the major source of Los Angeles smog, it had been clear that auto exhausts were a prime contributor to air pollution. Research in other cities had increasingly confirmed that the Los Angeles problem was not unique but was typical of most major urban areas. The Congress in 1960 passed legislation directing the surgeon general to make a study of the effects of motor vehicle exhaust fumes on the public health.[35]

During 1964 Muskie's Senate Subcommittee on Air and Water Pollution held hearings around the country on the air pollution problem. It became clear from the hearings that two major gaps in the existing federal authority were the regulation of automobile emissions and steps to improve the disposal of garbage and trash. In January 1965, Muskie thus introduced a bill providing for federal standards and enforcement for air pollution from new automobiles. The Muskie bill also contained a separate title initiating a federal program of support to deal with the solid waste disposal problem.

HEW, having followed the Muskie hearings, presented a similar proposal for auto regulation to the White House. The president reacted negatively, preferring to see if the automobile industry would cooperate voluntarily before subjecting it to federal enforcement. Two months after the president's reaction, James Quigley, assistant secretary of HEW, was called by the Senate subcommittee to testify on the Muskie bill. The Bureau of the Budget ruled that HEW was bound by the president's decision, and Quigley duly testified on April 6 that the administration opposed the major provisions of the Muskie bill. Muskie was appalled, and Quigley's April 6 testimony met with widespread denunciation in the press. *The New York Times, The Wall Street Journal, The Washington Post,* and the Los Angeles *Times* all editorialized against the administration stand. The president, realizing that a political error had been committed, reversed his position. Quigley reappeared before the subcommittee on April 9, and, stating that his previous testimony had been "completely misunderstood," volunteered to work with the committee to improve the language of the bill.[36]

Following Quigley's reversal, the air pollution provisions of the Muskie bill met with little opposition. The automobile industry did not object strongly, because it feared fifty diverse state standards far more than a uniform federal standard. The industry did succeed in having the House committee weaken some of the provisions, but the bill easily passed the Senate and the House and was signed by the president on October 20, 1965.

The 1965 act gave the secretary of HEW authority to establish regulations controlling emissions from all new motor vehicles. Although no deadline was set in the law for the establishment of the regulations, HEW agreed in the hearings that it would promulgate rules applicable to 1968 model automobiles. The state of California had already pioneered the way in establishing emission controls, and in fact the regulations which HEW was to apply to the 1968 models were the same regulations which

California had developed for 1967 models within the state. The 1965 act also contained several lesser amendments to the 1963 Clean Air Act. These included provisions for the abatement of U.S. air pollution sources which endangered the health or welfare of persons in Canada or Mexico, and authority for HEW to call a conference to focus attention on potential sources of air pollution.

THE AIR QUALITY ACT OF 1967

Public pressure on the federal government to control air pollution increased greatly between 1963 and 1966, and there was a widespread feeling both in Congress and the Executive Branch that satisfactory progress was not being made. Concern both within the government and outside it was given dramatic focus by a November 1966 pollution episode in New York City where a four-day inversion was estimated to have caused the death of eighty persons.

The month after the New York episode, four thousand people convened in Washington for the Third National Conference on Air Pollution. HEW planned to use the conference as a spring-board for new comprehensive air pollution legislation featuring regional control organizations and national emission standards. In his keynote address to the conference, John Gardner, the secretary of HEW, stated, "State and local governments have been slow in seizing the opportunities for action. In particular, they have failed to establish the regional approaches demanded by a problem that ignores traditional state boundaries. . . . Another matter which you will surely want to discuss at length is the question of standards. Lack of uniform air quality and emission standards serves as a deterrent both to states and communities and to industry." [37] Muskie also addressed the conference and, while agreeing that new approaches were needed, clearly indicated his opposition to national standards. "With the exception of moving sources of pollution (for example, automobiles)," he stated, "I do not favor fixed national emission standards for individual sources of pollution." [38] The administration chose to ignore Muskie's opposition.

On January 30, 1967, President Johnson delivered a message to the Congress on "Protecting Our Natural Heritage." The message gave primary emphasis to the air pollution problem and called for major new legislation to be known as the Air Quality Act of 1967. The proposed act was to include national emission standards for major industrial sources of pollution and the establishment of regional air quality commissions to enforce pollution control measures in "regional airsheds" which cut across state and local boundaries. The president also called for federal assistance to initiate state automobile pollution inspection systems, a major increase in the federal air pollution research effort, and federal registration of motor fuel additives such as tetra-ethyl lead.

Between February and May, Senator Muskie held an extensive series of hearings covering all aspects of the administration bill. Industry spokesmen were unanimous in their opposition to national emission standards, and Muskie indicated his own reservations about the proposal. The whole question of standard-setting was the subject of considerable confusion and dispute. In addition to the national standards for selected industries, the administration proposal gave authority to the regional commissions to set standards for their particular regions. The commissions were to be staffed and financed by the federal government, and the secretary of HEW was given complete authority to review and modify their proposed standards. Thus the bill envisioned a dominant federal role in the establishment and enforcement of air quality standards.

A further controversy which ran throughout the hearings and which had a significant impact on consideration of the bill in Muskie's committee was the problem of sulfur oxides. Early in March HEW had made a series of decisions which put the department on record as favoring sulfur standards so stringent that industry claimed they threatened to eliminate the use of coal in the nation's largest metropolitan areas. Jennings Randolph, the chairman of the Senate Public Works Committee, came from the coal-producing state of West Virginia and was not insensitive to the interests of the coal industry. Randolph was Muskie's chairman, the air and water pollution group being a subcommittee of the Public Works Committee. Thus Randolph was in a key position to influence the legislation. During April he submitted a set of extensive amendments to the bill which, among other major changes, would have removed the air pollution program from the Public Health Service and placed it under a separate Air Quality Administration.

On July 15, Muskie reported a bill which clearly bore the committee's imprint. National emission standards were relegated to a two-year study to be conducted by HEW. The regional commissions were retained, but instead of being instruments of the federal government their standard-setting function was made part of a process which rested heavily on state initiative. This process, developed by Muskie and clearly drawing on the precedent of the 1965 Water Quality Act, gave the states 90 days from the time HEW issued criteria for a specific pollutant to file a letter of intent stating that within 180 days they would establish standards for that pollutant, such standards to be applicable in air quality control regions which would be designated by the secretary of HEW for each state. The secretary of HEW would have the power to approve the state standards and to set such standards himself if a state failed to comply with the deadline. The Muskie bill passed the Senate by unanimous vote.

The House sharply reduced the large increase in appropriation authorizations contained in the Senate bill and made several other minor changes. Much of the House debate was concerned with whether California should be permitted to set more stringent emission standards on motor vehicles than the standards set by the federal government. The Senate bill had allowed California to retain its more stringent standards, but the House Interstate and Foreign Commerce Committee, in a move prompted by Representative John Dingell of Michigan and the automobile manufacturers, had deleted the Senate language. The Dingell amendment provoked an extraordinary degree of public opposition among California residents, and the California congressional delegation succeeded in having the House committee's decision reversed by a floor vote of 152-to-58, thus restoring the Senate language allowing California to set its own standards.

A conference committee had little difficulty in reconciling the

House and Senate versions, and on November 14 the compromise version was approved by both Houses. On November 21, 1967, President Johnson signed the Air Quality Act into law.

The act the president signed was a highly complex piece of legislation, which bore the marks of the powerful forces that had helped to shape it. Many of the president's original recommendations had survived the congressional process. Assistance for state vehicle inspection, registration of fuel additives, a greatly accelerated research effort, and a regional orientation for standard-setting were all contained in the final bill. The influence of Senator Randolph had also left its mark on the bill. A separate authorization for pollution research, a requirement that HEW reconsider its criteria for sulfur oxides and that all future criteria be accompanied by recommended control techniques, the establishment of several advisory committees to HEW to ensure that industry opinion would be heard, and changes in the enforcement procedure to ensure that all concerned parties would be represented were among the contributions made by the senator from West Virginia.

The greatest contribution to the bill had come from Senator Muskie. He had shaped the standard-setting procedures so as to place direct responsibility on both the states and the federal government. Before the states could act, HEW had to designate the regional air quality control regions and issue criteria and recommended control techniques. Furthermore, the secretary of HEW was given the power to seek a federal court injunction against any kind of polluter if he had reason to believe that an air pollution emergency existed in any particular city. The states were responsible for the actual setting of the standards, subject to HEW approval, and for devising and carrying out a plan for their enforcement.

THE 1970 CLEAN AIR AMENDMENTS [39]

The procedures contained in the 1967 act proved to be as time-consuming and ineffective as those contained in previous legislation. Few of the deadlines contained in the act were met. Between 1967 and December 1970 only 21 state implementation plans had been submitted, and none had been approved by the federal government.[40] Without the implementation plans there was no enforcement of state and federal standards. Meanwhile, public interest in pollution control was building to massive proportions, and by 1970 air and water pollution were top-ranking national issues.

Another factor which influenced the political climate in 1970 was public mistrust of the automobile industry.[41] Ralph Nader's book, *Unsafe at Any Speed*,[42] had cast doubt on the safety of Detroit's products. The subsequent attempt of General Motors to intimidate Nader backfired spectacularly, with the giant auto maker finally having to publicly apologize to Nader. At about the same time the Justice Department began an investigation to determine whether the automobile companies had conspired to prevent the installation of air pollution control devices. The investigation ended in 1969 with a consent decree which at least implied that the big three manufacturers had in fact illegally worked together to thwart air pollution control.

The authorizations contained in the 1967 version of the Clean Air Act expired in 1970 and, given the general climate and the lack of progress under the old act, it was clear that major revisions of the law would be proposed. The House Subcommittee on Public Health and Welfare of the Committee on Interstate and Foreign Commerce, spurred by Representative Paul Rogers, held hearings in December 1969 on new air pollution legislation. In January 1970 President Nixon delivered his State of the Union Message, and it was clear from the Message that the White House had jumped on the environmental bandwagon. Senator Muskie's prominence as a leading contender to oppose Nixon for the presidency in 1972 undoubtedly helped convince the president that it would be politically fruitful to become heavily involved in the pollution issue which was closely identified with Muskie.

The State of the Union Message was followed in February by a Special Message on the Environment. Along with the Special Message, the administration sent to Congress a strong series of amendments to the Clean Air Act. They called for the establishment of national air quality standards and national emission standards for new or hazardous air pollution sources. The proposal for national emission standards was similar to what the

Johnson Administration had recommended and Muskie had rejected in 1967. With respect to automobiles, the administration amendments strengthened the testing and enforcement provisions of the law and authorized the federal government to register and regulate fuels and fuel additives, such as lead in gasoline. However, they did not change the basic auto emission standard-setting procedures which had been established in 1965.

In March, Muskie introduced and held hearings on several amendments to the Clean Air Act, but they were minor changes compared to those contained in the Nixon bill. The joint federal-state standard-setting procedure was retained, Muskie apparently being no more favorable to national standards than he had been three years earlier. Meanwhile, the House subcommittee held further hearings, focusing primarily on the bill which had been submitted by the administration. On June 3, the full House committee reported out a bill which followed the general lines of the administration bill but which shortened several of the deadlines, added sections on aircraft emissions and federal facilities, declared each state to be an air quality control region, and contained other changes which generally strengthened the proposal. When the bill came to the House floor on June 10, an effort was made to make the provisions relating to automobile emissions more stringent but the House rejected most of these amendments and passed the committee version of the bill by a vote of 374-to-1.

By mid-June the pressure on Muskie was intense. Public concern over pollution had reached new heights on Earth Day in April and showed no signs of abating. The president appeared to be taking leadership on the pollution issue, threatening to undercut one of Muskie's strong points as a presidential contender. The usually conservative and slow-moving House had moved with considerable speed and passed a bill which was even stronger than Nixon's. As a final blow, in May one of Ralph Nader's task forces had published a report on air pollution which called into question Muskie's entire record in pollution legislation. "Muskie," the report said, "is, of course, the chief architect of the disastrous Air Quality Act of 1967. That fact alone would warrant his being stripped of his title as 'Mr. Pollution Control.' But the Senator's passivity since 1967 in the face of an ever worsening air pollution crisis compounds his earlier failure. Muskie has rarely interceded on behalf of accelerated pollution efforts . . . Perhaps the Senator should consider resigning his Chairmanship of the Subcommittee and leave the post to someone who can devote more time and energy to the task." [43]

Stung by these criticisms and spurred by the existing pressures, the Muskie subcommittee drafted a bill which far exceeded both the House and administration proposals in stringency. On August 25, 1970, it reported a bill to the full Public Works Committee which required automobile emissions by 1975 to be 90 per cent below 1970 emissions. It contained national air quality and emission standards for stationary sources, and required that the state implementation plans be designed to achieve the national air quality standards by 1975. The authorizations for appropriations were considerably higher than those in the House bill, a citizen suit provision had been added, and numerous other changes had been made to make the bill "tougher" than any air pollution measure which had ever been introduced.

Although subject to intense industry pressure to weaken the proposal, and especially to modify the automobile emission standards, the full committee made few changes in the Muskie bill and reported it out on August 25. It reached the Senate floor September 21, and passed unanimously the following day.

The conference committee appointed to reconcile the House and Senate versions was subjected to heavy lobbying by industry, the conservation groups, and the administration. The key question was the auto standards, and the administration, through Secretary of Health, Education, and Welfare Elliot Richardson, sent the committee a formal letter requesting that the auto standards be relaxed. But public opinion and the pressure of the environmental groups proved sufficient to counterbalance the auto industry and the White House. On December 16 the committee reached agreement on a bill which basically followed the lines of the Muskie proposal, including the 1975 auto emission standards. On December 18, the bill passed both houses by a voice vote. The president signed the bill into law on December 31, 1970. In a typically petty political move, the White House did not invite Muskie to attend the signing ceremony. A new set of ground rules for air pollution control thus went into effect, setting the stage for many battles to come.

THE ENERGY SUPPLY AND ENVIRONMENTAL COORDINATION ACT OF 1974

The first major battles which resulted in legislative changes in the Clean Air Act arose from the severe energy shortage that hit the country in the fall of 1973. Air pollution controls were a minor factor in the energy shortage, although they had made some contribution to the gasoline shortage by forcing power plants to switch from coal to oil. The power companies, the automobile industry, and the coal and oil companies saw the energy crisis as an opportunity to weaken the provisions of the Clean Air Act.

There was agreement in Congress that some modifications in the clean air rules were necessary to allow flexibility to deal with the energy problem. The question was how drastically to change the Clean Air Act, and the proposals ranged from outright repeal of large portions of the Act, to minor modifications affecting the timing of the law's provisions. Largely due to the strong position taken by Senator Muskie against the more drastic proposals, the bill that was finally enacted made few changes in the basic structure of the air pollution law.

The Energy Supply and Environmental Coordination Act of 1974, which was signed by the president in June of 1974, amended the Clean Air Act in two important ways. First, it allows EPA to temporarily suspend emission limits applied to stationary sources. The authority to give such suspension is hedged by several important restrictions relating to the timing of the suspensions and the situations in which they can be given. The law also prohibits suspensions that would result in a violation of the primary air quality standards. The suspensions must be decided for each particular source, i.e., a suspension can be given for a particular power plant, but not for all power plants.

The second important change made by the 1974 legislation

related to the automobile standards. The Act extends all of the 1975 interim auto emission standards through 1976; allows a one-year extension of the 1977 standards for hydrocarbons and carbon monoxide, subject to EPA approval and establishment of new interim standards for 1977; and limits nitrogen oxides emissions to 2 grams per mile in 1977.

The 1974 Act did not settle many of the controversies that have arisen as a result of the implementation of the 1970 Clean Air Act. For example, it is still unclear to what extent the Act allows air quality to be lowered in areas that are now cleaner than the EPA standards. It is also a matter of dispute whether power plants and other large stationary sources can use "intermittent controls," controls that go into effect only when weather conditions make it likely that the air quality standards will be violated. These and other matters will probably be the subject of further amendments to the Clean Air Act.

Part II

THE POLICYMAKERS

CHAPTER 3

Congress

CONGRESSIONAL ORGANIZATION AND ENVIRONMENTAL POLICY

THE WORK of Congress in formulating environmental policy can be divided into three areas: the formulation and approval of legislation; the conducting of oversight hearings and investigations; and the reviewing and approval of appropriations. In the environmental field the legislative function has been the most important congressional activity. The relevant congressional committees have not hesitated to rewrite proposed legislation submitted to them by the Executive Branch.

It is important to understand the way in which Congress is organized to deal with environmental policy. The work of the Congress is done almost entirely by committees. It is a rare occurrence for a committee decision to be overturned by the full House or Senate. Congressmen are assigned to committees by the Democratic Steering Committee and the Republican Committee on Committees in the Senate and by the Democratic Committee on Committees (comprised of the Democratic members of the House Ways and Means Committee) and the Republican Committee on Committees in the House. Members of both houses submit their preferences with regard to committee assignment to the above committees, but factors other than preference enter into the final assignment. Loyalty to the party leadership is an important criterion. For example, Senator Muskie of Maine was assigned to the Public Works Committee partially as a punishment for having voted against Lyndon Johnson, then the Majority Leader, on a controversy over the Senate cloture rule.[1]

Almost every committee of both the House and Senate exercises some role in environmental policy making. This multiplicity of relevant committees often delays or stalemates decision-making. As can be seen from Table 3.1., at least 22 congressional committees have important environmental responsibilities. Within each House there is also little communication among committees. To take the most significant example, the substantive committees responsible for formulating legislation and reviewing the progress and problems of the agencies administering the programs have little contact or influence over the appropriations subcommittees which give money for the same legislation and agencies.

The problems caused by the involvement of numerous congressional committees in pollution control legislation are accentuated by relations between the House and the Senate, which resemble the relations between two sovereign governments. Each House is jealous of its prerogatives and considers itself superior to the other. At times the rivalry manifests itself in an absence of contact and communication between the members or staffs of a committee in one House and its counterpart in the other. At other times it results in elaborate legislative maneuvers such as those that took place over water pollution legislation in the closing days of the 1968 Congressional session.

The numerous overlaps and conflicts among the committees with regard to the fragmented jurisdiction over environmental matters were clearly illustrated in 1972 when several important administration proposals were delayed because of jurisdictional disputes or overlaps between committees. The pesticides bill was referred to the Senate Commerce Committee after having been approved by the Agriculture Committee; the Noise Control Act was reviewed by both the Commerce and Public Works committees in the Senate; and the Environmental Financing Authority bill was referred to the Senate Banking, Housing, and Urban Affairs Committee after having been reported out by the Senate Public Works Committee. Looking at another aspect of the same problem, the EPA's activities are the responsibility of about fourteen different committees in the two houses of Congress. The Council on Environmental Quality is also faced with the same difficulty.

For the past five years Congress has ostensibly wished to create a Joint Committee on the Environment to have oversight responsibility over environmental problems in much the same way the Joint Economic Committee reviews economic policy. The proposed committee would not have authority to receive or report legislative measures, but it would receive and comment on the President's Annual Environmental Quality Report and it could also comment on legislative proposals submitted to standing committees. Thus, the committee would not significantly alleviate the problem of the variety of committees involved in environmental matters, but even this modest measure has been blocked by procedural trickery, a victim of committee rivalry for primacy in environmental policy.[2]

As in any institution, personalities are a critical factor in the operation of the Congress. Cooperation among the congressmen and among their staffs is often not visible to the outsider but it is undoubtedly what keeps the system functioning. More visible and spectacular are the conflicts and rivalries which mark certain aspects of environmental policy making in the Congress. Senators Henry Jackson and Edmund Muskie, chairmen of the two most important Senate environmental committees, have clashed frequently, most recently over the question of national land use policy. Even within the same committees, personal rivalries can cause problems. House action on the toxic substances bill was delayed for months because of a jurisdictional dispute between two subcommittee chairmen in the Interstate and Foreign Commerce Committee.

In the Senate, primary responsibility for air and water pollution control legislation is located in the Subcommittee on Air and Water Pollution Control of the Public Works Committee. The subcommittee is headed by Senator Edmund Muskie. In the House, the Subcommittee on Rivers and Harbors of the Public Works Committee deals with water pollution legislation, but air pollution matters are handled by the Committee on Interstate and Foreign Commerce.

In the ten years that Muskie has headed the Subcommittee on

Table 3.1. **Major Congressional Committees and Subcommittees Involved in Environmental Policy**

Committee	Chairman	Environmental Responsibilities
SENATE		
1. Agriculture and Forestry	Herman Talmadge	Agriculture and forestry generally; pesticides; soil conservation
Subcom. on Environment, Soil Conservation and Forestry	James Eastland	Soil conservation and forestry
2. Appropriations	John McClellan	Appropriations
Subcom. on Agriculture, Environmental and Consumer Protection	Gale McGee	USDA, EPA, FDA, and CEQ appropriations
3. Banking, Housing, and Urban Affairs	John Sparkman	Urban affairs generally, housing
4. Commerce	Warren Magnuson	Interstate and foreign commerce generally; fisheries and wildlife; marine pollution
Subcom. on Environment	Philip Hart	Toxic and hazardous substances; noise
5. Foreign Relations	J. W. Fulbright	Foreign relations
Subcom. on Oceans and Int'l Environment	Claiborne Pell	Int'l environmental treaties
6. Government Operations	Sam Ervin	General oversight; governmental organization; research
7. Interior and Insular Affairs	Henry Jackson	Public lands; supply of materials and fuels; water resources; parks and recreation; NEPA
8. Labor and Public Welfare	Harrison Williams	Health research and regulation; occupational health
9. Public Works	Jennings Randolph	Pollution control
Subcom. on Air and Water Pollution	Edmund Muskie	Air and water pollution; solid waste; noise

HOUSE

Committee	Member	Jurisdiction
1. Agriculture	W. R. Poage	Agriculture and forestry generally; pesticides; soil conservation
2. Appropriations	George Mahon	Appropriations
Subcom. on Agriculture, Environmental and Consumer Protection	Jamie Whitten	USDA, EPA, FDA, and CEQ appropriations
3. Banking and Currency	Wright Patman	Housing
4. Education and Labor	Carl Perkins	Occupational health
5. Government Operations	Chet Holifield	General oversight, governmental organization
Subcom. on Conservation and Natural Resources	Henry Reuss	Water pollution oversight
6. Interior and Insular Affairs	James Haley	Public lands; supply of materials and fuels; water resources; parks and recreation
7. Interstate and Foreign Commerce	Harley Staggers	Public health, air pollution
Subcom. on Commerce and Finance	John Moss	Toxic substances; consumer protection
Subcom. on Public Health and Environment	Paul Rogers	Air pollution
8. Merchant Marine and Fisheries	Lenonor Sullivan	Fisheries and wildlife; oceanography
Subcom. on Fisheries and Wildlife Conservation and the Environment	John Dingell	Fisheries and wildlife; NEPA
Subcom. on Oceanography	Thomas Downing	Oceanography, marine pollution, marine sanctuaries
9. Rules	Ray Madden	All legislation
10. Science and Aeronautics	Olin Teague	Research; technology assessment
11. Ways and Means	Wilbur Mills	Environment-related taxation

JOINT COMMITTEES

Committee	Member	Jurisdiction
1. Atomic Energy	Rep. Melvin Price	Atomic energy

Air and Water Pollution he has succeeded in becoming the dominant congressional figure in pollution control. He has not hesitated to revise drastically administration proposals, and it is now a matter of some pride on the part of his subcommittee that administration bills rarely emerge from committee in the same form in which they were submitted. Muskie has had no trouble in obtaining the support of the rest of the Senate for his proposals, and the House has generally followed his lead, especially on air pollution matters.

The House Interstate and Foreign Commerce Committee, which has jurisdiction over air pollution bills, probably deals with more legislation than any other congressional committee. Its responsibilities include public health, transportation, securities and exchange regulations, and numerous other matters. Air pollution legislation constitutes a very small part of the committee's workload, and Harley Staggers, current chairman of the committee, has not shown any particular interest in the subject. His constituents have a strong stake in protecting the coal industry, but Staggers has usually been able to rely on his fellow West Virginian, Jennings Randolph, the chairman of the Senate Public Works Committee, to watch out for the interests of the coal companies.

Until 1964, Ken Roberts headed the Health and Safety Subcommittee of the Interstate and Foreign Commerce Committee. Roberts was one of the leaders in promoting the early air pollution legislation and his subcommittee developed considerable expertise on pollution.[3] However, after Roberts's defeat at the polls in 1964 no member of the committee has shown similar interest, and in recent years the House has generally acquiesced in Senate decisions on air pollution. Representative Paul Rogers of Florida is now the member of the House subcommittee who is most knowledgeable about air pollution. Representing a conservative district, he has sometimes been protective of industry.

Water pollution legislation in the House is the responsibility of the Rivers and Harbors Subcommittee of the Public Works Committee, which, since 1955, has been headed by John A. Blatnik of Minnesota. Blatnik, a liberal Democrat, was the prime mover behind the 1956 and 1961 water pollution acts.

However, in recent years he has been somewhat overshadowed by Muskie in the Senate.

The relationship between the House and Senate Public Works Committees with respect to water pollution demonstrates the vital role played by individuals in shaping the orientation of a committee. At least until 1963, while Robert Kerr was head of the Senate committee, Blatnik took the lead in the formulation of water pollution legislation. Kerr was not fully convinced of the need for such legislation, and Blatnik played the role of the liberal initiator, fighting the Senate forces of conservatism. As illustrated by the battles over water pollution during 1967 and 1968, the roles have now been reversed. Kerr has been replaced by Muskie, and the Senate committee is now the initiating force. The House committee has become a conservative force, more protective of industry, although sometimes, as in 1972, compensating for this by urging greater spending for waste treatment grants.

LEGISLATION

Since the early years of the Truman Administration, most major legislative proposals have been brought to the attention of the public and the Congress by being included in the president's legislative program.[4] This program for each year is outlined in the State of the Union Message and then described in more detail in particular messages to the Congress dealing with selected policy areas such as environment, health, or energy. The messages are accompanied or followed by draft legislation which is usually introduced by the relevant committee chairman in each house, or by the ranking minority member of the committee if Congress is not controlled by the president's party. The president thus sets much of the agenda for congressional business at the start of each session.

The process within the Executive Branch for deciding on the president's legislative program has varied depending on the president and the types of issues under consideration. During the Truman and Eisenhower years the executive branch agencies suggested legislative proposals to the Budget Bureau, and the

Bureau along with the White House staff then wrote the presidential messages. Under Kennedy and Johnson, legislative proposals came primarily from special task forces established each year for the purpose of suggesting new legislative initiatives in particular policy areas. The composition of these task forces varied. In the Johnson Administration, one environmental quality task force consisted of nationally known figures from outside the government; another year the group was composed of "working-level" bureaucrats; and in several years the task force members were cabinet or subcabinet level bureaucrats.[5]

President Nixon relied primarily on White House staff and other executive office agencies for his legislative initiatives. His 1970 environmental legislative program was put together by an interagency task force headed by a White House staff member. With the creation of the Council on Environmental Quality (CEQ), the president turned to this new institution, and in 1971, 1972, and 1973 the Council was in charge of developing the environmental legislation and formulating the president's environmental message. The small size of the Council's staff made it heavily reliant on other agencies for expertise, but it also allowed the Council to prevent ideas from becoming diluted in the bureaucratic clearance process within an operating department, and CEQ's removal from operating programs freed it from entrenched agency positions and permitted it to develop new ways of solving environmental problems.

The path leading from an idea to a law is a long and tortuous one in the U.S. government. Usually there are lengthy negotiations in an agency or inter-agency group over the drafting of a bill. Once a bill is written, it must be reviewed and commented upon by all concerned federal agencies. When all the comments have been received by the Office of Management and Budget (OMB) there are further negotiations to try to settle differences. The process takes several months, and thus legislation which is to be sent to Congress in January or February must be drafted in September or October. The Congressional process of approving legislation takes much longer and the mortality rate for new proposals is high in both the executive branch and Congress. Of the 35 legislative proposals submitted by CEQ to OMB in 1972, only 8 finally became part of the president's program. Of the more than 25 environmental proposals submitted by the administration to Congress between 1970 and 1972, only 9 had become law by the end of the congressional session in October 1972.

It may be that the rapid pace of developments in the environmental area and the creation of new executive branch institutions have shifted some of the initiative for developing legislative ideas away from the Congress. Many of the presidential proposals are based on ideas or bills which have previously been introduced in Congress. However, of the five major environmental acts passed by the 92d Congress (water quality amendments, noise, pesticides, ocean dumping, and coastal zone management) all were based on bills developed almost entirely by the executive branch. One act (coastal zone management), however, was an executive proposal made to the prior Congress, and had been withdrawn to allow presentation of a broader land use bill. Several minor acts (marine mammals, the Tank Vessel Act Amendments in the Port and Waterways Safety Act, and the marine sanctuaries title of the Ocean Dumping Act) were initiated entirely by Congress.

Once the president has submitted draft legislation, the Congressional committees have not hesitated to mold it more to their own liking. The water quality amendments were completely re-written in the Senate by the Muskie subcommittee and in the House by the Public Works Committee. The pesticides bill was markedly changed by the Agriculture committee. However, the noise and ocean dumping bills emerged from the congressional process with few changes from the administration bills.

Partisan alignments have had little influence on congressional legislative action on environmental issues. Rarely have either the committee or floor votes on environmental measures divided along party lines. In the most dramatic instance of a potentially partisan issue in the past few years, Nixon's veto of the 1972 Water Pollution Control Act Amendments, a majority of Republicans in both houses voted to override the Republican President's veto.

The complexity of the legislative process can best be illustrated by examining an actual example. The idea for what eventually became the Toxic Substances Control Act originated within the Council on Environmental Quality. During the summer and early fall, the Council's staff collected information on hazardous chemicals not being controlled under the air and water pollution statutes, on the number of new chemicals being marketed annually, and on other matters related to the toxic substances problem.[6]

On October 1, 1970, the Council held a meeting with representatives of about a half dozen federal agencies to discuss the outlines of a proposed toxic substances bill. This was followed by a second similar meeting a few weeks later, and throughout October and November consultations were held with a variety of experts about the toxic substances problem. Simultaneously, the Council set to work drafting an actual bill. The bill went through a number of draft versions within the Council. By early December, the Council had a draft which was acceptable to it, and informal negotiations were initiated with the Department of Commerce, the agency most likely to oppose the bill within the administration. These negotiations were long and heated. A number of changes were made in the bill, but Commerce was still not satisfied with the proposal.

On January 7, the Council transmitted the latest draft of the bill to the Office of Management and Budget, which in turn circulated it for comment to all interested federal agencies. A copy was also sent to the White House. The agency and White House reactions precipitated a month of very intensive negotiations over the bill's content. Most of the negotiations were "refereed" by OMB. The pace of the negotiations can be illustrated by the fact that new drafts of the bill were prepared by the Council on January 22, 25, 28, February 2, and February 7. There were many points of controversy, but the key one was whether the Environmental Protection Agency (EPA) (which would administer the bill if it became law) would have the power to impose regulations on a new chemical before it was commercially produced. CEQ and EPA strongly favored this authority, while Commerce and the White House staff opposed it. Finally, on February 3, the question was appealed directly to the president. He decided against including any pre-marketing authority in the bill.

On February 8, 1971 the president delivered his second annual Message on the Environment. The toxic substances bill was supposed to be sent to Congress with the Message, but on the morning of February 9, meetings were still being held to decide on the wording of key sections of the bill. Finally, two days later, agreement was reached on all parts of the bill and it was sent by EPA Administrator William Ruckelshaus to the president of the Senate and the speaker of the House. The Administration bill was introduced as H.R. 5276 in the House by Representative Harley Staggers on March 1, and as S. 1478 in the Senate by Senator Philip Hart on April 1.

The staff of the Senate Commerce Committee went to work on the bill almost immediately. They produced a complete rewrite of the bill, containing much stronger and more sweeping provisions regulating both new and existing chemicals, introduced by Senator William Spong on July 27.[7] In August the Environment Subcommittee of the Senate Commerce Committee held two days of hearings on the Spong and Administration bills. In October and November the subcommittee met several times in executive session, and in February 1972 the staff produced a working draft of a new bill. The staff bill substituted for Spong's provisions, which would have required EPA approval of new chemicals, a requirement that new chemicals be submitted to EPA ninety days before being marketed. Unless EPA proposed a regulation restricting the chemical it could be marketed. After another executive session in which Spong accepted the language of the staff bill, the subcommittee reported a bill to the full Commerce Committee. In April the full committee met, and on May 5 it reported out a revised version of S. 1478 which closely resembled the February staff draft.[8]

Throughout this time, the House had taken no action. When first introduced, the bill had been referred to the House Committee on Interstate and Foreign Commerce. The House Commerce Committee had a busy schedule and did not consider the toxic substances legislation to have high priority. The committee was also faced with a jurisdictional dispute between the subcommittees chaired by Representatives John Moss and Pat Rogers. Each man believed that the bill should be referred to his subcommittee. Finally, prodded by the White House and the impending Senate action, the bill was given to Representative Moss. Once this obstacle was overcome, action was rapid.

The Moss subcommittee held hearings in May, and on August 7 it reported a bill to the full committee.[9]

Meanwhile, on May 30, S. 1478 had passed the Senate by a vote of 77-to-0. An industry sponsored amendment to soften the pre-market notification provision was defeated 42-to-28.

On September 28, the House Commerce Committee reported out its own bill.[10] Representative Staggers, the committee chairman, announced that there would not be enough time left in the 92d Congress for a conference between the House and Senate.

The House approved the bill on October 13 by a vote of 240-to-61. The next day the Senate voted 29-to-22 agreeing to the House bill with two amendments—one on pre-market clearance and the other on the relationship of the toxic substances bill to other laws. When the Senate bill reached the House the following day there was an objection to bringing it up under the unanimous consent provision. This foreclosed the possibility of further House action in the time remaining, and on October 18 the 92d Congress came to a close with the toxic substances bill still not enacted.

In January 1973, with the opening of the 93d Congress, the process started over again. The administration submitted a somewhat strengthened version of its original bill.[11] Both the House and Senate committees held hearings and then marked up their bills. When it became clear that both the House and Senate versions would contain some type of pre-market control by EPA, the administration finally reversed its position and endorsed a limited pre-market screening provision. The Senate bill was reported out of committee June 26,[12] and passed by the Senate July 18. The House bill was reported out June 29,[13] and passed the House July 23. A conference committee was formed to settle the differences between the House and Senate versions. The chances of the conference committee reaching agreement before the close of the 93d Congress seem slim. Industry pressure and the reluctance of the House conferees to compromise have prevented any serious attempt to agree on a bill.

APPROPRIATIONS

The power of the purse belongs to the Congress, although, as with legislation, the initial input to the appropriations process comes from the president. In February of each year the president submits to Congress his budget requesting money for each of the federal agencies for the fiscal year beginning in July. Under the congressional rules of the game, the House Appropriations Committee is the first to consider the budget requests, and only after it has acted do the proposed appropriation bills go to the Senate.

Traditionally, the House has reduced the president's requests and the Senate Appropriations Committee acts as an "appeals court", listening to the financial woes of the agencies and restoring funds cut by the House or adding amounts to the president's requests. Differences between the Senate and House committees are resolved in a conference committee appointed for the purpose.

The most influential actors in the congressional appropriations process are the subcommittees of the House Appropriations Committee. The review of the president's requests is conducted by the subcommittees, and the full committee only rarely changes a decision reached by the subcommittee. In 1971, the House Appropriations Committee reorganized the jurisdiction of its subcommittees, and responsibility for the budgets of EPA, CEQ, and the Food and Drug Administration was given to the subcommittee reviewing the Department of Agriculture budget. This subcommittee is chaired by Jamie Whitten, a congressman from Mississippi best known in the environmental community for his ardent defense of the utility of chemical pesticides. Initially, there were widespread fears that Whitten would sharply limit expenditures for environmental improvement. As can be seen from Table 3.2., these fears have not fully materialized, although the key position held by Whitten has undoubtedly imposed a degree of caution on the bureaucracy which otherwise would not have existed.

Whitten has increasingly used his position to criticize and to try to influence the work of EPA and CEQ. His committee's report on the fiscal 1974 EPA appropriations stated, "The hearing record this year shows strong evidence that actions by the Environmental Protection Agency . . . have contributed to the energy crisis, have increased the damage from floods because of the delay of flood and soil conservation projects, have increased the cost of production of food thereby contributing to higher consumer prices, and have greatly increased the danger to human health by banning DDT, which according to testimony has never injured a human being. In addition, actions by the agency have placed American industry and American agriculture at a competitive disadvantage both at home and abroad." [14] One might infer from this that Mr. Whitten does not fully support the actions which EPA has taken.

Table 3.2. **Appropriations for Pollution Control Programs**
(excluding waste treatment grants)
(in $ millions)

Fiscal Year	President's Request	House Mark	Senate Mark	Final Cong'l Budget	% of Cong'l Change from President's Request
1969	237	204	211	206*	− 13
1970	247	253	255	254	+ 3
1971	267	262	277	271	+ 2
1972	451	425	459	441	− 2
1973	446**	467†	492	467	+ 5
1974	490††	530	569	522	+ 6

* The final Congressional budget included an additional $16 m for other environmental control activities.
** Excludes $35 m proposed for later transmittal.
† Excludes $30 m appropriation in House bill for transfer to Department of Agriculture for REAP program.
†† Excludes $96 m in contract authority for Sec. 208 of the Federal Water Pollution Control Act.

Tables 3.2 and 3.3. show that congressional changes from the president's total budget figure for pollution control programs, with the exception of the water pollution waste treatment grants, have been minor. However, there have been a few significant shifts made among the programs that together make up the total. Also, the history of the waste treatment grant appropriations has been stormy, with the president traditionally trying to hold down expenditures and the Congress insisting on the need to give the localities more funds to treat their domestic sewage.

If measured in terms of dollar reductions in agency budgets, the Office of Management and Budget in the Executive Office of the President is probably a more influential budgetary force than the congressional appropriations committees. The OMB, in its consideration of funds for air and water pollution control, is not subject to the same degree of public pressure as is the Congress. It has therefore felt more at liberty to reduce agency requests.

The influence of public pressure was demonstrated in the fall

Table 3.3. **Appropriations for Water Pollution Waste Treatment Grants**
(in $ millions)

Fiscal Year	Authori- zation	President's Request	House Mark	Senate Mark	Final Cong'l Budget	% Cong'l Change from President's Request
1969	700	225	203	225	214	− 5
1970	1,000	214	600	1,000	800	+274
1971	1,250	4,000*	1,000	1,000	1,000	− −*
1972	2,750	2,000	2,000	2,000	2,000	0
1973	5,000	2,000	1,900	1,900	1,900	− 5
1974**	6,000	− −	− −	− −	− −	− −

* For fiscal year 1971, the President requested $4 billion in contract authority to be spent over a four-year period. The Congress rejected the proposal for contract authority.
** Comparable figures for fiscal year 1974 are not obtainable for several reasons: the Federal Water Pollution Control Act Amendments of 1972 contain several different authorizations related to waste treatment grants, and the primary authorization is in the form of contract authority; there is an ongoing dispute over Presidential impoundment of the waste treatment grant funds; and the Executive Branch and Congress follow different budgeting practices with respect to contract authority—the President's budget contains only the dollar amount of the authority which can be obligated whereas the Appropriations Committees' reports contain the amount appropriated to meet the obligations.

of 1969 by an extraordinary reversal of the trend toward more stringent review of pollution budgets. President Nixon had supported the Johnson Administration's budget request of $214 million in fiscal 1970 for waste treatment plant construction grants, the same level of funding as in 1969. Under intense pressure from a "Citizens' Crusade for Clean Water," 222 members of the House (including at least 38 Republicans) signed a petition calling for an appropriation of $1 billion, the full authorized amount. The House Appropriations Committee, responding to the same pressures, sent to the full House a recommendation of $600 million, almost three times the administration request. The White House announced that it was willing to compromise and agree to $750 million, but the proponents of the $1 billion figure, operating on the same faulty intelligence as the White House, rejected the compromise. When the vote came on the House floor, an amendment calling for the full $1 billion was defeated, 148-to-146, and the House approved the committee's recommendation of $600 million.[15] The Senate voted the full $1 billion, and the conference committee compromised on a final appropriation of $800 million.

Increasingly in recent years the president has been exercising the last word as well as the first with respect to appropriations. For many years the president's budget office has allocated appropriated funds to the federal agencies on a quarterly basis to insure that they do not spend more than they have been appropriated. At first on rare occasions, but now with increasing frequency, the allocation power has been extended to include the authority to withhold appropriated funds altogether and return them to the Treasury. Under the Nixon Administration funds had been withheld both because the president disapproved of a particular program and as a general economic measure to reduce or slow down the rate of expenditures. In effect, the president had gained, without the benefit of a specific statute, the right to have an item veto over appropriations. Such a veto has been exercised over a variety of environmental programs. In fiscal year 1973, the president withheld $400 million from the Department of Housing and Urban Development's appropriation for sewer and water grants to local communities, $270 million from land and water conservation activities of the Interior Department, and $210 million from the Department of Agriculture's Rural Environmental Assistance Program.

The most notable case of presidential impoundment has come with respect to funds authorized under the Federal Water Pollution Control Act of 1972. Sec. 205(a) and Sec. 207 of that Act authorize the allotment and appropriation of $5 billion for fiscal year 1973, $6 billion for 1974, and $7 billion for 1975 to be available to assist state sewage treatment works construction approved by EPA for federal funding. President Nixon originally vetoed the bill, and expressed concern that although the legislation conferred some technical spending discretion and flexibility on the executive, pressure for full funding would be so intense that funds approaching the maximum authorized amount would ultimately be paid out.[16] However, Congress passed the act over the president's veto. The president then ordered the EPA administrator to make available only $5 billion of the $11 billion appropriated by Congress for use over the next two years, and a regulation to that end became effective December 8, 1972.[17] In January 1974 he ordered EPA to commit only $4 billion of the $7 billion authorized for fiscal 1975, thus bringing the total withheld to $9 billion of the $18 billion authorized.

Numerous court cases have been filed challenging the allotment of less than the full sums authorized by the Act for treatment works construction grants. Two cases so far decided, order the full $11 billion allotment to be made; EPA in turn has filed a motion to stay those judgments pending appeal. In *City of New York* v. *Ruckelshaus*,[18] Judge Oliver Gasch held that the language and legislative history of the Act clearly indicated the intent of Congress to require allotment of the full sums authorized to be appropriated. A similar decision was reached in *Campaign Clean Water* v. *Ruckelshaus*,[19] with the effect of the Court's order restricted to Virginia. Neither decision deals with EPA's refusal to *obligate* (contract to pay out) the full amount of appropriated funds because the Federal Water Pollution Control Act was designed to grant executive discretion in controlling the rate of spending. Instead, the courts ordered only that the full allotments authorized must be made, so that the funds can be available for obligation to the states. The Supreme Court has agreed to hear the impoundment cases, but its decision will not come until late 1974 or early 1975.

By basing their decisions on the wording and legislative history of the specific statutes, the courts have avoided adjudicating the constitutional separation of powers issue of whether an appropriation is a mandate to spend or merely permission to spend. However, the impoundment issue has been partially settled by the enactment in June, 1974, of a budget reform act.[20] The act allows the president to impound funds temporarily unless the House or Senate passes a resolution calling for the funds to be spent. The president is not allowed to permanently withhold funds unless Congress passes a bill withdrawing the appropriations which provided the funds.[21]

CONGRESSIONAL OVERSIGHT

Aside from the legislative and appropriations functions, Congress reviews and oversees the activities of the executive branch. It may hold hearings to lay the basis for new legislation, undertake reviews of how existing legislation is working, or conduct investigations to uncover wrongdoing within the executive.

The oversight function has generally been neglected by Congress because it is considered less interesting and less politically fruitful than formulating and passing new legislation. Also, oversight is heavily dependent upon prying information out of the executive agencies which can be a difficult and painful process. Although a few congressmen have achieved spectacular political success through investigative hearings and other kinds of oversight functions, these men are the exception rather than the rule. Most committees are reluctant to spend much time on reviewing the implementation of laws, and when oversight hearings are held they tend to be rather shallow information-gathering sessions.

In recent years new pollution control legislation has been preceded by some oversight hearings to identify problem areas. Thus, for example, the 1972 Water Pollution Control Act Amendments were partially influenced by oversight hearings held by the House Public Works Committee during 1971. Similarly, the House Subcommittee on Public Health and Environment held several days of oversight hearings before considering what were to become the 1970 Clean Air Act Amendments.

Oversight hearings can also serve useful political purposes. When Muskie was the leading contender to run against Nixon in 1972, he announced a series of air pollution oversight hearings. As reason for the hearings he stated that he was "particularly concerned about the Administration's failure to support EPA as the leading agency for environmental protection. The Agency's efforts under the Clean Air Act of 1970 are being undermined in the White House." [22]

Congress is greatly assisted in its oversight duties by the General Accounting Office (GAO). GAO is the fiscal watchdog of Congress, and its primary mission is to review all government expenditures to insure that funds are not being misspent. For many years this mission was narrowly interpreted to mean that GAO should guard against fraud and other illegal acts. In recent years the concept of "misspent" has been broadened to include an examination of whether the funds are actually accomplishing the purposes for which they were appropriated. Thus the Office conducted an investigation of whether the waste treatment grant funds were significantly reducing water pollution.[23] It has also completed investigations of both air and water pollution enforcement and of agency compliance with the National Environmental Policy Act.[24]

The GAO reports are read carefully by the agencies under investigation and by the congressional committees with responsibility for the agency or program investigated. The changes brought about by GAO can be seen from the reports themselves, which usually include an account of agency actions taken during the course of the investigation to rectify the problems discovered by GAO.

The legislative process illustrates the wide dispersion of power brought about by the pluralistic political system. The president can attempt to bring some degree of centralization to the process of legislative formulation in the executive branch, but only at the cost of lowering the quality of the bills sent to the Hill. When the bills are considered by the Congress they are exposed to the many conflicting pressures of rival committees, differing legislative constituencies, and competing interest groups. A strong leader such as Muskie can serve as the central focus for such pressures and can exercise considerable influence on the final form of the legislation, but he must frequently defend his position against attempts to disperse his power, and he must constantly operate within the parameters set by the relevant political forces. The most important of these forces are public opinion and interest groups.

CHAPTER 4

Public Opinion and Interest Groups

THERE IS widespread agreement that the state of public opinion is one of the crucial factors in the campaign for cleaner air and water. In any society, the attitudes held by the general public form the ultimate parameters of governmental action. As Ido de Groot states, "After all, it is these attitudes, be they expressed as perceptions, opinions, beliefs, hopes, desires, wishes, or feelings, that, stably and in change, ultimately accrue into political decisionmaking and socially imposed ordered change. These collective societal attitudes . . . dictate what is feasible and necessary in society." [1]

In some situations the voting public may be the actual decisionmakers, and in such cases public opinion is obviously of crucial importance. The most common situations of this type are referenda on local or state bond issues for the construction of waste treatment plants and other water pollution control facilities. Water pollution control usually demands significant capital investments, and in most localities public approval is a requirement for such investments. If public opinion has not been educated to realize the need for pollution control, the control effort is doomed to failure.

Public opinion may also be considered an important factor in weighing the costs and benefits of pollution control. Decisions about pollution will inevitably be made in the political arena where public opinion weighs heavily, but even for the person who attempts to evaluate control decisions apart from political factors, people's opinions are an important consideration. The fact that people worry about pollution is a significant cost of pollution. Public opinion may also be the most reliable available indicator of the aesthetic and recreational costs of pollution.

We shall look at public opinion and the political process in terms of three stages—"wants," "demands," and "decisions." [2] A "want" in this context is some perceived dissatisfaction potentially within the sphere of governmental remedy. The perception of such wants does not in most cases lead to any political action. A "demand" occurs when a want is translated into a request or demand that the government take action to alleviate the problem. Thus a housewife may be annoyed by the soot which collects on her windowsill each morning. If she rests content with a few grumbles and the use of some soap she possesses a want. But if she writes her congressman or joins a citizen's group in an attempt to eliminate the cause of the soot, she has translated her want into a demand. The third stage in the public opinion process is the "decision" stage, which is the action or lack thereof taken by the government.

WANTS

Public concern over both air and water pollution has been rising rapidly. About three-fourths of the people in the United States today consider pollution to be a problem. The increase in this concern is shown in the polls conducted by the Opinion Research Corporation (ORC). For the past several years ORC has asked a nationwide sample, "Compared to other parts of the country, how serious, in your opinion, do you think the problem of water (air) pollution is in this area—very serious, somewhat serious, or not serious?" Whereas in 1965 only 13 per cent of the population thought that water pollution was a very serious problem, 38 per cent thought so in 1970.[3] The corresponding figure for air pollution rose from 10 per cent to 35 per cent.[4]

Table 4.1. **Public Opinion of Seriousness of Water Pollution Problem**

	Percentage of Population				
	1965	**1966**	**1967**	**1968**	**1970**
Very Serious	13	19	24	27	38
Somewhat Serious	22	30	28	31	36
Not Serious or No Opinion	65	51	48	42	26
	100	100	100	100	100
(n)	(1,077)	(2,308)	(1,047)	(2,079)	(2,168)

Source: Opinion Research Corporation, "Public Opinion Index" (Princeton, N.J., 1966, 1967, 1968, 1969, 1970).

Table 4.2. **Public Opinion of Seriousness of Air Pollution Problem**

	Percentage of Population				
	1965	**1966**	**1967**	**1968**	**1970**
Very Serious	10	19	27	25	35
Somewhat Serious	18	29	26	30	34
Not Serious or No Opinion	72	52	47	45	31
	100	100	100	100	100
(n)	(1,051)	(2,033)	(1,047)	(2,079)	(2,168)

Source: Opinion Research Corporation, "Public Opinion Index" (Princeton, N.J., 1966, 1967, 1968, 1969, 1970).

The percentage of the population concerned about the pollution problem ranks it as one of the major worries of the general public. Responses to questions asking people to rank pollution in comparison to other problems have varied widely, depending on when the question was asked, how it was phrased, and what kind of sample was questioned. In several studies of local areas, unemployment and juvenile delinquency outranked air pollution as a perceived community problem, but pollution was still considered one of the half dozen most serious problems.[5] In a study of St. Louis, except for the central-city area, air pollution outweighed problems associated with race.[6]

The major determinant of public concern with air pollution is the actual level of pollution prevalent in the area of residence.[7] Studies of both Buffalo, New York, and St. Louis demonstrated a high correlation between the level of pollution in the neighborhood and the seriousness with which people viewed the problem. The 1970 ORC study found that whereas only 18 per cent of rural people and 20 per cent of persons in small towns (pop. 2,500–99,999) thought that the air pollution problem was very serious, 31 per cent of persons in communities with populations of 100,000–999,999 and 65 per cent of those living in cities with populations over 1 million ranked air pollution as very serious. Since there is generally a correlation between the size of the community and the degree of air pollution, this would tend to confirm the Buffalo and St. Louis findings.

It is more difficult to measure the degree of water pollution which exists in particular communities or neighborhoods and there are no very good data to indicate whether public concern with water pollution correlates with the severity of the problem. One would not expect a significant association between place of residence and water pollution because exposure to water pollution is not normally experienced in the home, except in those rare instances when the taste or quality of drinking water is affected.

For both air and water pollution, concern with the problem increases as one moves higher up the socio-economic scale. The higher a person's income, the more education he has had, and the higher the status of his occupation, the more likely he is to view air and water pollution as serious problems.[8] The explanation for this lies partially in the varying degrees of exposure to information media, at least in the case of air pollution. People have to be taught that air pollution is bad for their health. One may even have to be taught to consider air pollution aesthetically unattractive. Thus, unlike such problems as unemployment or crime or poor housing, perception of air pollution as a problem is heavily dependent upon exposure to channels of information; and numerous studies have shown that those with higher incomes or education are exposed to more information.

One irony of the air pollution situation is that if control efforts become more successful, public opinion will be increasingly more difficult to arouse. The public responds to air pollution in the form of smoke and odor, the two forms of pollution which are perceptible to the senses, but probably not the two most damaging to health.[9] Sulfur oxides, nitrogen oxides, carbon monoxide, and other highly dangerous pollutants are neither seen nor smelled in the amounts usually found in ambient air.

Table 4.3. **Perceived Seriousness of Air and Water Pollution Related to Education and Income, 1968**

	Air Pollution % "very serious" % (n)	Water Pollution % "very serious" % (n)
Education		
Less than high school completed	23 (475)	21 (475)
High school completed	27 (363)	23 (363)
Some college	35 (199)	32 (199)
Income		
Under $5,000	21 (312)	17 (312)
$5,000–$6,999	24 (237)	19 (237)
$7,000–$9,999	31 (234)	29 (234)
$10,000 or over	33 (246)	32 (246)

Source: Opinion Research Corporation, "Public Opinion Index" (Princeton, N.J., 1968).

Thus, as initial control efforts reduce the smoke and odor problems the public may begin to believe that the problem has been solved, whereas in reality the most injurious forms of pollution may remain as prevalent as ever.

Perception of the water pollution problem probably arises from somewhat different factors than that of air pollution. Most forms of water pollution can be either seen or smelled and little education is necessary to be offended by a filthy river or angered by a sign which states that swimming is not allowed because of pollution. The correlation between high education and income and concern about the water pollution problem may relate to the differing degree of demand for various forms of recreation—swimming, fishing, sightseeing—which are likely to be endangered by pollution. Those with higher incomes engage in such activities more than those with lower incomes and thus they are more concerned about the pollution problem. In short, one might say that perception of air pollution is dependent on degree of education, whereas perception of water pollution is more dependent on amount of income.

This is not to say that perception of water pollution as a serious problem does not also depend on exposure to channels of communication. Governments at all levels and several nationwide private groups have devoted considerable time and energy in recent years to trying to convince the public of the dangers of pollution. Their success is demonstrated by the great increase in public concern in the past few years. Although degree of pollution may be the greatest single determinant of *variations* among different groups in the degree of concern about the problem, educational efforts and publicity given to the problem would seem to be the best explanation for the overall *amount* of public concern. Neither air nor water pollution has gotten so much worse in the past few years as to account for the great increase in public awareness.

What we have seen in the past few years is a common phenomenon of governmental bureaucracies supported by various interest groups utilizing large amounts of resources to bolster their own strength. The process is circular, at least up to a point, because as the bureaucracies gain support, they increase their ability to command resources of men and money, which in turn increases their ability to stimulate still further support. As the water pollution budget grows, the amount of money spent educating the public about the water pollution problem also increases. And as the educational effort succeeds, it results in pressure applied to Congress and the administration to devote still more funds to water pollution control. There is nothing necessarily evil about this; it is done by almost every unit of the federal government and by most agencies of state and local government.

The growth of public concern over the pollution problem may also involve some psychological factors. At a time when America is deeply divided on fundamental political questions, an issue like pollution which at least verbally unites everyone is not only of political value to officeseekers but also of psychological value to members of the general public. Thus people may stress concern with pollution as a way of avoiding thinking about more divisive matters. The unifying aspects of the issue are reinforced by perceptions of who or what is responsible for pollution. For many persons, at least among the more sophisticated segments of the public, pollution is a result of "technology." When technology is named as the villain nobody is offended, and "man against technology" seems to have much the same appeal that "man against nature" held in past years.

If public concern with pollution is to result in anything being done about the problem, then those who are concerned must also take some sort of constructive action. In most cases this action involves making demands upon some level of government. The wants, in other words, must be translated into demands.

DEMANDS

It requires a much higher degree of commitment and sophistication to do something about pollution (or any other public problem) than simply to worry about it. The problem must be seen as one which government or some other group can do something about; there must be knowledge about what kind of action an individual can take; and there must finally be a willingness to give the time and effort to take the action. Even if the action is only writing a letter to a congressman, these requirements are very difficult for the average American to meet.

In almost all the studies of public opinion on pollution a significant gap was found between those who were very concerned about pollution and those who had done anything about their concern.[10] The latter category was a very small percentage of the former. People were simply unaware of what could be done to control pollution. This same phenomenon probably helps to explain some of the seemingly inconsistent results obtained in various national opinion polls. When the Gallup Poll asked people in February 1968: "What do you think is the most important problem facing the country today?", the category of "sanitation: garbage, sewage" ranked a poor eleventh, considerably behind education, transportation, housing, and other issues.[11] But when people are presented with a specific list of governmental programs, air and water pollution consistently come out at or near the top in the public list of priorities. Thus the Harris Survey in April of 1967 found that more people favored expanding air and water pollution control than any other Federal programs, including aid to education, medical care, housing, and poverty.[12] The same results were obtained in a Trendex Poll in December 1967 and a Gallup Poll in October 1969.[13] In all of these polls the respondents were presented with a list of programs. It seems that when people are "cued in" to considering pollution control as a governmental activity they rate it very highly, but they do not ordinarily consider it in this light.

Although specific data for pollution issues are lacking, it is probably those with more education and higher incomes who are most likely to take some kind of action to promote clean air and clean water. Studies of other issues have indicated that this is generally the case, and the anti-pollution pressure groups which have been formed in recent years seem to be made up primarily of upper- and upper-middle-class individuals.[14]

Data are not available to make any direct correlation between the state of public opinion and governmental action taken to control pollution. Even if such data were available, one would not be justified in drawing any cause-effect relationship between opinion and action. It is possible that those communities which have the most active control programs also have the most active programs to educate the public about pollution. Thus the state of public opinion might be more an effect than a cause of active local efforts to curb pollution.

It is possible to correlate data on the severity of the air pollution problem in particular localities with the amount spent by the local government for control. The result of this comparison can be seen in Table 4.4. There is little relationship between the severity of the air pollution problem and per capita local expenditures.[15] If, as we stated above, level of pollution is the major determinant of public concern, then it is clear that there are many factors other than public concern which influence the actual decisions taken by the government.

GROUPS FAVORING POLLUTION CONTROL

The most effective way for the private citizen to influence governmental action is usually through group action. The translation of individual wants into group demands is at the heart of the political process in a democratic society. Interest groups not only provide a channel for demands but may also help to stimulate wants and to foster the translation of wants into demands.

The major groups involved in the politics of pollution control have been conservation groups, such as the National Wildlife

Table 4.4. **Severity of Air Pollution Compared to Expenditures for Control**

1. SMSA	2. Cents Per Capita for Control (non-Federal funds only)	3. Expenditure Rank*	4. Severity of AP Rank
New York	29.77	2	1
Chicago	21.69	4	2
Philadelphia	13.38	10	3
Los Angeles-Long Beach	58.94	1	4
Cleveland	27.63	3	5
Pittsburgh	16.14	9	6
Boston	4.7	11	7
Newark	0	12	8
Detroit	17.25	7	9
St. Louis (city & co.)	16.79	8	10
Gary-Hammond-E. Chicago	20.34	5	11
Akron	18.32	6	12

Source: Col. 2: 1967 expenditures from U.S. Senate, Committee on Public Works, *Air Pollution 1967*, Vol. III, pp. 1160–1283, divided by 1960 population figures taken from the U.S. Census of Population. The absence of any expenditures in Newark is due in part to the dominant role played by the state government in controlling air pollution in New Jersey. Col. 4: Ranking of severity of air pollution from U.S. Public Health Service data, reprinted in *The New York Times*, August 4, 1967, 34:2. For an explanation of the basis of the ranking, see National Center for Air Pollution Control, "A Listing of the 20 Areas with the Most Severe Air Pollution Problems," mimeographed, n.d.

* This refers to ranking among the 12 cities listed, not among all cities.

Federation and the Izaak Walton League; groups representing particular levels of government, such as the National Association of Counties; and the industries affected by pollution control regulations.

The conservation or environmental interest groups at the national level can be divided into two kinds. There are the older, usually larger and more stable, groups which have had a long interest in the preservation of fish and wildlife; and there are the newer groups, which have been formed in the past few years explicitly to deal with pollution and other environmental problems.

The backbone of the two largest older groups, the National Wildlife Federation and the Izaak Walton League, consists of hunters and fishermen. Because water pollution and pesticides are the two forms of pollution which tend to be most injurious to fish and wildlife, these groups initially focused on these areas. However, in recent years, they have concerned themselves with air pollution and the whole gamut of environmental problems.

All of the conservation groups, and especially the groups devoted to the interests of fishermen, have been ardent advocates of strict water pollution control. The principles of the Izaak Walton League of America, one of the most active groups, are representative. The official policy of the League is: "There is no sound justification for water pollution. The people of the United States are entitled to wholesome water, usable for all human needs . . . the public goal should be maximum removal of pollutants from all streams, rather than use of streams to carry an 'acceptable maximum' load of wastes." [16] This policy, it should be noted, runs contrary to the cost-benefit, community-use approach which we discussed in the first chapter.

The various conservation groups differ in their tactics and their effectiveness. The Izaak Walton League is probably the most active in lobbying for water pollution control. Its local chapters and state divisions have been quite effective in pushing for state regulation and enforcement, particularly in the Midwest.[17] Washington lobbying is left to the national headquarters, which is located in Illinois but which maintains an office in Washington.

The National Wildlife Federation is the largest of the conservation groups, although its estimate of 3,500,000 "supporters" represents several times the number of its actual members. The Federation issues several regular publications which are widely distributed, and it testifies frequently before congressional committees. Resolution Number One adopted at the Federation's 1968 annual convention states:

> This organization emphasizes its urgent concern about contamination of the environment by water and air pollutants, by toxic chemicals used as pesticides and for other purposes, by solid wastes, and by noise. It is believed that these conditions in the light of the human population increase, and considered collectively, constitute the most serious and pressing conservation problem of the time.[18]

The Sierra Club is the oldest of the environmental groups, having been founded in 1892 by naturalist John Muir. Despite its age, it is also among the most militant and aggressive of the pro-conservation groups. Its original purpose, and still its abiding interest, is the protection of wilderness areas against any encroachment. However, it has come to view pollution as just as great a threat to wilderness as dams, roads, or other more obvious insults, and it has been an ardent supporter of almost all the recent anti-pollution measures considered at the national level. It succeeded in its court fight to have EPA interpret the Clean Air Act as forbidding the lowering of air quality anywhere in the United States (see Chapter 6).

Another one of the older conservation groups which has been very active in the anti-pollution fight is the Audubon Society. Originally concerned with saving birds from extinction, the Society extended its concern to all types of wildlife and then, like the Sierra Club, concluded that pollution control was an integral part of its primary mission. It has been particularly concerned with pesticides but has joined with other environmental groups in a wide variety of anti-pollution battles.

All of the groups discussed above are membership organizations whose members are organized in local and state chapters. The relationship between the national headquarters and the local chapters varies from organization to organization and sometimes over time within the same organization. Usually the local chapters are bound by the policy established nationally, but they are also free to pursue issues arising within their own area and often have significant impact at the state or local level.

The great increase in environmental awareness which occurred during 1969 and 1970 was accompanied by a proliferation of environmental interest groups at all levels. A nationwide survey of environmental groups by the Council on Environmental Quality discovered that more than half the groups had been founded during or after 1969.[19] At the national level, the beginning of the "environmental decade" saw the birth of such groups as the League of Conservation Voters, Friends of the Earth, Environmental Action, and the Natural Resources Defense Council.

Several of the newer groups, notably the Natural Resources Defense Council and the Environmental Defense Fund, have concentrated largely on bringing court cases to stop environmental abuses. Many of the suits they have initiated have been against government agencies to force the halting of particular projects or to get the agencies to comply with the provisions of the National Environmental Policy Act. Some of their frequent successes are described in Chapter 6.

The newer groups do not have the large membership base of the older groups, and some of them have chosen not to seek members at all but to focus instead on lobbying or on providing information to other groups and the general public. Thus the League of Conservation Voters compiles and publishes the environmental voting records of Congressmen and other public figures. It also contributes money and support to the campaigns of pro-environmental Congressional candidates. Environmental Action, which grew out of the *ad hoc* organization which coordinated Earth Day in 1970, lobbies at the national level and distributes information on national issues to a large network of other environmental groups. The Council on Economic Priorities does in-depth studies of corporate involvement in social problems and has conducted and distributed detailed analyses of pollution control efforts in the paper and steel industries. The non-membership groups obtain their funds primarily through individual contributions and foundation grants.

A few of the newer groups have patterned themselves on the membership-base type of organization of the older groups. However, the newer groups are more intensely devoted to direct political action, such as lobbying, and have generally eschewed the tax-exempt status of the older organizations. Examples of such organizations include Friends of the Earth, established in 1969 by David Brower who resigned as Executive Director of the Sierra Club, and Fisherman's Clean Water Action, recently set up by Ralph Nader as a follow-up to his task force reports on the water pollution problem.

The impact of the environmental groups has been felt in the halls of Congress, in the bureaucracy, and in the polling booth. The environmental legislation of the past several years is one indicator of this. Another is the outcome of elections. In the 1972 elections, of 57 gubernatorial and congressional candidates endorsed by the League of Conservation Voters, 43 were victorious. Bond issues for environmental improvements, which totaled more than $1.5 billion, were passed throughout the nation. Other victories, such as defeat of the Colorado winter olympics, and passage of a stringent California coastal protection act, were also won in the 1972 elections.

The conservation groups have been supported in their fight

for water pollution control by numerous groups interested in outdoor recreation and by several major women's groups, notably the League of Women Voters. The interests of the conservation and the recreation groups tend to merge, and in fact the distinction between the two is not a very sharp one. However, certain groups, such as the Outboard Boating Club of America, the Federation of Fly Fishermen, and numerous local sportsmen's clubs, have interests which are much narrower than those of the conservation groups.

The League of Women Voters in 1956 chose water resources as a major subject for study and action. League members undertook "Know Your River Basin" surveys throughout the country, and many of the League chapters were quite influential in pushing for stronger state and local pollution control. The national League headquarters testified before Congress on a wide variety of water resource matters, including the various amendments to the Water Pollution Control Act. In 1966 the League voted to retain water resources as one of its major concerns.[20] And in 1969 the League demonstrated that it was one of the most effective of all the groups favoring pollution control. It spearheaded a "citizens' Crusade for Clean Water" which enlisted the support of 38 organizations, including the AFL-CIO and the major conservation and municipal groups, 22 governors, and 222 members of the House of Representatives. The Crusade was aimed at getting Congress to fund the full $1 billion authorization for waste treatment grants and, although it did not succeed in getting the full authorization, it was successful in having the appropriation significantly increased.

The U.S. Conference of Mayors, the National League of Cities, and the National Association of Counties are the other major set of interests, aside from the conservation groups, supporting pollution control legislation at the national level. The cities and suburbs have been faced with the necessity of undertaking major expenditures for the laying of sewer lines and the construction of waste treatment plants. Thus their major stake in federal legislation has been to get Washington to commit more federal funds for these purposes. This interest coincides with that of the conservation groups, who tend to see federal resources as the only hope for stimulating sufficient investment to curb water pollution significantly. The municipal and county groups have also looked upon federal action as the primary means of ensuring that the pollution control efforts of one municipality will not be undercut by the lack of such efforts in a neighboring upstream community.

The groups representing local officials have had even more impact on the federal air pollution effort than on water pollution legislation. They were the major forces pushing for strong federal legislation, and the drafting of the 1963 Clean Air Act was done in part by Hugh Mields, who was the chief lobbyist for the U.S. Conference of Mayors.[21] Air pollution is more uniquely an urban problem than water pollution, and thus the major efforts for strong control measures have come from the big cities.

The interests of the cities have sometimes conflicted with those of the states, and state prerogatives in the pollution field have been zealously guarded by two groups of state officials—the Association of State and Territorial Health Officers and the Conference of State Sanitary Engineers. Both groups have an obvious stake in the expansion of pollution control efforts and they have been effective partners with the federal government in promoting the cause of clean air and water. However, they have looked with disfavor on federal encroachments into state responsibilities, particularly enforcement, and they have also discouraged attempts by Washington to deal directly with local governments.

As the relationship between air pollution and certain diseases has become clearer, several health groups have taken an active interest in air pollution control. The American Medical Association has been concerned with the problem for some time. In 1967 the National Tuberculosis Association announced the establishment of the National Air Conservation Commission, an arm of the Association devoted to the control of community air pollution. The aims of the Commission include the urging of "nationwide action for control of air pollution" and support for "the establishment of strong and effective legislation and enforcement procedures." [22]

Organizations of scientists have also taken considerable interest in pollution matters. The American Academy for the Advancement of Science established an Air Conservation Commission to study air pollution, and other scientific organizations have urged their members to become involved in pollution control. The Scientists Institute for Public Information, a group of scientists originally concerned with nuclear warfare problems, has turned increasingly to environmental problems. The large role of scientific questions in pollution controversies has attracted the interest of many individual scientists, and the impact of modern technology in both causing pollution and perhaps providing a cure for it has made the issue appealing to those scientists concerned about the social implications of technological advances.

The groups discussed above have not had pollution control as their sole concern. They are groups founded for other purposes which have developed an interest in pollution control as the need for regulation became apparent. But in both air and water pollution control there have been some national groups and numerous local groups which have been founded on the basis of a concern with pollution.

The Water Pollution Control Federation brings together all those who are professionally involved in the water pollution field. It includes government officials at all levels, scientists working on pollution problems, and representatives of firms manufacturing pollution control equipment. The Federation has provided a valuable forum for the exchange of views, but because of its mixed membership it has refrained from taking any stand on controversial matters. It does not engage in lobbying activities and does not testify before congressional committees.

The Air Pollution Control Association was founded in 1907 by twelve municipal smoke inspectors who banded together under the imposing title of the International Union for the Prevention of Smoke. The membership was originally limited to smoke inspectors for fear of an industry takeover, but by 1915 the organization felt confident enough to open its ranks to all comers. In recognition of the broader scope of the air pollution problem, the organization dropped "Smoke" from its title in 1957 and became the Air Pollution Control Association. It now has 6,500 members.[23] The Association does not engage in lobbying activities, but it promotes the cause of air pollution control through various educational and publicity techniques and also provides technical assistance.

On the local scene numerous groups have been formed to combat pollution. In water pollution such groups are often concerned with water resource management generally and are organized to cover an entire watershed. However, there has been less need in water pollution than in air pollution to form local groups. Established groups, such as sportsmen's clubs and the League of Women Voters have provided the major local support for clean water. There have not been, until recently, existing organizations with strong local roots to support the cause of clean air. This gap has been largely filled by the environmental groups created since 1969, although in some of the larger metropolitan areas groups dedicated to air pollution control existed prior to the new wave of environmental concern.

There are probably about 5,000 environmental organizations in the United States today.[24] Most of them devote the bulk of their time to disseminating information and to holding meetings and discussions. About half the groups which replied to a National Center for Voluntary Action questionnaire reported that they testified at public hearings, and 17 per cent stated that they engaged in lobbying activities.[25]

Some of the most influential groups at the local level are those created to deal with a specific project. For example, the Upper French Broad Defense Association (UFBDA) was created to oppose the construction of fifteen reservoirs in western North Carolina. During the 1972 elections, it worked actively for Board of County Commissioners candidates who were unsympathetic to the reservoir plans. Members of the organization served as campaign chairmen and workers for these candidates. The UFBDA sponsored public meetings to provide a forum for the candidates and mailed information about the candidates to its members. All its candidates won seats on the Board. Official support for the project diminished, and shortly thereafter the Tennessee Valley Authority withdrew the proposal.[26]

INDUSTRY

No group opposes pollution control per se. Clean air and clean water have joined the ranks of motherhood and apple pie in the American political pantheon. However, some groups are clearly more in favor of pollution control than others, or pollution control would not be a political problem. Industrial polluters tend to be at the core of much of the opposition to stringent pollution controls.

The dilemma of the polluting industry is not difficult to understand. Pollution control equipment is expensive, and it adds nothing to the value of the goods produced. Insofar as a company is in business to make money, pollution control is generally bad business. But counterbalancing the profit incentive are the forces of law and public opinion.

The power of industry to foster or retard pollution control is tremendous. This derives not primarily from its political sophistication or monetary resources, but from the simple fact that the ultimate decision whether or not to cease polluting lies with each individual firm. Government can set standards and can enforce them against particularly recalcitrant firms, but without widespread cooperation on the part of industry significant pollution abatement will not be achieved. Pollution laws, like all other laws, require a high degree of voluntary compliance for their success, and thus the private sector, considered collectively, has a veto power over the progress of much pollution abatement.

The attitude of industry toward complying with pollution control regulations depends heavily on the quality and effectiveness of the regulating agency. If the agency is willing and able to enforce the regulations against polluting industries, and if the industries are reasonably sure that all competitors in the area are to be treated alike, then there will probably be a high degree of voluntary compliance.

Aside from the effectiveness of the regulatory agency, the likelihood of any particular firm abating its pollution is dependent primarily on three factors: (1) The cost of abatement in comparison with the company's resources; (2) the sensitivity of the firm to public opinion and the amount of adverse public opinion aroused by the firm's activities; and (3) the political influence possessed by the firm. The first of these factors is the most important. Public opinion and political influence will be unimportant considerations if the cost of abatement is so small as to be insignificant. If the cost is so great as to entail the bankruptcy of the business, public opinion will not be a significant factor but political influence may be very important.

Industry investment in pollution control during 1972 was estimated at more than $2.5 billion for air pollution control and more than $1.5 billion for water pollution control. About half this amount was capital investment in equipment, the other half was for operation and maintenance. Private investment in air and water pollution control facilities has been growing at an annual rate of more than 30 per cent between 1967 and 1973. However, despite this dramatic increase, it is anticipated that pollution control equipment will still account for less than 6 per cent of total private investment in plant and equipment in 1973.[27]

The Council on Environmental Quality estimates that between 1972 and 1981 a total of $227 billion will have to be spent to meet current air and water pollution control requirements.[28] From this $227 billion, $121 billion will be for water pollution and $106 billion for air pollution. About $80 billion will have to come from the private sector to deal with stationary sources of air pollution. An additional $60 billion will be required to finance control of air pollution from automobiles, both for the cost of emission control devices and the higher operating costs resulting from use of non-lead or low-lead gasoline. Although the cost of environmental improvement is obviously very great, studies by the Council and others indicate that spending these amounts will not have any significant adverse effects on the economy.[29] It will, of course, mean the sacrifice of other desirable goals, and thus a premium must be put on spending the money most effectively.[30]

Industry has lobbied intensively for governmental subsidies to offset the costs of pollution control equipment. It has been quite successful in obtaining exemption for such equipment from state taxes, and many localities have also passed legislation exempting pollution control equipment from property taxes.[31] At the federal level the efforts for tax writeoffs or other forms of subsidy have met with more limited success because of the combined opposition of the Treasury Department and the powerful head of the House Ways and Means Committee, Wilbur Mills. The Treasury Department and Mills have both expressed the opinion that the tax structure should not be made any more complex than it now is, and that taxes should be used only as a method for raising revenue, not for any other purpose.

Most economic experts argue that tax subsidies are an inefficient method of encouraging pollution control. Such subsidies would pay only for waste treatment, but in the case of many industries it would be far more efficient to prevent the wastes from being produced by changing the manufacturing process. For example, the amount of water used in manufacturing paper or steel can be reduced by 95 per cent if certain manufacturing processes are used.[32] But since a tax subsidy would not pay for such a process change, a subsidy system would encourage the plants to produce twenty times as much pollution and then build a large "end-of-the-line" treatment plant. The treatment plant approach would be much more expensive for the government and for the society as a whole, but it might be less expensive for the manufacturer who could not get a tax writeoff for employing the more efficient process.[33] Also, most methods of giving tax credits help those who need it least by providing more credit for firms making large profits than for firms making small profits or no profit at all.

The sensitivity of firms to public opinion depends heavily on the character of the corporate managers and thus is difficult to generalize about. Large firms which sell to the public under their own name are generally more conscious of public relations, and such firms have often taken the initiative in publicizing the need for pollution controls.[34]

A conspicuous exception to the generalization about companies which sell to the public under their own name is the automobile industry, which has generally taken a rather callous attitude toward the pollution problem. In January 1969, the Justice Department filed suit against the four major auto manufacturers and their trade association, charging that the companies had conspired to delay the development and use of devices to control air pollution from automobiles. In September, the federal government announced that it had agreed to settle the suit through a consent decree which would not impose any penalty on the manufacturers and would seal the grand jury records, thus closing off information that might be used in other damage suits. The case illustrates both the attitude and the power of the automobile companies.[35]

Political influence is generally a function of the size of the firm, its importance to the economy, and also probably the degree to which it is normally involved in dealing with governmental agencies. Industrial firms employ a wide variety of political strategies. For some, the best defense is a good offense. Thus thirty-seven corporations in the Ohio River Valley between Ohio and West Virginia banded together as the West Virginia-Ohio Industry Committee, drafted an interstate air pollution control compact, and succeeded in having it passed by the Ohio and West Virginia legislatures.[36] While the public spiritedness of these firms is praiseworthy, there is also little doubt that one of the major reasons for the industry initiative was to ward off the federal government, which had already held one abatement conference in the area, had promised two more, and had acquired the power to establish interstate commissions under the 1967 Air Quality Act.

The variety of defensive tactics is well illustrated by the efforts of the coal industry to combat regulations on sulfur oxide emissions. The National Coal Policy Conference used a number of tactics within the executive branch, including the threat to push for the transfer of the air pollution function to the Department of the Interior. Having failed in the executive branch, the industry representatives succeeded in having Congress make several significant alterations in the 1967 Air Quality Act, including the requirement that HEW reconsider its criteria for sulfur oxides and the addition of various provisions for greater industry representation in the enforcement and standard-setting functions. The battle then shifted to the state and local arena where the industry resorted to the courts to block sulfur regulations. In New Jersey and St. Louis the coal interests were successful in getting the courts to delay application of the regulations.

It should be clear from what has been said above that industry cannot be considered any more monolithic in relation to pollution control than it is in relation to any other major public issue. This point is underscored by the growing role of industries engaged in the manufacture of pollution control equipment. For firms which contribute to pollution, government regulation and the installation of control equipment is at best a necessary evil. However, for firms manufacturing control equipment, the more regulation the better. For example, while the automobile industry dragged its heels on the question of controlling pollution from motor vehicles, American Machine and Foundry and other potential manufacturers of afterburner equipment were lobbying for more stringent regulations which, they hoped, could be met only by the installation of the additional equipment they would produce.[37]

Pollution control is now a major industry and expanding rapidly. To the more than $2 billion spent in 1972 by industry for control equipment must be added the approximately $4 billion spent by municipalities for treatment plants and sewer lines. These figures represent a major increase over the previous year's expenditures, and there is no reason to question the statement of one authority on investments that "The overall pollution-control market may be developing into one of the most rapidly growing segments of the economy." [38]

There are, in addition to the manufacturers of control equipment, other entire industries which benefit from the regulation of pollution, and these other industries are of even more political significance and economic importance than the control equipment producers. For example, the natural gas and nuclear power industries have been beneficiaries of the campaign against high-sulfur coal and oil. Many sectors of the economy, such as commercial fishing and certain types of agriculture, are dependent on clean air and water for their continuance. All of these interests have not hesitated to push for more stringent regulation of pollution when it is in their interest to do so.

INTEREST GROUP IMPACT ON DECISIONMAKING

Given the multitude of interest groups representing all shades of opinion on questions of pollution control it is almost impossible to isolate the effects of interest groups per se. An administrator who appears to be acting totally independently may simply be anticipating the reaction of some group or set of groups to his decision. However, we can hazard a few generalizations about interest group influence.

The influence of polluting industries tends to be greater at the state and local level than at the national level. Such industries are more important to the economy of the locality or state than to the national economy and thus have more bargaining power. They can threaten to leave the locality but they are not likely to threaten to leave the United States. The state and local governments are generally less sophisticated and have fewer political resources to draw on than does the federal government. Also, the state and local governments must carry on a continuing relationship with the industries involved, and it is the states and localities who must take specific actions directed for or against specific groups. In contrast, the federal government is more often involved in laying down rules of a general nature, and when it does deal with specific industries (in enforcement actions, for example) it can anticipate withdrawing from the involvement after a period of time and thus does not have to be as sensitive to the interests of the polluters.

The greater vulnerability of the state and local governments to polluters carries over to the national level by way of the local orientation of the Congress. The industries affected adversely by pollution regulation can generally get a sympathetic hearing from Congressmen whose districts or states may also be adversely affected. However, the outcome of legislative struggles in the Congress are determined largely by the senior members of the key committees. The Air and Water Pollution Subcommittee of the Senate Public Works Committee has been remarkably free of industrial influence and thus has spearheaded much of the fight for stronger anti-pollution legislation. The strong public sentiment in favor of such legislation has been sufficient to win the Subcommittee the support of the rest of Congress.

The federal bureaucracy is a microcosm of the competing interests in the private sector. The Commerce Department protects the interests of private business generally, the Bureau of Mines defends the coal and oil industry, the Federal Power Commission promotes natural gas and electric power, and the Environmental Protection Agency and the Council on Environmental Quality represent the environmentalists. Who wins among these competing interests depends on the strength of the players, the state of public opinion, and reflecting both these factors, the opinions of the president and the White House staff.

Although the opinions of the president are rooted partially in his personality, they are, like any man's opinions, highly dependent on circumstances. The Richard Nixon who in August of 1970 stated, "We should set ourselves a higher goal than merely remedying the damage wrought in decades past. We should strive for an environment that not only sustains life but enriches life, harmonizing the works of man and nature for the greater good of all," [39] is the same president who, in December, 1973, stated, "I'm going to have to propose some things that will drive the environmentalists up the wall, and they're half-way there already. How are we going to get the coal out of the ground without driving them out of their trees?" [40] Whether the president harmonizes the works of man and nature or drives the environmentalists out of their trees depends heavily on the strength of competing interest groups and the state of public opinion.

CHAPTER 5

The Executive Branch

SINCE 1970 the institutions for the development and implementation of federal environmental policy have undergone remarkable change. Particularly within the executive branch, new organizations, such as the Council on Environmental Quality and the Environmental Protection Agency, have been created. Existing agencies, such as the Department of the Interior, have been reorganized to deal with new environmental responsibilities. The enactment of the National Environmental Policy Act[1] has markedly influenced the role of the executive branch in dealing with environmental problems.

PRE-1970 EXECUTIVE BRANCH ORGANIZATION

Before 1970 there was no single agency in the federal government with overall responsibility for pollution control. Each of the major categories of pollution control (water pollution, air pollution, solid waste, radiation, occupational health and pesticides) was embodied in a separate administrative unit, and between 1966 and 1970, the two most important units—the National Air Pollution Control Administration and the Federal Water Pollution Control Administration—were located in different departments, the former in the Department of Health, Education and Welfare (HEW), the latter in Interior. The federal air pollution control effort dates back to the early part of this century when the Bureau of Mines in the Department of the Interior began conducting research into means of controlling excess smoke emissions. The Bureau of Mines established an Office of Air Pollution and then later abolished it, but the Bureau has continued to maintain an interest in controlling pollution from coal and oil.[2]

As we have seen, the efforts by Los Angeles to control its pollution and the Donora episode focused national attention on air pollution. In December 1949, President Truman requested the Secretary of the Interior to organize an interdepartmental committee which would call the first United States Technical Conference on Air Pollution, and in May 1950 the conference was held in Washington.[3] The first resolutions in Congress calling for research into the health hazards of air pollution were introduced in 1950. As the problem came to be viewed primarily as a threat to health, the Public Health Service (PHS) was increasingly considered to be the proper agency to take the lead in research and control efforts.

In the early post-World War II years the PHS's concern with air pollution was centered in its Division of Industrial Hygiene. In 1960, PHS combined two existing units and created a Division of Air Pollution headed by Vernon G. MacKenzie, a sanitary engineer. In 1966 the name of the division was changed to the National Center for Air Pollution Control (NCAPC) but the Center still suffered from an acute case of bureaucratic layering. It was one of five units under the Bureau of Disease Prevention and Environmental Control, which in turn was one of four bureaus under the PHS, which in turn was one of eight independent units reporting to the secretary of HEW. This situation did not prevent, indeed it encouraged, the Director of NCAPC to by-pass the hierarchy and deal directly with the secretary's office.

In the 1968 reorganization of HEW, the Public Health Service as an organizational entity was abolished and the problem of layering somewhat relieved. The National Center for Air Pollution Control became the National Air Pollution Control Administration (NAPCA), and was one of three major units in a newly created Consumer Protection and Environmental Health Service. The head of the service reported through the Assistant

Secretary for Health to the secretary of HEW. Despite this change, the air pollution problem still did not receive high priority within the vast, sprawling HEW bureaucracy.

In looking at the federal water pollution program, we find that it also dates back to the early twentieth century. In 1912, the Public Health Service was explicitly authorized by Congress to investigate the pollution of navigable streams and lakes. The investigations were prompted by the frequent outbreaks of typhoid fever in urban areas attributed to water supplies.[4]

Until passage of the 1956 Water Pollution Control Act, almost all of the water pollution control work remained at the state level. As Murphy states, "Through the 1950s the federal government largely confined itself to congratulating states upon their work and their compacts, to conducting river basin surveys and other research work to assist the existing state agencies, and to carrying on a program of public education."[5] The only significant exception to this was the financial help in the construction of waste treatment facilities which the federal government provided during the New Deal period.

When the 1948 federal act was passed, PHS established a Division of Water Pollution Control. The division quickly acquired certain characteristics and ways of doing business which were to characterize it at least until its transfer to the Department of the Interior in 1966. The division, like most of the rest of PHS, believed in working primarily through the state health departments. It did not believe that the federal government should work directly with localities, and it was convinced that the initiative in controlling water pollution should rest with the states, not with the federal government. The internal administrative workings of the division reflected this philosophy. Emphasis was placed on field installations, and the central headquarters in Washington was small and exercised little control. Partly as a result of this, there was little coordination among the component units of the division. The enforcement people did not talk to the technical assistance people, the research program was not tied to the control program, the grants were distributed without much thought being given to the operating needs of the agency.

The division both benefited and suffered from a considerable amount of congressional interest in its administration. The large component of public construction in the water pollution program was bound to attract congressional interest, but such concern went beyond the waste treatment grant construction program. For example, beginning with the 1948 act's authorization of a water pollution control laboratory in Cincinnati, Ohio, the Congress in succeeding acts specified the number and location of the field laboratories of the water pollution agency. The 1961 act authorized seven such laboratories, with the relevant committees informing PHS of exactly where the laboratories were to go. Not surprisingly, several of the "recommended" locations coincided with the districts of key congressmen.[6]

The reluctance of PHS to come into conflict with the state health agencies, as well as the low status of the Division of Water Pollution within the HEW hierarchy, led to congressional agitation to change the status of the water pollution agency. There was pressure for the creation of a separate Water Pollution Control Administration within HEW in 1961; but, deferring to the views of Secretary Abraham Ribicoff, Congress contented itself with the modest change of transferring the authority under the Water Pollution Control Act from the surgeon general to the secretary of HEW.[7]

As the Congress began to consider the water quality standards provisions which were to become law in 1965, pressure for administrative change increased. If the federal government was to review and approve state water quality standards, it was clear that the agency doing the reviewing and giving the approval would have to be willing to bargain and to risk antagonizing the state agencies. A number of other changes in the nature of the water pollution control program had also reinforced the desire for change. It had become clear that health considerations were a comparatively insignificant factor in the contemporary problem of water pollution, and it thus seemed anomalous to have the authority for the program vested in the nation's health agency. Some critics charged that the doctors who ran PHS slighted the water program because of its lack of importance for public health. It was also becoming clear, at least to the administration, that more emphasis should be placed on organizing the program on a river basin basis and tying it more closely to the other water resource activities of the government. The Public Health Service had been conducting studies of entire river basins for years, but the impact of such studies on the pollution control program was minimal.

The combined pressure of these considerations led to the authorization in the 1965 amendments to the Water Pollution Control Act of a Federal Water Pollution Control Administration (FWPCA) which would remain in HEW but would report directly to the secretary and be independent of PHS. (This proposal had been made as early as 1959 by Representative Blatnik.)[8] Both the secretary of HEW and the White House remained silent on the merits of the new organizational arrangement.

It was destined to have a short life. The act was signed by the president on October 2, 1965. Five months later, on February 28, 1966, the president submitted to Congress a reorganization plan transferring the newly created FWPCA from HEW to the Department of the Interior.[9] The reorganization plan took effect, with the assent of Congress, on May 10, 1966.

There are numerous conflicting accounts of how and why the transfer proposal was made. It seems clear that the initiative for the move come directly from President Johnson, under prodding from Interior Secretary Stewart Udall.[10] The president gave his full backing to the transfer despite opposition from Senator Muskie, the Budget Bureau, and other influential sectors. HEW Secretary Gardner, who had assumed office only six months before the decision, indicated that he was not prepared to fight to retain the agency. After leaving office he reportedly stated that he regretted this decision more than any other he had made during his tenure as secretary.

The Environmental Protection Agency

In December 1969 President Nixon responded to the growing public concern about pollution by requesting the President's Advisory Council on Executive Organization, better known as the Ash Council for its chairman Roy Ash, to examine whether the federal pollution control programs should be reorganized.

The Council and its staff rapidly came to the conclusion that the pollution programs should be consolidated. However, there ensued a long internal debate as to whether the pollution programs should be put in a new separate agency or made a part of the Department of Natural Resources which the Ash Council was also proposing. The Department of Natural Resources was to include the government's timber, mineral, and parks programs, water resource development, energy, Indian affairs, and several other programs. Ash, whose guiding principle was to minimize the number of federal agencies reporting to the president, favored including pollution control in this package. The Council's staff believed that this would submerge the pollution control programs and result in decisions favoring resource development at the expense of improved environmental quality. Finally, Ash agreed to a separate independent pollution control agency. Accordingly, in April, 1970, he sent to the president a memorandum detailing the plans for what was to become the Environmental Protection Agency.

The White House did not make any changes in the Ash Council proposal, and it was sent to the Congress as Reorganization Plan Number 3 of 1970. The plan proposed the creation of an independent Environmental Protection Agency (EPA) headed by an administrator who would report directly to the president. The new agency would incorporate the major federal programs for controlling air and water pollution, environmental radiation, pesticides, and solid waste. (Offices dealing with noise and toxic substances were added to EPA in 1971 and 1972 respectively.) Although there was some quibbling over which organizations would be included in EPA and some Congressmen who felt that natural resources and pollution control should be combined, the proposal was never in serious danger of being rejected by Congress. In September the 60 days for Congressional rejection expired, and on December 2, 1970, EPA came into being.

All reorganizations cause some confusion and trauma for the individuals and agencies involved, but the creation of EPA was unprecedented in terms of the number and size of disparate agencies brought together under a new organizational structure. In many cases parts of different agencies which had been rivals or opponents for years found themselves suddenly part of the same organization. Single programs within EPA were made up of personnel and procedures acquired from two and sometimes more federal departments. To take perhaps the extreme example, the EPA pesticide program was composed of parts of HEW's Food and Drug Administration, the Department of Agriculture, and the Department of the Interior, three agencies which had had numerous disputes about pesticide regulations over many years. Even the HEW portion of the program was for all practical purposes divided into two organizational units which approached the pesticide problem very differently.

The problems of joining disparate parts of other agencies have been aggravated by EPA's internal organization. The Ash Council staff considered how the new agency should be organized, and generally concluded that the basic structure should be along functional lines such as enforcement, research, and standard-setting. This was a departure from the traditional programmatic approach focusing on air and water pollution.

The EPA budget structure, designed before the agency formally came into being, was therefore based on the functional principle. (see Table 5.1.) Also, three of the five assistant administrators were given functional responsibilities: research, enforcement, and planning and management. However, because of the pressure to move rapidly in response to legal deadlines contained in EPA's statutes, which are written on the basis of particular programs, it was decided that the programmatic approach would have to be partially retained, at least as an interim measure. Accordingly one of the two remaining assistant administrators was given responsibility for air and water programs and the other was designated Assistant Administrator for Hazardous Materials Control[11] (see figure 5.1.). In April, 1974, the air and water programs were split between the two Assistant Administrators so that one is now responsible for water pollution, pesticides, and toxic substances, and the other is responsible for air pollution, noise, radiation, and solid waste.

The half functional, half programmatic organization continues to form the basic internal structure of the EPA. The result is that almost every EPA activity can be equally the responsibility of at least two different parts of the organization, and a long

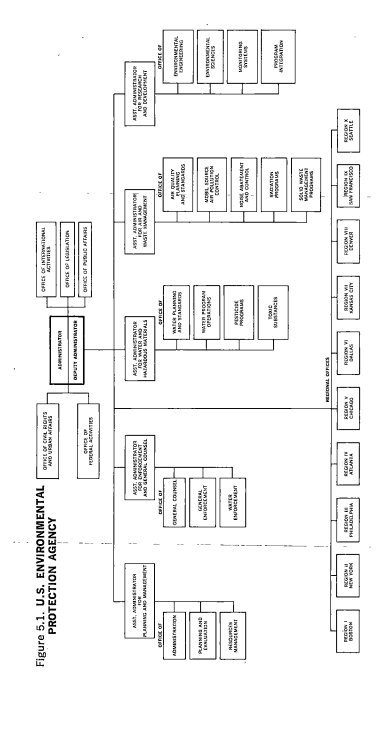

Figure 5.1. U.S. ENVIRONMENTAL PROTECTION AGENCY

series of decisions have had to be made dividing responsibilities among the assistant administrators. Thus, for example, air pollution research has been given to the research office while air pollution monitoring is the responsibility of the air pollution office. The continuing need for such Solomon-like decisions has tended to perpetuate the internal struggles which marked the creation of the agency. Many key decisions are made only after debate among members of a steering committee or an intra-agency task force. However, many of the issues have been satisfactorily resolved, and there is general agreement that the present organization is a definite improvement over the situation which existed prior to EPA's creation.

As of April 30, 1973, there were 8,255 full-time EPA employees. They were divided as follows among the seven major divisions of the organization: Air and water programs 897; hazardous materials programs 969; research and monitoring 1,895; enforcement and general counsel 375; planning and management 1,008; office of the administrator 273; and the regional offices 2,838. About 2,800 of these people are located in the Washington, D. C. area. The remainder are scattered throughout the ten EPA regions. The number of employees given for air and water programs is deceptively low because most of those listed under regional offices are responsible for air and water pollution control.

The ten EPA regional directors report, at least in theory, directly to the EPA administrator, and there has been a concerted effort within the agency to decentralize decision-making to the regional offices. Most of the major regulatory decisions, such as approval of state air and water quality implementation plans and review of discharge permit applications, are made initially in the regional offices. They are then reviewed in Washington. Although this arrangement has succeeded in placing increased policy responsibility in locations nearer to where the problems are, it has also at times created problems of insuring uniformity among the various regions and of getting the regions to adhere to policies or instructions from Washington. Such problems are common to all of the federal agencies which have large numbers of personnel in the field.

Because of the unpredictable allocation of functions between the programmatic and functional divisions, the budget numbers provide a better picture of the activities of the agency than do the personnel figures. (There is one notable exception to this statement: The largest item by far in the budget is the grant program for the construction of municipal waste water treatment plants. But this program accounts for a relatively small portion of the agency's internal attention and effort.) What the budget reveals is that EPA, since its creation, has conceived of itself primarily as a regulatory and enforcement agency. The 1974 budget submitted by the president calls for a major cut in the research budget.

The role of enforcer and regulator was partially thrust upon EPA by the pressure of legally established deadlines. The Clean Air Amendments of 1970 and the 1972 Water Pollution Control Act Amendments required the agency to take an extensive series of far-reaching and politically sensitive actions (see Chapter 2). Most of these actions entailed establishing regulations for specific industries and for the implementation of air and water standards, and the two acts established tight timetables for the execution of these functions. The acts also contained lengthy sections dealing with research, but there were no deadlines pertaining to the research activities.

Table 5.1. **EPA Budget**
(in $ thousands—budget authority)

	1973 (estimate)	1974 (estimate)	Increase or Decrease (−)
Research and development	173,145	148,700	− 24,445
Abatement and control	262,034	339,100	77,066
Enforcement	35,574	47,400	11,836
Agency and regional management	46,184	50,800	4,616
Construction grants	1,900,000	−−*	−1,900,000
Construction contract authority	5,000,000	−−*	− 5,000,000
Other	3,552	2,952	− 600
Total	7,420,489	588,952	− 6,831,537

Source: The Budget of the U.S. Government—Fiscal Year 1974.

* No FY 1974 funds were included for the municipal waste treatment program because the grant and contract authority allocated in FY 1973 was intended to fund the program for several years.

Even if the statutes had not required regulatory action, the temper of the times demanded it. The press and the attentive public were tired of excuses and weary of pleas for more research. Visible and dramatic action was called for. The man President Nixon selected to head the agency, William Ruckelshaus, was well suited to meet this demand. His previous position as Assistant Attorney General and his training as a lawyer predisposed him to look at environmental problems as adversary proceedings and to consider court-enforced regulatory action as a logical path of action. His experience as a state legislator and senatorial candidate from Indiana had given him a sensitivity to the political aspects of environmental issues.

Thus several factors combined to give EPA the role of anti-pollution policeman. It has maintained and strengthened this role up to the present time. It has faced several critical policy choices—notably implementation of the 1975 automobile air pollution emission standards and the banning of DDT—and has decided in favor of a tough anti-pollution stance.

In the wake of the Watergate scandal, Nixon asked Ruckelshaus to temporarily assume the directorship of the FBI. To succeed Ruckelshaus at EPA the President, in August 1973, named Russell Train, the first Chairman of the Council on Environmental Quality (see below), to be Administrator.

The change in EPA leadership, combined with a lowering of the priority which the White House and perhaps the public accorded to pollution control, have given rise to fears that EPA, like so many of the independent regulatory commissions, will change its tough posture and will eventually be 'captured' by the interests which it is supposed to regulate.[12] This will probably occur to some degree as the initial enthusiasm for pollution control declines, but EPA is unlikely to go the way of the Interstate Commerce Commission or the Civil Aeronautics Board. Unlike most of the independent regulatory commissions, EPA's constituency includes a number of well organized and moderately powerful groups which favor strong regulatory control over polluters. These groups provide a counterbalance to the power of the polluting industries. Also, EPA's functions are not purely regulatory. As we have seen, a large portion of its budget is devoted to the distribution of grants and the conduct of research. The distribution of grants, as well as the regulatory activities, make EPA and the state and local pollution control agencies highly interdependent, and the state and local agencies provide additional counterbalance to the polluters. The research efforts are important because one of the primary ways in which the regulators have been captured by the regulated is through the monopoly of information and expertise held by the regulated. The EPA will always have to be somewhat dependent on industry for economic and technical information, but its independent research capability is essential if it is to maintain its freedom of regulatory action.

THE COUNCIL ON ENVIRONMENTAL QUALITY

A second organization with a central role in environmental policy making was created in 1970—the Council on Environmental Quality. The Council comprises a chairman and two members who, organizationally, report directly to the president. The legislative authority for the Council stems from two related measures, the National Environmental Policy Act of 1969 (NEPA)[13] and the Environmental Quality Improvement Act of 1970.[14] These acts became law after a lively strategic minuet among the president and two pairs of competing congressional committees.

In May 1969, the president responded to the growing development of and concern over environmental problems and the apparent lack of a coordinated federal approach to them by creating a Cabinet-level interagency Environmental Quality Council.[15] Concurrently, the House Merchant Marine and Fisheries Committee and the Senate Interior Committee were considering bills "to provide for the establishment of a Council on Environmental Quality",[16] on the model of the Employment Act of 1946, which created the Council of Economic Advisers. Senate passage of a bill creating a Council on Environmental Quality was quick; it was placed on the consent calendar and passed on July 10, 1969 by a voice vote.

After the House passed the bill on September 23, 1969, a

jurisdictional conflict between the Senate Interior and Public Works committees sharpened. The Senate Public Works Committee members felt that they should have a major voice in determining the content of the legislation because they were responsible for the federal air and water pollution statutes. They felt that they should have at least an equal voice with the Interior Committee in shaping and overseeing the work of any new environmental institution. A compromise was reached early in October. Under the compromise, the bill establishing the Council on Environmental Quality (CEQ) would be accompanied by a new title to another bill pending in the Senate Public Works Committee, the Water Quality Improvement Act of 1970. The new title, the Environmental Quality Improvement Act of 1970, would create an Office of Environmental Quality to provide staff support for the Council. The conferees reached agreement on the NEPA bill and both Houses agreed to the conference report just before Christmas 1969. The president signed the bill on January 1, 1970, as his first official act of the 1970s. Passage of the Public Works Committee bill followed, and it was signed into law on April 4, 1970. The Office of Environmental Quality has in practice been totally merged with the Council and had no separate existence except in the statute.

The two acts gave CEQ a broad range of formal responsibilities to:

Receive from all federal agencies statements on the impact of each major action which significantly affects environmental quality.

Coordinate all federal agencies with respect to their actions which affect the environment.

Review existing environmental monitoring systems.

Collect, analyze, and evaluate information on environmental quality.

Promote knowledge of the effects of actions and technology on the environment and encourage means to prevent or reduce adverse effects on the environment.

Prepare an annual report.

Analyze conditions and trends in the quality of the environment.

Make recommendations to the president on policies to improve environmental quality, and make such studies as the president may request.

Recommend to the president and federal agencies priorities among environmental enhancement programs.

Conduct public hearings or conferences.

Advise and assist the president and the agencies in achieving international cooperation for dealing with environmental problems.

Despite its broad authorities, the Council is and will probably remain a small organization. Its current total staff consists of about fifty people, divided evenly between professionals and clerical personnel. The professional staff represents a wide variety of disciplines, ranging from ecology and chemistry to law and economics. The Council's 1973 budget was $2,550,000, which was reduced slightly to $2,466,000 in fiscal 1974. About half of the budget is for contracts to investigate particular policy problems with which the Council is concerned.

Starting as a totally new organization, CEQ has had to define its functions and create a role for itself within the government. The broad nature of its legal authorities has generally made it possible for the Council to deal with those environmental problems which in its own opinion were most important. However, some of its functions, such as involvement in controversies over environmental impact statements and the preparation of an annual report to the Congress on the status of environmental quality, have been determined by its statutory mandate.

The question of role has been more difficult. The location of the Council within the Executive Office of the president implies that it should serve as an adviser to the president and that it should be a loyal and integral part of the administration. However, the expectation of some Congressmen and of a number of the environmental interest groups has been that CEQ should be a sort of "environmental ombudsman" speaking out in public for the environmental cause regardless of administration policy.

For the most part the Council has chosen the role of presidential adviser, in the belief that this gives it more influence within the government and thus enables it to be more effective in pursuing its policy views. In fact, it is doubtful that the Council could have power in any other way because its location in the Executive Office is the only leverage it has over the actions of the government. The Council was given no real muscle in the laws which created it, and it is doubtful that the support of environmental groups could provide the Council sufficient power to influence the bureaucracy or withstand the blows of a hostile president.

The CEQ has been criticized for this role choice by many environmentalists. Typically the criticism has arisen from a situation where CEQ fought for the environmental viewpoint within the confines of the executive branch, lost the battle, and then publicly supported the Administration position. The Supersonic Transport (SST) and the Alaskan pipeline were among the most spectacular such instances. However, in other cases the criticism resulted from misunderstanding or simply a difference of opinion between the Council and the environmental interest groups. Stream channelization and modification of NEPA to deal with nuclear power plants initiated prior to NEPA's enactment are examples of such cases.

Perhaps the major task undertaken by the Council is the coordination and development of a unified annual presidential environmental message and legislative program. In 1971 and 1972, over 25 environmental legislative proposals were submitted by the executive branch to Congress. Nine were enacted during the 92d Congress. In 1973, five additional measures were submitted along with revised versions of the unenacted bills from the previous two years and several treaties for Senate ratification. Many of these proposals were generated by the CEQ staff. Others stemmed from proposals made in earlier years either by the executive branch or by individual Congressmen. Still others came from the operating agencies. But all of them were carried forward through the drafting and agency review process by the Council. Among the major proposals originated by CEQ and now enacted into law are comprehensive measures dealing with noise, pesticides, and ocean dumping. The CEQ has also had the responsibility for implementing the procedural aspects of the environmental impact statement process required by the National Environmental Policy Act. (The process is described below in the section on coordination.) The Council has done this by issuing guidelines to the federal agencies which state what kind of information must be included in the statements, what kinds of projects should be covered, and when and how they should be circulated to the public and relevant government officials. The CEQ has no way it can enforce these guidelines other than by persuasion, and its staff members spend considerable time with agencies working with them (and sometimes against them), interpreting the application of the guidelines and cajoling compliance with the spirit as well as the letter of the National Environmental Policy Act.

The Council is not required to comment on the impact statements, and given its very small staff only about a third of the statements are even read within CEQ. But the Council does comment to the agencies on the more important statements, and a shift in decision on a major project is occasionally attributed to the Council. Publicized examples are the halt to construction of the Cross-Florida Barge Canal, rejection by the secretary of Transportation of the California Minarets Road proposal, and delays in funding the Tocks Island project in the Delaware River Basin. The Council's opposition to the Cannikin nuclear test also surfaced in the context of the court action which unsuccessfully sought to block the test blast.[17]

About half of the Council's budget is spent on research, usually social, economic, or legal research related to immediate policy questions. The results of these efforts often are published in the Council's Annual Report, which has become a valuable reference document, or in special published reports. Examples of the latter include reports on toxic substances, ocean dumping, integrated pest management, and land use control.

In mid-1973, CEQ reached a turning point. Russell Train, who had guided the Council through its first three years, left to become EPA Administrator. At about the same time, most of the Council's senior staff members departed for a variety of reasons. Whether CEQ's enemies within and outside the executive branch will take advantage of these events to reduce the Council to a clerical organization for processing impact statements remains to be seen.

OTHER EXECUTIVE BRANCH AGENCIES

Although the creation of EPA consolidated the primary federal agencies involved in pollution control, there are still many agencies outside of EPA which play a significant role in pollution control efforts. These agencies were not incorporated in EPA because their missions were considered more related to other programs than to pollution control. For example, the Bureau of Mines does extensive research on coal and other fuels and this research is often directly related to air pollution control. But it is clear that the Bureau's primary mission relates to its concern with mineral resources, not with air pollution control. Other such agencies include the National Institute of Environmental Health Sciences in HEW, the Geological Survey in the Department of the Interior (which conducts more water quality monitoring than does EPA), and the National Oceanic and Atmospheric Administration in the Department of Commerce.

The involvement of many different federal agencies in carrying out pollution control policy should not be surprising. Given the complexity and interrelatedness of contemporary American society, there is no major policy area which can be neatly contained within the jurisdiction of one agency. The tendency to create even larger and more encompassing federal departments is an effort to deal with this difficulty, but the only total 'solution' would be the creation of a single Department of Government.

A good example of the interrelatedness among seemingly disparate policy areas is provided by a letter to the *Washington Post* from the wife of a Kansas wheat farmer.[18] She complained that the farm might not be able to produce much wheat because of a shortage of fertilizer. The fertilizer was in short supply because of a shortage of natural gas. In turn, the shortage of natural gas was due in part to air pollution regulations which encouraged the burning of non-polluting natural gas instead of coal or oil. Thus, a housewife might have to pay higher prices for bread because of the impact of air pollution regulations. In bureaucratic terms, EPA regulatory actions directly affected the problems of the Agriculture Department through the intermediary of the Federal Power Commission's allocation of natural gas.

COORDINATING MECHANISMS

Given the numerous federal agencies involved in pollution control, coordination within the executive branch is a constant and troublesome problem. Much effort is expended in trying to resolve conflicts among agencies and attempting to harness the collective power of the federal government to work for common ends.

Much of the communication between federal agencies takes place informally at the working levels of the bureaucracy. The off-the-cuff phone call to an acquaintance in another agency or the chance meeting at a professional conference may be what keep the system functioning. But more formal mechanisms are also required to permit the formulation of policy and to arrive at official solutions to problems.

The creation of both EPA and CEQ were in part motivated by a desire for closer coordination. The EPA represents the application of the common sense belief that the best way to coordinate closely related programs is to make them the responsibility of a single agency. Unfortunately, if each of the programs is carried out by powerful bureaucratic organizations the belief may not prove true in practice. The CEQ represents a different approach—an overhead staff agency which can serve as a mediator and supervisor among interrelated operating line agencies. Here the problem is twofold. The operating agencies almost always know more about their programs than does the overhead agency and thus has a distinct advantage in resisting change. Second, the overhead agency may not have enough power to force action upon a reluctant operating agency. The Council on Environmental Quality has suffered from both of these problems and thus has had only minimal success in coordinating the actions of diverse agencies. The Office of Management and Budget, with its potent authority to cut agency budget submissions, has been more successful in this regard.

Perhaps the most common mechanism for coordination has been the interagency committee. The shortcomings of such committees have been well explored.[19] The most important issues tend not to be discussed, and those that are considered are resolved by resorting to the lowest common denominator of agreement. The federal agencies are, for the most part, legal and political equals with no incentives to influence each other's business. There is considerable incentive, from the standpoint of insuring bureaucratic stability and freedom of action, not to try to meddle in the business of a sister agency. Thus, any serious attempt at regular coordination runs so counter to the general characteristics of the federal government that the cards are heavily stacked against its success.

Up to now we have been discussing coordination in the sense of trying to maximize cooperation and minimize duplication among those agencies engaged in environmental improvement activities. This is coordination in the usual public administration sense. But there is a second type of coordination which is of equal importance and which has been uniquely highlighted in the environmental area by the National Environmental Policy Act. This is the problem of trying to prevent the actions of one agency from inadvertently undermining the efforts of another. In the case of the environment this means trying to insure that agencies do not cause excessive environmental damage in the pursuit of their primary missions.

Section 102 of the National Environmental Policy Act requires that any federal agency undertaking any action which will significantly effect the environment must prepare a statement describing the impact that the action will have on the environment and alternative courses of action which might minimize adverse environmental effects. These statements must be made public and must be circulated for comment to relevant federal, state, and local agencies. The courts have ruled that the requirement for environmental impact statements is judicially enforceable, and numerous court decisions have put real teeth into the impact statement process (see Chapter 6).

The environmental impact statements (or "102 statements" as they have come to be called) are, in a sense, a perverse coordinating mechanism because unlike most coordinating techniques they are designed to create and focus controversy rather than minimize it. But this is true only in a sense, because the conflicts which, under the 102 process, are now bureaucratic conflicts between two agencies are the reflection of real conflicts in the non-bureaucratic world. If a highway proposed by the Department of Transportation would create an air pollution problem and thus conflict with EPA's programs to control air pollution, this would be a real conflict in the natural world. Prior to the existence of the 102 process it probably would have gone unrecognized in the bureaucratic world. It is now likely to be translated into a conflict between Transportation and EPA, and the result is the recognition of the need to coordinate programs and the existence of a mechanism to allow such coordination to take place.

As of September 1973, impact statements had been filed on more than four thousand separate federal actions.[20] The effect on improving federal coordination and decision-making could be seen in the behavior of agencies such as the Atomic Energy Commission and the Corps of Engineers.[21] However, the success of the 102 process has resulted in strong sentiment for its modification. The analysis needed for the preparation and review of the impact statements requires considerable manpower and time, which is considered as a waste and a threat to the projects by Congressmen whose primary concern is getting roads, pipelines, or dams built. The agencies undertaking the actions predictably resent the entering wedge which the statements provide for the courts, environmental groups, and other federal agencies to become involved in the fate of a project.

The impact statement process shows that innovations which improve coordination among agencies can be introduced. But the basic problems of coordination are rooted in the pluralistic pattern of American politics, the general complexity of policy issues in an urbanized, industrialized society, and the particular complexities of pollution control. Although improvements in administrative efficiency and coordination can be made, these underlying factors of pluralism and complexity are not likely to change.

CHAPTER 6

The Courts

THE FLURRY of environmental activity which affected the legislative and executive branches of the government had a dramatic impact on the courts as well. The number of environmental cases increased markedly and judicial decisions became significant determinants of policy. Many of the court decisions affecting air and water pollution policy were based on cases involving a wider range of environmental issues. Thus, it becomes necessary to trace the growth of the courts' role in the environmental area, as a whole, to delineate their influence on pollution control policy.

The increase of environmental cases over the last decade was due to many factors. In the past, the courts played a very limited role in federal enforcement, but in 1971 the Environmental Protection Agency rediscovered the 1899 Refuse Act and for the first time began to bring a significant number of enforcement actions against polluters. Although the courts had for centuries been involved in suits between private parties, as environmental groups organized they increasingly brought a new kind of suit directed not against private parties but against the government. The courts, aware of public concern, re-examined and expanded their interpretation of standing (the right to bring suit). The public concern was felt by the lawmakers as well, and they enacted new environmental legislation (see Chapter 2) which would eventually appear before the courts for interpretation.

Some of this legislation affirmed the courts' view of standing and contained clauses granting citizens the right to sue for enforcement. All of these factors combined to greatly increase the courts' role in the policy process.

The recent role the courts played in environmental issues can best be analyzed if we look at their decisions in several different areas. First, we shall briefly glance at the suits citizens brought against private parties in the past. Then we will examine the gradual change in court opinions regarding standing because, in determining who may bring suit, the courts have expanded the number and types of environmental issues brought before them. We will then turn to the National Environmental Policy Act because the courts' interpretations of this act have greatly influenced the administrative procedures of the executive branch of government. From there we shall go on to examine the cases brought against the federal government under the 1970 version of the Clean Air Act.

CITIZENS IN THE COURTS

For hundreds of years there have been private cases brought to court against polluters. In 1611, William Aldred's case was heard in the English Courts. The defendant in the case had built a pigsty which interfered with the view from Aldred's window. The "stench and unhealthy odors emanating from the pigs drifted on to Aldred's land and premises and were such that Aldred and his family and friends could not come and go without being subjected to continuous annoyance, to the destruction of the use and benefit of the premises by Aldred." [1] Aldred requested forty pounds in damages. The Chief Justice awarded damages to Aldred for the stopping of both light and air, and went on to state, "And the building of a lime-kiln is good and profitable; but if it be built so near a house, so that none can dwell, an action lies for it." [2]

Until the second half of the twentieth century, most suits resembled the Aldred case in that they were suits brought by a private party against another private party. These suits basically fell into the categories of negligence and liability suits, nuisance suits like Aldred's (where damage must be proved) and trespass suits in which damage need not be proved.

Citizen suits against private parties have had many shortcomings in the field of pollution control. Often in the case of air and water pollution it is difficult for a plaintiff (the person making the complaint) to establish which among several polluters had caused the harm, since multiple sources may contribute to the pollution of a particular area or body of water. It is also difficult for the plaintiff to prove the necessary causal relationship between the pollutant and his particular problem. Also, in the case of nuisance suits, it is not easy for the plaintiff to prove that the "defendant was negligent or that his conduct was intentional or unreasonable." [3]

Aside from the difficulty of winning a suit against a private polluter, the very high cost of litigation has kept the number of such suits very small. Even if such a suit is brought and won, it is usually less expensive for the polluter to pay claims than to install pollution control devices. Thus, these suits against private parties have not been a very effective tool in the fight against pollution.

One attempt to overcome this problem was the class action suit. In these suits, a number of people, each injured too little to justify the expense of an individual lawsuit, pooled their resources and aggregated their claims to sue as representatives of an injured class. A large number of class action suits were filed in the last few years. But on December 17, 1973, in *Zahn* v. *International Paper Co.,*[4] the Supreme Court ruled that each plaintiff in a class action suit must be able to allege the $10,000 worth of damages usually required to establish federal court jurisdiction over the controversy. Until this decision, the courts had considered the $10,000 damage requirement met if any one party in the class action suit was seeking damages of that amount or more.

The Zahn decision struck a blow to the class action suit. One effect the class action suit might have had was to encourage polluters to install anti-pollution devices rather than face the large number of claims brought against them in the class action suit. The court, in deciding to limit class action suits and prohibiting one plaintiff from "riding on another's coattails," [5] has reduced the number of claims that will be made and has probably destroyed class-action cases as an effective threat against polluters.

In other areas of environmental law, where damages are not claimed, the courts have taken a broader view of who may bring suit. The greatest shift in court attitude has been with regard to the kinds of stakes an individual is required to have in order to sue the federal government. Three legal decisions in the last decade have greatly expanded the citizen's right to seek judicial review of federal action.

In the 1965 case of *Scenic Hudson Preservation Conf.* v. *Federal Power Commission*,[6] a large breakthrough occurred. The case involved the Federal Power Commission's (FPC) approval of construction of a reservoir and pumping station on New York's Hudson River at Storm King. A statute existed which permitted review of this type of FPC decision by any aggrieved party. A group of conservation organizations, concerned about the effect the project might have on the scenic value of the area, sought review of the FPC action on aesthetic and conservation grounds. The second circuit court granted standing to this group maintaining that other than economic interest could be the basis for being an "aggrieved person." It also noted that "associations of individuals could have standing to protect the environmental interests of the individuals themselves as well as the interests of the association." [7] The recognition of non-economic stakes broke ground for a flood of citizen suits against potentially harmful administrative decisions, and it was this interpretation along with subsequent court decisions which paved the way for the citizen-suit provisions in the air and water pollution statutes. The part of the decision relating to individuals and associations, although further refined in later cases, established the grounds upon which all the new environmental organizations and industry could seek standing.

In 1970, the Supreme Court, in *Data Processing Service Organizations* v. *Camp*,[8] decided there no longer had to be specific language in the statute authorizing "adversely affected or aggrieved persons" to bring suit if the defendant were "(1) suffering injury in fact and (2) arguably within the 'zone of interests' protected by the statute in question." It specifically stated that the zone of protected interests may reflect " 'aesthetic, conservational, and recreational' as well as economic values." [9]

In 1972, the Supreme Court further defined standing in *Sierra Club* v. *Morton* (the Mineral King case).[10] Here the Sierra Club charged that the proposed development of a ski resort on federal land in the Mineral King Valley in California violated federal statutes governing National Forests and National Parks. The court held that the Sierra Club did not have an adequate stake in the preservation of the Valley to have standing to bring the suit, because the club had not asserted that its activities or those of its members would be affected by the development. The court maintained that the environmental impact of Mineral King would "not fall indiscriminately upon every citizen but would fall only on those who used the area." However, the court added that once a citizen or group showed its stake in the environmental decision, the plaintiff could assert the interest of the general public as well. It went on to state, "Aesthetic and environmental well-being, like economic well-being, are important ingredients of the quality of life in our society and the fact that particular environmental interests are shared by the many rather than the few does not make them less deserving of legal protection through the legal process." [11]

This decision failed to establish who had standing when federal action adversely affected the general public as a whole rather than a specific user group. However, in 1973, in *Scrap* v. *United States,*[12] the Supreme Court agreed to hear its first National Environmental Policy Act (NEPA) case, and resolved the issue of standing in environmental law. The plaintiffs, a group of George Washington University Law School students among others, had opposed the Interstate Commerce Commission's (ICC) approval of a temporary railroad freight rate increase where no environmental impact statement had been filed. The plaintiffs claimed that the rate increase would decrease the use of recycled goods, thereby producing more litter and other harmful effects on parks in the Washington, D.C. area. The ICC argued that the harm alleged by the plaintiffs was too vague and unsubstantiated for them to be granted standing. The Supreme Court, however, upheld the plaintiff's right to sue. Unlike the Mineral King case, which affected a specific geographical area, the Scrap case involved potential harm to anyone who made use of the country's scenic resources and all who breathed the air. The court stated "To deny standing to persons who are in fact injured simply because many others are also injured would mean that the most injurious and widespread Government actions could be questioned by nobody." [13]

In these two cases, the Supreme Court has made clear that in order to have standing to sue, a plaintiff must show that he personally, or the group of which he is a member, will be affected by the potential harm. If the potential harm will affect a narrow group of people, he must be able to prove that he will be one of those affected but if the potential harm affects all citizens, any citizen can bring suit.

This broad view of citizen-standing can have an important impact on environmental problems. First, it must be noted that it can be nearly impossible for a citizen's group to get a dispute on the agenda of an executive agency or congressional committee. The courts become his major means of access to the government. By filing suit, most environmental groups have found they also gain publicity for their cause which may help them to get action in both the executive and legislative branches. These cases, based on citizen initiative, usually reflect a range of citizen concern not represented in the bureaucracy and may encourage administrators to take a harder look at the alternatives to and the cost and benefits of their decisions. If plaintiffs were permitted to sue only on economic grounds, the pressures on the bureaucracy would be such that it would give much less weight to such non-economic factors as aesthetics and wildlife. In short, these standing decisions give more leverage to citizens and "the more leverage citizens have, the more responsive and responsible their officials and fellow citizens will be." [14]

The question of "standing" in the courts has been defined not only by judicial review but by legislation at both the state and federal level. Numerous states have attempted through legislation to guarantee citizens the right to challenge activities that might be harmful to the environment.

One of the early and most publicized of these acts was Michigan's Environmental Protection Act of 1970 which permits any private or public entity to sue any other private or public entity for equitable relief from "pollution impairment or destruction" of the "air, water, and other natural resources and the public trust therein." The Michigan law goes on to direct the courts "to develop a common-law of environmental degradation through case-by-case definition of pollution of the environment." [15] The courts are also authorized to review state pollution standards (if challenged) and to substitute their own standards for any that may be found deficient. This type of legislation involves both citizens and the courts in standard-setting and leaves the final word in the hands of the judges, rather than the administrators. This opens the way for the courts to play a new and major role in environmental policy. In the past, the courts have tried to restrict their decisions to interpretations of the law and the legislative procedures required. Michigan's law is an invitation for the courts to make substantive policy, when the decisions made by the bureaucrats are found lacking.

To overcome the problem of standing, other states have also enacted legislation authorizing citizens to bring suits. However, most of these leave standard-setting within the administrative agencies, and the role of the courts is confined to enforcing these standards. As of mid-1972, five other states besides Michigan had enacted one or the other type of citizen-suit laws.[16]

Opponents of these citizen suit laws had argued that the courts would be swamped with frivolous law suits which would cause immense delay in essential projects. However, a recent survey of states with these laws, showed that in the first two years of their existence, only fifty citizen suits had been filed.[17]

The United States Congress also realized the need to legislate standing, and included citizen-suit clauses when it amended the Clean Air Act in 1970 and the Water Pollution Control Act in 1972. However, before examining the effects of these statutes, we will turn to some prior federal legislation which did not contain citizen-suit clauses.

THE NATIONAL ENVIRONMENTAL POLICY ACT OF 1969

Thus far we have dealt primarily with the courts' expanding interpretation of standing. But the role of the courts in environmental policy also expanded with its new interpretation. Citizens who were granted standing now had their cases heard and these cases were brought to force the government to enforce its own laws. The courts' willingness to grant standing had opened the door for its role in review of administrative decision making.

Of all federal environmental legislation the National Environmental Policy Act of 1969 (NEPA)[18] has probably led to the greatest increase in environmental court cases. Although NEPA does not contain a citizen-suit clause, the courts have ruled that NEPA's "102" impact statement procedure is enforceable by citizen suits. In brief, section 102 of NEPA requires all agencies of the federal government to prepare environmental impact statements on "major actions significantly affecting the quality of the human environment" [19] (see Chapter 5). By June of 1973, less than four years after NEPA's enactment, there had been more than four hundred lawsuits which challenged agency compliance with NEPA.[20]

The bulk of the first NEPA cases were suits to compel the filing of 102 statements, where none had been prepared. The job of the courts was to define the meaning of "major actions" and "significantly affecting" as used in the statute, so as to determine which actions required an impact statement. In *Scherr* v. *Volpe*[21] the court stated, "It is the court which must construe the statutory standards ('major' and 'significantly affecting') and, having construed them, then apply them to the particular project and decide whether the agency's failure [to prepare a statement] violated the congressional demand." [22]

A sampling of cases illustrates the wide range of areas affected by the courts' decisions. The courts upheld agency decisions that 102 statements were not required, under the circumstances of particular cases, for a military practice maneuver in Reid State Park in Maine, for federal approval of a lease of lands held by the government in trust for Indians in New Mexico, for erecting a federal office building to house Corps of Engineers staff in

Mobile, Alabama, and for grants to assist construction of a 66-unit apartment project in Los Angeles and a lower income housing project in Houston. They have held that 102 statements were required for a grant to assist construction of a college high-rise housing project in Portland, Oregon, for Interstate Commerce Commission approval of a temporary boost in railroad freight rates, for federal aid for widening a Wisconsin State highway, and for a Soil Conservation Service project to channelize sixty-six miles of Chicod Creek in North Carolina.[23]

A large number of the early NEPA cases concerned projects which had been initiated before the enactment of NEPA. The question for the courts was whether NEPA applied to these projects, and if so, at what stage of the bureaucratic process was an impact statement required.

One of the earliest and most significant NEPA cases raised these issues. In *Calvert Cliffs Coordinating Committee v. Atomic Energy Commission,*[24] an impact statement was filed, but the plaintiffs charged that four of the regulations devised by the Atomic Energy Commission (AEC) to meet the requirements of NEPA violated section 102 of that act. Two of the challenged AEC provisions concerned AEC's attempt to delay compliance with NEPA. One of these provisions prohibited the raising of non-radiological environmental issues at any hearing if notice for the hearing appeared in the *Federal Register* before March 4, 1971.

The Atomic Energy Commission defended this provision by arguing that the March, 1971 date was set to provide for an orderly transition period and to avoid delays in meeting the urgent needs of the country for electrical power. They also pointed out that NEPA did not have an "inflexible timetable." The court held that, although NEPA indeed had no "inflexible timetable," it had a clear effective date and that "the effective date of it demands that they [the agency] strive, 'to the fullest extent possible,' to be prompt in the process." [25] Addressing itself to this same point, the court stated, "Again, the Commission's approach to statutory interpretation is strange indeed—so strange that it seems to reveal a rather thoroughgoing reluctance to meet the NEPA procedural obligations in the agency review process . . ." [26]

The second challenged provision stated that if a permit for construction had been granted prior to the date set for NEPA compliance and if an operating license was not yet issued, the agency would not consider environmental factors or require modifications in the facility prior to the issuance of the operating license. The court found that this provision also failed to comply with NEPA. "By refusing to consider environmental alterations until construction is completed, the Commission may effectively foreclose the environmental protection desired by Congress . . . If 'irreversible and irretrievable commitments of resources' have already been made, the license hearing may become a hollow exercise." [27] The court went on to suggest that the AEC consider a temporary halt in construction while it carried out a pre-operating license review. The court admitted this would cause delay but found it more consistent with the purpose of NEPA "to delay operation at a stage where real environmental protection may come about than at a stage where corrective action may be so costly as to be impossible." [28]

Two other AEC provisions were challenged in the Calvert Cliffs case in addition to the two time-delay provisions. One was the ruling that required environmental factors to be considered by the agency's regulatory staff, but not by the hearing board which conducted a review of staff recommendations, unless such issues were raised by outside parties or members of the staff.

The court again upheld the plaintiff on the grounds that section 102 of NEPA required that the detailed statement accompany proposals through the agency review process. "What possible purpose could there be in requiring the 'detailed statement' to be before hearing boards, if the boards are free to ignore the contents of the statement?" [29] The court went on to point out that "Beyond Section 102 (2)(C), NEPA requires that agencies consider the environmental impact of their actions 'to the fullest extent possible.' . . . Compliance to the fullest possible extent would seem to demand that environmental issues be considered at every important stage in the decision making process concerning a particular action . . ." [30]

The fourth AEC provision that was challenged prohibited the hearing board from conducting an independent evaluation of environmental factors if other responsible agencies had already certified that their own environmental standards had been met by the proposed action. The AEC hearing boards had assumed that if proposed nuclear plants met EPA's water quality standards, no further consideration of water pollution was necessary.

Again the plaintiffs were upheld. The court said, "NEPA mandates a case-by-case balancing judgment on the part of the federal agencies. In each individual case, the particular economic and technical benefits of planned action must be assessed and then weighed against the environmental cost; . . . Certification by another agency that its own environmental standards are satisfied involves an entirely different kind of judgment. Such agencies, without overall responsibility for the particular federal action in question, attend to only one aspect of the problem . . ."[31]

The Calvert Cliffs case made it clear to agencies that NEPA would be enforced to its fullest by the courts, and that the environmental impact of a proposed action had to be balanced against the benefits of that action. The role of the courts in relation to NEPA was of critical importance. For NEPA requires both a significant increase in workload for all federal agencies and a new substantive approach which may conflict with an agency's specific goals. One could hardly expect that NEPA's 102 process would be eagerly complied with by these agencies. The court's strong decision in Calvert Cliffs forced the AEC, and presumably other agencies, to stop dragging their feet and establish a realistic approach to dealing with the environmental implications of the decisions which now faced them.

The Calvert Cliffs decision was made after the Council on Environmental Quality had issued its 1971 Guidelines. Before these guidelines were issued, court decisions concerning 102's retroactivity had not been consistent. The CEQ guidelines provided that "to the maximum extent practicable" impact statements should be applied to further major federal actions even though they arise from projects or programs begun before NEPA became law. This is to minimize the adverse environmental consequences of the further actions that may not have been fully evaluated at the outset of the project or program.[32] The question became not so much one of retroactivity, but rather one of applying the '102' process to all ongoing projects if major actions remained to be taken. Calvert Cliffs cited these guidelines in its decision and most courts have subsequently used this approach in decisions concerning projects already underway.

The question of retroactivity was an important one for environmental groups, but not nearly as important as how the 102 process would relate to all the projects begun after NEPA's enactment. In many of the citizen suits where agencies were challenged for failing to file 102 statements, the court's task was not merely to decide whether an impact statement was required, but also to interpret at what stage of a project the impact statement had to be filed.

Some of the timing requirements of NEPA in regard to impact statements were spelled out by the courts in *Scientists Institute for Public Information, Inc. (SIPI)* v. *Atomic Energy Commission*.[33] Here, the question before the courts was whether an impact statement was required for a research and development project as a whole, or whether impact statements need only be filed for individual facilities as they were developed. The AEC had filed an impact statement on a pilot facility for the breeder reactor, but had not considered the environmental impact which would result if the pilot plant were successful. The breeder technology became an accepted method for generating power. The court ruled that an impact statement was necessary at the research stage for "development of a technology 'serves as much to affect the environment as does a Commission decision granting a construction permit for a specific plant . . .' " The court further noted, "Once there has been, in the terms of NEPA, 'an irretrievable commitment of resources' in the technology development stage, the balance of environmental costs and economic and other benefits shifts in favor of ultimate application of the technology." [34] The AEC did not contest this decision and the overall effect of it will be to force agencies to consider environmental factors at a still earlier point in the decision making process. The decision also has the effect of making the 102 process a major tool for assessing the impacts of new technologies before they are widely adopted.

As we saw in the Calvert Cliffs case, the courts' interpretations of 102 procedural requirements have not been restricted to when or whether impact statements are required. Several important court decisions, besides Calvert Cliffs, have spelled out what an impact statement must contain to comply with NEPA. In *Committee for Nuclear Responsibility* v. *Seaborg*,[35] the courts ruled that an agency (in this case AEC), must discuss within its 102 statement, opposing views of responsible scientific opinion. This way the ultimate decision could be made in the light of "the full range of responsible opinion on the environmental effects." In *Natural Resources Defense Council* v. *Morton*,[36] the court held that an impact statement filed by the Interior Department was unacceptable because it had not adequately discussed alternatives to the proposed action. The court further held that the 102 statement must gather in one place a discussion of "the relative environmental impact of alternatives" and that alternatives meant those reasonable courses of action available to the government as a whole not just a single agency.[37] The Calvert Cliffs decision had stated that an impact statement also required a balancing of the costs and benefits of the project. "In some instances environmental costs may outweigh economic and technical benefits and in other instances they may not. But NEPA mandates a rather finely tuned and 'systematic' balancing analysis in each instance." [38] Similarly in *Natural Resources Defense Council* v. *Morton,* the court stated that an impact statement provides "a basis for (a) evaluation of the benefits of the proposed project in light of its environmental risks and (b) comparison of the net balance for the proposed project with the environmental risks presented by alternative courses of action." [39]

In all the above decisions, the courts have restricted themselves to defining the procedures an agency must follow to comply with NEPA, rather than addressing themselves to the particular substantive decision made by the agency. The question has been, "Have the agencies performed all their obligations under NEPA?" not "Is the agency's decision right or wrong?" This does not mean, however, that the courts' decisions have not had a wide impact. As the CEQ guidelines seemed to have an effect on the court's decisions, the court's decisions have had an effect on the executive agencies. There can be no doubt that the first alterations in the agencies were procedural, but the procedural changes have caused agencies to also change their substantive decisions.

One obvious effect of the courts' decisions can be seen in the number of impact statements filed. Although agencies are undoubtedly still not filing all the "102" statements required by NEPA, there can be no doubt that the threat of court action, with the possible consequence of halting projects, has acted to encourage agencies to file statements. There was a dramatic increase in the number of statements filed after the courts' early decisions. However, beginning in 1972, the number of impact statements began to drop off. This can be explained by the fact that many of the agencies had, by this time, caught up with their backlog of statements due on projects initiated before NEPA's enactment.[40]

The preparation of these statements required a large expenditure of agency money, staff and time, and caused delay in projects. According to William Doub, an AEC Commissioner, the Atomic Energy Commission alone expanded its regulatory staff from 600 at the time of Calvert Cliffs to 1,200 in 1973. Similarly, their regulatory expenditures increased from $15.7 to $46.5 million over the same period. It should be noted, however, that not all of these increases were directly due to the NEPA process. Doub has further estimated that before Calvert Cliffs it took one half a man-year of AEC staff time to complete an impact statement. After Calvert Cliffs, he estimated an impact statement required five AEC staff man-years.[41] The AEC responded to Calvert Cliffs by issuing guidelines which halted the issuance of new licenses before impact statements were prepared. The regulations, however, permitted temporary licenses which the courts halted in *Izaak Walton League* v. *Schlesinger* (Quad Cities).[42] The result of these two decisions was a period of seventeen months during which no major nuclear plant licensing actions were taken.[43]

The AEC has been affected more than most agencies by NEPA and the court decisions arising from the act. But almost all agencies have changed their procedures to some degree to adjust to the impact statement requirement. However, procedural changes are not the same as substantive changes, and in most agencies the impact statements still serve as justifications for decisions already made rather than as important inputs into the decision-making process.

There is evidence that some agencies have adopted the spirit and purpose of NEPA as well as its letter. AEC has shelved two proposals to store radioactive wastes until further studies are made of the environmental consequences of the proposals. The Corps of Engineers has dropped several construction proposals because of the environmental harm they might cause. None of these actions have been taken directly because of court rulings; and many other examples of voluntary compliance with NEPA could be cited.[44]

There is no doubt that the courts' decisions have played a critical role in this "voluntary" compliance. The immediate effects of Calvert Cliffs could be seen in the AEC's "102" regulations and in their actions, but it is important to note that the Scientists Institute for Public Information case was brought two years after Calvert Cliffs, and that with all the voluntary compliance, citizen groups and the courts were not satisfied that AEC was truly considering the environmental impact of its actions at every stage of the decision-making process. The AEC's stakes are not primarily environmental and it is, therefore, apt to shortchange environmental considerations, unless citizens maintain their vigilance and the courts their strict interpretation of NEPA.

A number of court decisions have addressed the question of whether section 102 applies to actions of the Environmental Protection Agency. The legislative history of NEPA is unclear as to whether the Congress intended to exempt proenvironmental regulations and actions from the 102 requirement, and the court interpretations of this question have been inconsistent. However, the question is no longer an important issue because the 1972 Amendments to the Federal Water Pollution Control Act exempted EPA's water pollution regulatory actions from NEPA and the Energy Supply and Environmental Coordination Act of 1974 gave a similar exemption for actions taken under The Clean Air Act. Thus, the only EPA decisions for which impact statements may be required are waste treatment grants and actions taken in areas other than air or water pollution. This does not mean that citizens are prevented from suing EPA for failing to comply with the air and water pollution statutes.

THE CLEAN AIR ACT

As we have mentioned earlier, the 1970 Amendments to the Clean Air Act specifically authorized citizens to bring suits against the administrator of EPA for failing to perform a duty required by the Act. Citizens were also authorized to bring suits against polluters, if they failed to comply with standards established pursuant to the Act.[45] The court could award litigation costs to either party, thereby easing the financial burdens of plaintiffs but also deterring them from bringing frivolous suits. The 1972 Amendments to the Federal Water Pollution Control Act contained similar provisions.[46]

Due to the strict but complex time requirements of these amendments, litigation under these acts has only begun and court interpretation in this area is in its infancy. In this section, we shall restrict ourselves to court decisions under the Clean Air Act, because not enough time has elapsed since the 1972 water amendments for the courts to have played a significant role. However, we can be sure that in the future there will be a large number of important issues which will be raised under the water amendments and that, in many cases, the courts will base their decisions on the precedents established under the Clean Air Act.

Cases under the citizen suit provisions mentioned above represent only a portion of the items which appeared on the courts' agenda under the Clean Air Act. The Clean Air Act had authorized the EPA administrator to set a variety of pollution control standards (see Chapter 8) and, as these standards were established, industry challenged them in the courts. The courts for the most part remanded the cases back to EPA.

Portland Cement Association v. *Ruckelshaus*[47] serves as an example of the cases in which new source performance standards were challenged.[48] Here the plaintiffs argued that the standards set down for Portland Cement plants economically discriminated against them in comparison with standards promulgated for power plants and incinerators. They also argued that EPA had not adequately demonstrated the achievability of the standards and the Association produced expert testimony showing errors in the EPA data and the possible significance of these errors. The court dismissed the first count on the grounds that the administrator is not required to justify different standards for different industries. But the case was remanded to EPA on the grounds that the achievability of the emission standards had not been demonstrated since they were based on erroneous data.

Kennecott Copper v. *EPA*[49] challenged EPA's secondary ambient sulphur oxides standards, again on the grounds that EPA had erred in the calculations on which the standard was based. The court remanded the case to EPA and EPA rescinded the relevant portion of its secondary standard.

In *Annaconda Company* v. *Ruckelshaus*,[50] a Federal District Court again remanded the case to EPA. This case dealt with the ability of Annaconda's copper smelter, which emitted sulfur oxides, to conform with EPA standards. The court found that since EPA's standards only affected Annaconda, Annaconda should have been consulted more in the standard setting process and that once again there was insufficient evidence to support the standards. However, the Court of Appeals overturned the District Court's decision, finding that EPA had followed due process.[51]

The industry case, which has received the most publicity to date and has probably had the widest impact, is *International Harvester Co.* v. *Ruckelshaus*.[52] The case is technically different from the preceding cases, because here the plaintiffs challenged the date by which emission standards had to be met rather than the standards themselves. The 1970 Amendments to the Clean Air Act required the administrator to set emission standards for light duty vehicles in order to reduce emissions of hydrocarbons and carbon monoxide ninety per cent by 1975. Congress had allowed an escape for industry, by permitting industry to petition for a one-year suspension of the 1975 requirements. Congress also called upon the National Academy of Sciences to conduct a study of the feasibility of meeting the emission standards established by the administrator.[53]

In *International Harvester* v. *Ruckelshaus*, the three major auto companies, General Motors, Ford and Chrysler, joined with International Harvester to bring suit after EPA had denied their petition for a one-year suspension of the standards on the grounds that the auto makers had failed to show that effective control technology was not available. The National Academy of Sciences in its study, concluded that the necessary technology to meet the 1975 requirements was not at that time available, but it noted that it was not impossible that the larger manufacturers might progress rapidly enough to produce cars that would be in compliance by the deadline. They suggested, however, that there might also be "severe driveability problems" in these vehicles which "could have significant safety implications." [54]

The court's decision in this case was based on a number of complex factors. The manufacturers' suspension request was based on actual test data showing that no car had actually been driven 50,000 miles and achieved the 1975 emission standards. When the administrator refused the extension, he relied on what the court referred to as a "technological methodology" to predict that the standards could be met. The plaintiffs argued in court that their opinions on the administrator's technological methodology and their data had not had a fair hearing in EPA since they had been denied the right to cross-examine. The court ruled that cross-examination was not required in this instance, where time was limited by statute.

The plaintiffs also argued the administrator could base his determination of "available technology" only on the technology that was available at the time of petition, and not on his prediction of future technological developments. The court disagreed and ruled that it was legitimate for the administrator to base his determination on the probable sequence of technology during the two-year lead time.

However, the court then carefully examined the substance of the prediction and the basis for EPA's rejection of the petition. The court was particularly bothered by the fact that the National Academy of Sciences study had supported the industry test data and had concluded that the technology was not available. The court found that unless EPA could demonstrate that its technological methodology was more reliable than the

Academy's,—which it had failed to do—EPA could not reject the Academy's conclusion.

The court also found that the technology was not available when the auto-makers conducted the test on actual vehicles, and that the administrator had failed to show that his methodology was indeed reliable enough to offset the petitioner's actual data. The court's decision on this point was reached in a framework that considered the potential costs of a wrong decision both economically and environmentally, and came to the conclusion that the environmental costs of a wrong decision would be quite low, whereas the economic costs in terms of jobs and the economy as a whole could be quite high. It concluded that "the risk of an 'erroneous' denial of suspension outweighed the risk of an 'erroneous' grant of suspension." [55]

The court, however, refused to grant the manufacturers' request to suspend the 1975 deadline and instead remanded the case to EPA for further proceedings so that the "Administrator may render a decision based on the best information available which extends to all the determinations which the statute requires as a condition of suspension." [56] Although the court did not preclude further consideration of available technology, it went on to suggest that EPA might choose to conditionally suspend the deadline and establish interim standards that would result in higher standards than an outright suspension.

On April 11, 1973, a year after the administrator had originally refused the extension, EPA, taking the court's advice, suspended the 1975 standards for a year and established standards for the interim. Thus, although the court did not order EPA to suspend the standards, its decision had the same effect.

The pattern of the courts' role in the pollution policy area becomes clear as we look back at the above cases. In each of the cases, the court found the burden of proof lay on EPA to show that its standards were based on reliable data and that the available technology had been adequately demonstrated. In most of the cases the court found that EPA could not sustain the burden of proof. The court, however, never ordered that the standards be overturned, but rather remanded each case back to EPA.

The courts discovered that in the area of pollution control, when attempting to ascertain whether reasoned judgments had been made, they could not restrict themselves to procedural matters, but rather became entangled in the substantive aspects of highly technical administrative decisions. The courts were not completely comfortable dealing with these substantive aspects nor in passing judgment on the relative worth of conflicting scientific opinion. Therefore, the cases were remanded. However, in *International Harvester* v. *Ruckelshaus,* the remand came very close to being a command to EPA to reverse its administrative judgment, a command based on the technicalities of controlling automobile air pollution. Although EPA's technical judgments undoubtedly will always be challenged by industry representatives, the degree of court intervention will depend on the agency's technical competence. The cases reviewed above indicate that there will be a large role for the courts to play unless there is an improvement in EPA's technical abilities.

Although these highly technical industry cases, in which the courts become involved in substance, may represent the courts' most arduous and complex task, some more traditional cases (from the viewpoint of the judiciary) have had an even greater impact on air pollution policy. *Sierra Club, et. al.* v. *Ruckelshaus*[57] is such a case.

The first stated purpose of the Clean Air Act was "to protect and enhance the quality of the nation's air resources so as to promote the public health and welfare and the productive capacity of the population." [58] The law also required EPA to promulgate air quality standards and the state to submit plans for implementing those standards.

On April 30, 1971, when EPA announced its preliminary guidelines for state plans to implement the national air quality standards, the administrator had warned that the standards "shall not be considered in any manner to allow significant deterioration of existing air quality in any portion of any state." [59] However, EPA reconsidered this nondegradation policy and concluded that its effects would impair efforts to move pollution sources out of areas that were already severely polluted. Therefore, the nondegradation provision was eliminated when EPA issued its final guidelines for state programs.

The Sierra Club then joined with three other environmental groups to enjoin the administrator of EPA from approving any implementation plan which allowed degradation of existing air quality, even if the existing air quality was better than the national standards. The EPA contended that more pollution, not less, would result if the states were prevented from relocating industry from high pollution sites where health and life were endangered to areas where the air quality was better than federal standards.

The District Court disagreed and found that the Clean Air Act required that all state implementation plans provide for nondegradation of the air, "no matter how presently pure that quality in some section of the country happens to be," and, therefore, ordered the administrator to review all plans and disapprove those which failed to provide maintenance or betterment of the present air quality. The EPA appealed the decision and the Circuit Court affirmed the judgment of the District Court.

On November 7, 1972, a year and one half after the standards were first announced, EPA disapproved all pending state plans because they did not forbid degradation of air quality. However, EPA went on to appeal the decision to the Supreme Court, on the basis that states retained the option to strengthen the federal standards. The environmental groups were then joined by eighteen states who claimed that the power of each state to set stricter standards was inadequate to protect them from pollution drifting from other states and from the competition between states for industry. The Supreme Court deadlocked in a four-four vote, and thus EPA was bound by the District Court ruling.[60]

The EPA then developed four plans to keep the nation's clean air from getting dirtier, and conducted public hearings on the plans. The Sierra Club found the proposals fell short of the legal requirements and that three of the proposals would not prevent significant deterioration of present air quality.

In this case, the courts, by interpreting the law, made a policy decision with far-reaching effects. The court's interpretation of the Clean Air Act, which was solidly grounded in the legislative history of the act, inescapably forced EPA to consider the relationships among land use, economic development, and air quality. If the air cannot be degraded, where will new economic development take place and what kinds of controls will be necessary on new and existing sources of potential pollution to insure that existing air quality is maintained? There are no easy answers to these questions, but the courts have clearly rejected EPA's first attempt at a solution.

State implementation plans have been challenged by environmental groups on a number of grounds. The administrator of EPA has been brought to court for permitting states to delay submission of portions of their implementation plans,[61] and for approving state plans that were deficient because: they failed to provide for required reviews, allowed for variances from the mandatory attainment dates, permitted the state air pollution director to consider economic and social factors and technical feasibility when issuing abatement orders, or allowed emission reports to be held confidential.[62] The courts have generally stuck to a strict interpretation of the law and the environmental groups have won a good many of their cases.

The EPA was also challenged in court for failing to prepare a state implementation plan. Section 110 of the Clean Air Act requires the administrator of EPA to promulgate regulations to replace any portion of a state plan he disapproves within two months of the disapproval. On May 31, 1972, EPA disapproved a large portion of the California implementation plan. On September 6 of that year, the City of Riverside began proceedings[63] to compel EPA to prepare an implementation plan for the South Coast Air Basin. On September 22, EPA proposed regulations to correct deficiences in the California plan for the South Coast Air Basin, but did not set forth the necessary transportation controls to meet the photochemical oxidant standard. However, the administrator announced at the same time that he would propose the appropriate transportation controls by February 15, 1973. The administrator moved to stay action on the above grounds, but the court denied the motion. Rather the court ruled that EPA's failure to file an implementation plan within the two month period following the rejection of California's plan violated a nondiscretionary duty. It, therefore, ordered EPA to publish in the *Federal Register* by January 15,

1973, an implementation plan for attaining the standard for photochemical oxidants in California including all necessary transportation and land use controls.

The court's decision not to stay the action in this case had little real effect on the date the implementation plans would be published. But the court wanted the opportunity to set precedent to show that the courts would not turn aside when the administrator violated specific duties assigned to him in the act, and that the time requirements of the act could not be disregarded.

On January 15, Ruckelshaus duly revealed EPA's plan to reduce photochemical oxidants in the Los Angeles area. The plan called for gasoline rationing and for a more than eighty per cent reduction in summer automobile traffic. As the administrator stated, "If the only way to meet the 1977 standards is to cut traffic eighty per cent, I don't know if that's feasible and still have a viable community." Noting that despite his doubts about the plan's feasibility, he was under a court order to promulgate the plan, Ruckelshaus stated, "This is the result of this law in this community at this time. Maybe the law has to be changed." [64]

THE ROLE OF THE COURTS

Almost all of the cases discussed above have been suits by a private party against the federal government. This comparatively new kind of suit has replaced suits between private parties as the most significant way in which the courts influence environmental policy. This change in the role of the courts reflects the ever greater intervention of the government in dealing with environmental problems. In this concluding section, we will therefore limit ourselves to the role of the courts in suits to which the government is a party.

Definitions of law evolve over a period of time through the many court decisions handed down. Cases are decided on the basis of the relevant decisions which have come before, and eventually a body of legal precedent is established, thereby easing the court's task in making decisions. Precedent will often determine what cases the court will agree to hear, what the court's approach to the case will be, and how the court will decide the case. Precedent contributes to the myth that there is no judicial discretion, that the law is certain and unchanging, and that judges are confined to finding the applicable law.

In the field of environmental law, the courts are presently engaged in establishing new precedents. The opportunity is always there for the courts to set new precedent by selection and construction of the old, but first the courts must be willing to free themselves from the constraints of the past. Since the courts do not operate in a vacuum, the time they are most apt to do this is the time when the public is demanding new solutions to problems.

The court interpretation of standing is a good example of this. One can trace the evolution of the new doctrine from the *Scenic Hudson* decision, which broke with the past, through the Supreme Court's SIPI ruling, which will undoubtedly be cited as precedent for some time to come. These decisions occurred at a time when the population was feeling particularly incapable of having an effect on government policy and when a small but vocal minority were becoming increasingly angry about the disregard for our environment. In a highly populated society where legislators are often not responsive to the concerns of individuals and small minorities, the courts become another avenue for affecting decisions and making concerns known. By granting citizens the right to complain about government misconduct, the courts opened the door for new kinds of cases to be heard, thereby permitting environmentalists to get their issue on the national agenda and reducing the frustration felt about environmental policy. In addition, court decisions sometimes result in identifying for Congress areas where new legislation is needed, as illustrated by the citizen suit provisions in the Clean Air and Water Acts.

The courts can not only control who brings cases before them, but also the grounds on which they will decide a case. In most cases, there are several different kinds of issues involved, and the court determines for itself which kinds it may properly address and which it may not. Sometimes the facts of a case, when a single straightforward aspect of the law is in contention, will determine precisely the approach the courts will take. But frequently, the facts of the case permit the courts a number of different approaches. The plaintiff argues the case from as many different angles as he can, in the hopes that the court will accept at least one of his arguments. The court then must decide which approach it will take. In the past few years, the courts have begun to approach cases in ways which allow them to exercise more influence over administrative decisions. How they have done this can best be explained by considering some of the different grounds on which the courts base their decisions.

Traditionally, judges feel constrained to enforce plain legal rules and are most comfortable deciding cases where the government has clearly taken an affirmative action that violates the law, or has failed to perform a procedural obligation spelled out under that law. For the most part, in the past, courts have looked at environmental cases against the government in one of the two ways mentioned above. But these are rarely the underlying issues that are in contention. Rather, they are simply the legal arguments used by the adversaries in the hopes of winning their case.[65]

To clarify the point let us look again at *Sierra Club* v. *Ruckelshaus*. The real underlying issue in this case was the extent to which air pollution control should impinge on economic development. The court did not deal with this issue and instead chose an approach based purely on the grounds that EPA was acting in violation of the Clean Air Act. In cases where the statute has been violated the court orders the agency to reverse its decision. In this case, the court's order coincided with the goal of the plaintiffs, but in many cases, the court's ruling may not coincide with the true goals of either party.

If we turn back to the NEPA cases where no impact statements were filed, we find the true cause for contention was usually the desirability of the proposed action. However, the courts in many cases ignored this issue and addressed themselves only to the procedural aspects of the act. The cases were remanded to the agency with the order that they perform the procedural obligation which had been overlooked or ignored. Neither party to the suit had really had his problems addressed. The agency could perform the required procedure, and then go ahead with the action, unless the action was again contested.

The plaintiff obtained temporary relief, while the agency was delayed by the time it took to perform the duty, but the true issue at stake was not resolved.

Slowly the courts have begun to expand their approaches to environmental cases that come before them. We may say that their decisions can be placed on a continuum shading very gradually from purely procedural judgments, through interpreting the procedural meaning of the wording of a statute, to outright substantive ruling which may have a major impact on the policy contained in the statute.

Another common approach the courts have used in examining cases is to review the administrative action to determine whether it is "arbitrary and capricious" or unsupported by the evidence. In theory this approach should allow the courts greater flexibility than they have when they use the straight violation of statute approach. However, quite frequently in the past if the defendant could show that he had followed the conventional procedures in arriving at his decision or that his decision was based on evidence arrived at in the conventional way, the court would rule that the action was neither arbitrary nor capricious.

Calvert Cliffs demonstrated that the courts would not always settle for the conventional procedures. The court in this case was concerned with the spirit of the law as well as the letter, and approached the case from the aspect of interpreting the procedural meaning as intended by Congress. The court interpreted the act to require more than "*pro forma* ritual," and thus did not restrict itself to ascertaining whether each step of the procedure as spelled out in the statute was followed. It went on to examine whether the procedural process did in fact serve the environmental goal of the act. This approach came closer to resolving the issues under contention than did the straight procedural approach discussed above.

The Calvert Cliffs decision addressed itself to the propriety of the courts reviewing an agency's substantive decisions and concluded that the courts could not reverse a substantive decision on its merits "unless it be shown that the actual balance of costs and benefits that was struck was arbitrary or clearly gave insufficient weight to environmental problems." [66]

However, in looking at the cases brought under the Clean Air

Act, we find that the procedures of the law were in most cases followed strictly and that it would be difficult to find that EPA had acted arbitrarily or capriciously in arriving at its decisions. These cases were decided on the basis that the decisions were not supported by the evidence.

In *International Harvester* v. *Ruckelshaus,* the question becomes whose evidence? The courts were confronted with the prospect of becoming technological umpires. The question for the courts was whether they were willing to get into highly technical scientific evidence and what purpose would be served by so doing. Judge David Bazelon wrote a concurring minority opinion to the case in which he stated, "Socrates said that wisdom is the recognition of how much one does not know. I may be wise if that is wisdom, because I recognize that I do not know enough about dynamometer extrapolations, deterior factor adjustment, and the like to decide whether or not the government's approach to these matters was statistically valid." [67] He would have remanded the case on procedural grounds rather than examining the data on which the decision was based.

The majority, however, did not opt for the procedural approach, but rather delved into the methodological considerations and the degree of expertise of EPA and the National Academy of Sciences. The court carried forth a meticulous probe of the substantive issues involved in the case, and even addressed itself to the possible economic consequences of an incorrect decision. [68] The court also commended EPA for its diligence, clearly eliminating the possibility that EPA had acted arbitrarily. This case thus represents a significant departure from the ones considered above. It is to be noted again that the case was remanded, thus allowing the court to avoid making any final decision but, given the constraints established by the court, EPA was more-or-less forced to reverse its original decision.

In the *International Harvester* decision, the court came quite close to making a major environmental policy decision on its own. We have traced above how the courts' decisions in environmental suits have increasingly tended to get the judges into the substance of a dispute and how the courts have used their flexibility in deciding cases to render decisions based on the spirit of the law and the basic underlying controversies as against the letter of the law and the procedures followed by the agency.

Whether increasing judicial intervention is desirable has been hotly debated for years. In the environmental area, the courts' willingness to address more than the legal technicalities has resulted in making NEPA a meaningful instrument of government reform instead of a lifeless political gesture. It has also resulted in giving environmentally concerned citizens an opportunity to influence many decisions made by agencies which were not inclined to base their decisions on citizen input. Finally, the courts have served a valuable watchdog function by questioning the validity of decisions in an area where decisions are often arrived at on the basis of political pressures. The courts have begun to question the validity of scientific evidence. It has become apparent that bureaucrats choose the evidence on which they base their decisions, and this choice may be only a justification for a decision already reached. Despite these clear gains from the courts' activities, one must keep in mind that the judges are not technical experts, nor are they politically responsive in any direct way. Thus, if the current trend continues and the courts actually begin to make the decisions instead of remanding them to the agencies, it may turn out that some of their decisions will be as arbitrary and as contrary to good public policy as the executive branch decisions they strike down. Our experience with an interventionist Supreme Court in the early 1930s lends some historical validity to these fears.

Regardless of how interventionist the federal courts become, it must be kept in mind that they constitute only one of the three branches of the federal government, and their actions are intertwined with those of Congress and the Executive. The relationship among the three branches is not a separation of powers but a separation of institutions sharing powers.[69] In particular, the Congress retains the right to override most of the court's decisions, and in the environmental area it will probably not hesitate to do so.

CHAPTER 7

State and Local Government

POLLUTION CONTROL at the state and local level must function in a setting of numerous governments competing for economic advancement and divided between polluters and the victims of pollution, between central cities and suburbs, and between Republicans and Democrats. All of the governments are short of funds and thus reluctant to invest in the public facilities necessary to curb pollution. The financial squeeze also intensifies the competition for industrial ratables, a competition which in many cases results in a reluctance to impose strict pollution control regulations.

The difficulty of achieving stringent pollution control at the local level and the regional nature of the pollution problem have resulted in a steadily greater assumption of responsibility by higher levels of government. The federal government has assumed the major responsibility for establishing air and water quality standards, but the states retain important powers to set air pollution emission standards and to issue water effluent permits. Despite increasing federal powers and authority, the states, and to some extent the localities, are now and will likely remain key actors in the compliance process. Aside from the political influence of the state and local governments, the federal government will simply never have sufficient manpower to assume most of the burden of enforcement.

RESPONSIBILITY FOR WATER POLLUTION CONTROL

Attempts to control water pollution in the United States date back almost to the beginning of the new nation. During the colonial period cities passed regulations governing the disposal of sewage, and a few of the more progressive communities invested in municipal sewer lines.[1] In the first half of the nineteenth century numerous state statutes and local ordinances were passed, dealing with nuisances and hazards to navigation arising from floating debris and other forms of water pollution. And in the 1870s and 1880s, as the relationship between contagious diseases and water pollution became known, states created boards of health which devoted much of their effort to water purification and the prevention of pollution.

Throughout the nineteenth century, although most state legislatures enacted water pollution statutes, the primary responsibility for pollution control rested with the local governments. The states delegated to local units of government the power to prevent or abate pollution and authorized local officials to enforce the state pollution laws through criminal prosecution. The authority of local government was supplemented by state authorization for aggrieved individuals to institute civil suits for damages caused by pollution.[2] These approaches to pollution control proved inadequate. The localities were unable to control pollution coming from upstream, and they had no incentive to control their own pollution. Individuals found it almost impossible to bring civil suits because of the difficulty of proving who was responsible for the damage.

The failure of local control efforts and the concern with typhoid and other waterborne diseases began to lead toward the centralization of pollution control responsibility at the state level. By 1948, every state had assumed responsibility for water pollution and most states had placed the administration of the program in the state health department. Beginning about 1950, the increased emphasis placed on water pollution control and the lessened importance of the health aspects of pollution began to affect state administrative arrangements. Independent pollution control agencies were created, or separate statutory agencies within the health department were established. By 1968, only twenty-one state health departments retained authority for water pollution control. Most of the New England and Southern states had established separate commissions or boards to deal with the water pollution problem, whereas the Midwest and Western states were more likely to retain responsibility in the state health department.

The authority of state water pollution control agencies is often limited by the same kinds of interagency jurisdictional problems which plague the federal government. In almost all states, the health department retains some responsibility for municipal water supplies. The fish and game department has a stake in the control of pollution, as does the parks or recreation department. Several states have created water resource agencies, which in some cases have jurisdiction over water pollution and in other cases do not. In many states coordination is attempted by the creation of a water pollution control board which includes representatives from the interested agencies; but many such boards also have significant industry representation, a practice which does not encourage strong enforcement efforts.[3]

Interagency problems at the state level were ameliorated in a number of states by the trend which began around 1970 to create comprehensive state environmental agencies. The trend was spurred by a growing realization of the interdependence of different aspects of environmental policy and was given specific impetus by the creation of the federal EPA in 1970. As of mid-1973, twenty-four states had comprehensive agencies with jurisdiction over both air and water pollution control. In thirteen additional states pollution control was still the responsibility of the Health Department, while in the remaining thirteen one agency was responsible for water pollution control and a different agency for air pollution control.[4]

The comprehensive state agencies take a variety of forms, but the most important distinction among them is whether they are limited to pollution control activities, as for example in New Jersey, or whether they also include recreation-oriented activities such as parks, hunting, and fishing, as in New York State. The latter type of agencies are likely to be somewhat less zealous in pursuit of pollution control because of a more conservative and divided constituency.[5]

In recent years a significant portion of the funds spent by state water pollution control agencies has come from the federal government. In 1972 about 20 per cent of the funding to support state agencies was federal funds (see Table 7.1.). The federal grants go entirely to state and interstate agencies, not to local agencies.

The trend has also been toward an increasing federal share in paying the cost of construction for municipal waste treatment plants. Both the total amount of federal funds appropriated for such construction and the percentage of construction costs which the federal government can pay have been increasing rapidly. The 1972 Amendments to the Federal Water Pollution Control Act allow federal funds to cover 75 per cent of construction costs. State and local investment in water pollution treatment facilities has jumped from $600 million in 1958 to over $1.7 billion in 1971. However, the rate of inflation has been high in the construction industry: if this increase is measured in constant dollars one finds that the "real" investment by state and local governments increased very little between 1963 and 1971.[6]

The states have been shouldering an increasing portion of the non-federal costs of waste treatment plant construction. This is due in part to the 1966 Clean Water Act which increased the federally funded percentage of costs if states agreed to pay 25 per cent of construction costs. It is also due to "pre-financing," a scheme first applied in New York State.

Table 7.1. **Funding and Manpower for State Water Quality Agencies, 1972**

State	Fiscal Year 1972 Budgeted (in $ thousands)			Fiscal Year 1972 Man-Years
	Federal	State	Total	
Alabama	185	159	344	30
Alaska	20	128	148	7
Arizona	77	81	158	12
Arkansas	113	346	458	44
California	672	4,934	5,606	315
Colorado	91	341	432	25
Connecticut	168	388	555	49
Delaware	86	238	324	32
Dist. of Col.	87	398	485	48
Florida	277	837	1,113	87
Georgia	214	675	889	55

Table 7.1. **Funding and Manpower for State Water Quality Agencies, 1972**

State	Fiscal Year 1972 Budgeted (In $ thousands)			Fiscal Year 1972 Man-Years
	Federal	State	Total	
Hawaii	69	331	400	31
Idaho	44	217	260	17
Illinois	431	1,791	2,222	154
Indiana	234	535	769	63
Iowa	123	170	294	31
Kansas	96	478	574	38
Kentucky	164	345	509	41
Louisiana	180	429	608	50
Maine	64	522	585	33
Maryland	184	1,794	1,978	111
Massachusetts	268	1,132	1,400	58
Michigan	360	1,557	1,917	117
Minnesota	158	1,385	1,543	85
Mississippi	137	174	311	23
Missouri	197	250	447	32
Montana	40	195	235	16
Nebraska	68	173	241	17
Nevada	26	36	62	6
New Hampshire	65	556	620	56
New Jersey	312	913	1,225	105
New Mexico	53	184	237	23
New York	645	4,665	5,311	216
N. Carolina	258	615	873	65
N. Dakota	37	31	69	7
Ohio	448	1,085	1,533	87
Oklahoma	118	264	382	34
Oregon	99	650	748	49
Pennsylvania	489	4,052	4,542	373
Rhode Island	109	219	328	27
S. Carolina	151	469	620	55
S. Dakota	39	58	97	9
Tennessee	204	778	982	60
Texas	425	3,668	4,093	275
Utah	56	137	193	15
Vermont	44	340	384	35
Virginia	208	1,178	1,387	114
Washington	137	1,158	1,295	74
W. Virginia	108	531	638	40
Wisconsin	200	1,710	1,909	88
Wyoming	24	48	72	4
Guam	74	66	140	14
Puerto Rico	193	144	337	36
Virgin Islands	73	37	110	11
Total	9,400	43,592	52,992	3,495

Source: Based on Council on Environmental Quality, *Environmental Quality—1972*, pp. 198–99. Figures may not add due to rounding.

In 1965, Governor Rockefeller developed and the New York State voters approved a $1 billion "Clean Waters" bond issue. The size of the bond issue was impressive enough, but it was the method of financing that proved most influential. The Rockefeller plan in essence put New York in the position of prefinancing the federal government's contributions to waste treatment construction within the state. The state agreed to make funds available to the localities as if the federal government had paid its full share; the state would then attempt to recover the amount of the federal share when Congress appropriated sufficient funds.

The Rockefeller plan was designed to meet two problems—the lag in federal appropriations and the rapidly rising costs of waste treatment plant construction. It permitted the localities within a state to proceed immediately with construction rather than waiting until federal funds were available. The New York State approach was adopted by several other states, and it received indirect sanction in the 1966 and 1972 federal acts which authorized states to collect retroactively on construction grants.

From the beginning of the federal waste treatment grant program in 1956, through the end of 1973, federal grants have amounted to almost $7 billion and local and state contributions have totaled an additional $12 billion. Although these figures indicate that the states and localities are spending almost two dollars for every federal dollar, the actual ratio varies considerably from state to state. Until 1966 the Federal grant formula favored smaller communities and more rural states. The 1966 amendments to the Federal Water Pollution Control Act made the formula more equitable, and the 1972 amendments go even further in aiding the more urbanized states. This has already provoked some controversy, and in its report on the 1974 EPA budget the conference committee of the House and Senate Appropriations Committees commented that under the new formula "clearly, rural America was the big loser." [7] Coming from the U.S. Congress this language was not a neutral observation, and EPA subsequently made modifications in its formula to give more money to the rural states.

The allocation of federal waste treatment construction grants within any given state is supposed to be done in accordance with a state water pollution control plan.[8] However, state plans for water pollution control are more fiction than reality. The federal government does not review the state plans, and within many states political pressures are more important than planning in determining which localities receive priority for the grants. In most states arbitrary formulas, such as "first come, first served," are used in approving grant applications in an attempt to minimize local political pressure on the state government. Little or no attempt is made to determine which treatment plants produce the most benefits or will be most effective in controlling pollution.[9]

The local governments have little incentive to build the necessary treatment plants. The situation existing in most states was vividly portrayed by the state of Maryland in its explanation to the federal government of why a state priority plan for grants had not been adhered to:

> "Almost without exception, every sewerage project in Maryland has been undertaken at the suggestion, urging, insistence, formal order, and, when administrative procedures are exhausted, by court action initiated by the Health Department . . . In Maryland's situation it would be the height of folly to tell some community, after a long and bitter struggle to get them to act, that they would have to wait for financing not because the money wasn't available, but because someone higher on the predetermined priority list has not yet caved in. In Maryland we have not reached the point where applicants are eager and competing for grants to build sewage treatment works. There are too many other competing needs . . . making demands on their limited capacities to borrow and spend to do anything that is not necessary. They build only what they are forced to build and only then if there are Federal and State grants immediately available . . ." [10]

Although the 1972 Amendments to the Water Pollution Control Act contain much stiffer requirements which must be met before a locality can receive a waste treatment grant, nothing in the act reverses the lack of incentive to actually undertake construction.

RESPONSIBILITY FOR AIR POLLUTION CONTROL

Until quite recently the interest of most state governments in controlling air pollution was minimal or nonexistent. Insofar as control efforts were made they were made by local government, usually in the large cities where the problem was most acute. The first state air pollution act authorizing enforcement at the state level was passed by Oregon in 1952, and only eighteen states had passed legislation before 1963.[11]

The lack of state interest in air pollution was due in part to the problem being considered nothing more than an unaesthetic nuisance. It was also due to the more localized nature of air pollution compared with water pollution. In one sense air pollution is the least localized of problems, because air flows freely and knows no terrestrial boundaries. But in a sense which is more meaningful from the standpoint of abatement action, air pollution, with the exception of pollution from motor vehicles, is highly localized. The problem arises from a large number of stationary sources, and if it is to be corrected it must be corrected at each of these sources. It cannot be centrally collected and treated like water pollution. The local nature of air pollution was even more apparent before the role of the automobile was realized and before communities considered the imposition of general restrictions on the use of certain types of fuel.

Before 1950, air pollution control at the local level was directed almost exclusively at the problem of smoke. Several communities, notably Pittsburgh, achieved considerable success in reducing the amount of smoke emitted into the local atmosphere. The Pittsburgh drive on air pollution started in 1946 with a decision by financier Richard Mellon to renew the declining industrial city. The heavy pall which had given Pittsburgh the nickname of "The Smoky City" was obviously one of the major factors inhibiting new development. Mellon, with the cooperation of Mayor David Lawrence, launched a vigorous control effort which succeeded in sharply reducing the amount of smoke and soot coming from the stacks of the city's heavy industry.[12] However, the limited nature of the city's accomplishments is indicated by the fact that in 1967 the Public Health Service still listed Pittsburgh as the sixth most polluted city in the nation.

Despite the more localized characteristics of air pollution, the same difficulties that local control experienced in water pollution began to be encountered in the air pollution control effort. The lines of political jurisdiction did not coincide with the flow of dirty air, and control efforts in one community were frustrated by the lack of controls in neighboring communities. However, the fact that air pollution was confined primarily to urban areas made the states less willing to assume responsibility than they had been for water pollution. There was thus a shift of responsibility not to the state level but to the county or regional level. This shift began in the early 1950s, and by 1965 half of all local programs had jurisdiction over an entire county or several counties.[13]

The growing realization of the health effects of air pollution led to local governments increasingly placing responsibility for air pollution control in the local health department. Originally the control function in many communities was the responsibility of the buildings department because of the emphasis placed on inspection of boilers. By 1965 more than half of the local air pollution agencies were located in the health department, only 10 per cent were in the buildings department, and the remainder were either independent or under some other department. Over 80 per cent of the agencies created between 1961 and 1965 were placed in the health department.[14] The trend toward locating air pollution control functions in the health department has now been overtaken by the creation of comprehensive pollution control or environmental agencies, discussed above in relation to water pollution control.

In 1967, with the introduction and passage of the Air Quality Act, a great shift began in the locus of air pollution control efforts. The primary responsibility up to this point had rested with local governments. But the threat of large-scale federal intervention and the responsibility for standard-setting placed on the states by the new legislation stimulated the states to take action. During 1967, twenty state legislatures enacted comprehensive air pollution control laws, and six other states adopted amendments to strengthen earlier legislation.[15] All states now have broad air pollution control laws on the books. In 1963 only three states (California, New Jersey, and New York) had air pollution budgets exceeding $100 thousand. By the end of 1967, twenty-two states had budgets over $100 thousand. By 1971, all but a few state air pollution budgets exceeded this amount, and at least five states (California, New Jersey, New York, Illinois, and Pennsylvania) had budgets exceeding $1 million. (See Table 7.2. for some indicators of state and local air pollution control efforts.)

The few studies of actual attempts to control air pollution have been mostly examinations of the efforts of local governments.[16] Crenson, in a study of Gary and East Chicago, Indiana, explored the factors which contribute to air pollution becoming (or not becoming) a local political issue.[17] The "collective" nature of the benefits to be derived from air pollution control was found to significantly inhibit the interest of traditional local political parties in making air pollution an issue. As Crenson says, "Clean air is a 'favor' which can be dispensed only in wholesale lots. It is an individual benefit which does not lend itself to the machine politician's way of doing business, and for that reason it is probable that machine politicians were less likely to make an issue of clean air than reform politicians." [18] Also, not surprisingly, Crenson found that in Gary (which is dominated by the U.S. Steel Company), U.S. Steel was an important factor in discouraging action on air pollution, although its power was exercised passively rather than actively. The "anticipated reaction" of the giant company was sufficient to prevent strong action from being taken.[19] In contrast with the relatively concentrated opposition to air pollution control, "support for anti-pollution proposals tends not to be consolidated within identifiable interest groups. It is diffuse." [20]

A study of the San Francisco Bay Area Air Pollution Control District (BAAPCD) found that, "Over the years, the BAAPCD (especially the staff) has evolved a very close cooperative relationship with industry, an arrangement which is beneficial to both sides, in that communication channels are kept open and information flows freely in both directions. At the same time, no such cordial relationship has existed with citizens' groups; contact has tended to be antagonistic more often than cooperative." [21] However, "the Board [of the BAAPCD] has showed . . . signs of moving its alliance away from industry and more toward the public. This change . . . is the result of direct

Table 7.2. **Funding: Air Pollution Control Agencies, Fiscal Year 1971**

State	Federal Funds	State Funds	Local Funds	Total Funds	Man-Years 1971	Man-Years 1972
Alabama	14,642	– –	18,851	33,493	12	24
Alaska	120,334	38,800	51,470	210,604	6	6
Arizona	350,490	235,128	189,221	774,839	47	54
Arkansas	276,729	136,000	– –	412,729	10	12
California	2,440,604	6,399,601	8,104,315	16,944,520	635	700
Colorado	615,996	378,651	234,491	1,229,138	56	72
Connecticut	709,523	291,911	263,981	1,265,415	56	87
Delaware	234,314	173,931	– –	408,245	21	21
District of Columbia	234,134	117,068	– –	351,202	19	24
Florida	902,370	572,392	376,754	1,851,516	123	146
Georgia	532,460	313,793	89,508	935,761	65	71
Hawaii	– –	– –	– –	– –	14	14
Idaho	60,000	137,808	– –	197,808	2	11
Illinois	1,412,000	947,200	1,883,375	4,242,575	291	364
Indiana	298,781	– –	437,409	736,190	71	94
Iowa	367,485	141,717	29,916	539,118	29	39
Kansas	354,658	104,011	65,232	523,901	31	32
Kentucky	514,870	335,902	202,062	1,052,834	76	76
Louisiana	399,208	225,535	– –	624,743	16	46
Maine	96,000	60,750	– –	156,750	5	9
Maryland	1,425,688	430,657	558,642	2,414,987	169	191
Massachusetts	1,240,000	207,500	367,028	1,814,528	61	60
Michigan	1,821,978	348,273	705,473	2,875,724	116	164
Minnesota	216,708	– –	229,358	446,066	46	50
Mississippi	80,000	64,000	– –	144,000	6	13
Missouri	948,062	161,745	623,908	1,733,715	85	93
Montana	239,007	103,834	34,934	377,775	17	30
Nebraska	123,359	25,824	25,613	174,796	8	14
Nevada	191,827	15,163	131,634	338,624	26	28
New Hampshire	81,381	51,140	– –	132,521	7	7
New Jersey	2,081,923	1,212,602	133,243	3,427,768	177	180
New Mexico	127,591	– –	45,405	172,996	23	40
New York	2,628,565	3,192,314	5,592,112	11,412,991	630	632
North Carolina	805,503	271,036	299,751	1,376,290	81	121
North Dakota	45,000	19,660	– –	64,660	4	5
Ohio	1,047,840	– –	1,240,000	2,287,840	129	201
Oklahoma	223,479	82,005	220,465	525,949	21	61
Oregon	569,181	385,784	317,855	1,272,820	57	77
Pennsylvania	2,974,300	1,454,332	1,523,613	5,952,245	256	332
Rhode Island	117,107	86,233	– –	203,340	12	16
South Carolina	356,173	332,125	70,155	758,453	44	68
South Dakota	21,000	7,000	– –	28,000	3	6
Tennessee	879,118	334,830	317,533	1,549,481	100	103
Texas	1,637,634	394,184	531,858	2,563,676	182	394
Utah	176,778	135,252	– –	312,030	17	24
Vermont	128,625	69,200	– –	197,825	6	8
Virginia	628,974	247,899	169,355	1,046,228	42	97
Washington	1,108,719	818,345	567,090	2,494,154	85	116
West Virginia	387,308	396,250	14,322	797,880	25	51
Wisconsin	100,000	224,000	13,220	337,220	14	77
Wyoming	68,016	34,722	– –	102,738	4	6
Guam	42,714	23,507	– –	66,221	1	3
Puerto Rico	– –	– –	– –	– –	25	32
Virgin Islands	72,094	41,168	– –	113,262	4	6
Total	32,548,250	21,780,782	25,679,152	80,008,184	4,068	5,208

Source: Council on Environmental Quality, *Environmental Quality—1972* (Washington: GPO, 1972), p. 197.

pressure on the Board, by a variety of citizens' groups which have become better organized in recent months." [22] The San Francisco study, as well as the Crenson study, note that new federal and state regulations have influenced local air pollution control agencies to move away from their pro-industry orientation.[23]

In his study for Ralph Nader's group, John Esposito examined air pollution control efforts in Houston, New York City, and Washington, D.C.[24] After painting a picture of unrelieved incompetence and inaction in all three communities, Esposito concludes, "Of the three cities discussed, only New York is atypical. Despite a shocking indifference for margins of safety, a breakdown of environmental law and order, an eleven-year tradition of corruption, and a penchant for unimaginative stopgap programs, New York's Department of Air Resources must certainly be ranked among the best control agencies in the country." [25]

COMPLIANCE AT THE STATE AND LOCAL LEVEL

The existence of numerous local governments, each jealously guarding its prerogatives and each diligently ignoring or working at cross-purposes with its neighboring governments, is one of the major underlying problems of the American polity. The problems posed by pollution accentuate this pattern and reveal some of its adverse consequences.

The classic conflict in water pollution is between the upstream polluter and the downstream victim of pollution. The upstream community receives all the benefits of being able to use the river as a sewer but pays none of the costs of pollution. The downstream victim receives none of the benefits but pays all the costs of dirty water. The limited jurisdiction of the local governments thus creates a disincentive to take any action to control pollution. The same disparity between who bears the costs and who gains the benefits exists in almost all metropolitan areas with respect to air pollution.

The effect of the "externalities" caused by the flow of air and water are reinforced by the rivalry among communities for industrial ratables. In most communities the desire for clean air and water is weighed against the fear of losing out in the race to attract new business and industry and to retain the industries which have already located in the town. If a community sets more stringent control standards than its neighbors, the plant looking for a new location may choose one of the neighbors to avoid the cost of installing control equipment. Thus this rivalry creates a further incentive for lenient enforcement.

Data are not available to indicate the actual effects of pollution regulations on plant location or relocation. Local officials probably exaggerate the impact which such regulations have, but industry groups do take advantage of the rivalry of local communities and the fragmentation of metropolitan areas. Where industry has already established its own enclaves within a metropolis, the industrial community is unlikely to do much in the way of controlling pollution, and will be reluctant to disturb the status quo. A state air pollution official in Missouri observed that

> . . . in the Kansas City area, which is smaller and more homogeneous than the St. Louis area, and where there are fewer of what might be called special purpose municipalities, the industrial community has supported the formation of a regional authority, whereas in the St. Louis area where little industrial villages abound, industry has maintained a silence on the subject, which one can only regard as hostile.[26]

The lack of cooperation among local governments interferes with sound planning for the installation of sewers and treatment plants, and results in the wastage of large amounts of funds for such facilities.[27] Individual communities build separate treatment plants when a combined plant would be far more efficient, suburbanites invest in individual septic tanks which must then be replaced by sewers and a treatment plant, towns build facilities which rapidly become obsolete because sufficient allowance has not been made for population growth. The obstacles to pollution control are compounded by a failure to work together and to plan.[28]

The state-local compliance process is characterized by negotiation, as is the federal process. The federal government negotiates primarily with the state control agencies, but the state and local control agencies in their turn must carry out negotiations with the polluters. Matthew Holden, Jr., summarizes the state-local situation when he says:

> In reality, regulatory decision-makers will not usually have this ability to ordain, because the parties who must comply have sufficient ability to "filibuster" that the agency loses much of its potentiality for success. Successful regulation thus depends on the consent of the regulated. Such consent is achieved by a process of bargaining—both explicit and tacit—which induces the regulated parties to agree (even reluctantly) to that which the regulator proposes.[29]

There are numerous opportunities for polluters to "filibuster" during the steps which lead to compliance. They may take steps to weaken the pollution control agency or deprive it of necessary powers. When a case is brought against a specific polluter, he can negotiate with the control agency about the nature of the remedial measures he must take and the length of time allowed for compliance. If negotiations with the control agency are unsatisfactory, the polluter can go to court where a good lawyer will be able to delay any effective action for several years.[30]

There are a number of factors which influence the effectiveness of a state or local control agency in getting polluters to comply with established standards. Obviously the resources and competence of the control agency itself will be crucial. The availability of technologically feasible means for controlling the pollution form another limiting factor. However, the economic and political characteristics of the polluter and the legal and public relations aspects of the control program will also significantly influence the final outcome. We have already discussed some of these factors in relation to industrial polluters.

The range of tactics and the political muscle available to the polluter are often crucial determinants of the pace and ultimate outcome of compliance efforts. The threat to move or close down is a useful political tactic, especially in communities heavily dependent on the polluting industry. The cases in which it is most difficult to achieve compliance are those where an industry or firm is economically marginal and politically influential. E. F. Murphy, illustrating this point, cites the case of the

Wisconsin dairy industry which consists of a large number of small firms who, banded together, exercise considerable political influence.[31]

Municipal governments are often among the most flagrant violators of both air and water pollution standards. Their failure to construct adequate sewage treatment facilities or to place proper controls on municipal incinerators contributes significantly to the pollution problem. While most municipalities must be credited with good intentions concerning pollution control, compliance is made difficult because they fall into the category noted above of being hard-pressed for funds but politically influential. Most local budgets are very tight, but it is difficult to force the local government to take action because it has influence with the governor and the state legislature.

The competence of the state and local agencies is also often questionable. In 1973, the U.S. General Accounting Office concluded that, "In general, the States' enforcement programs were not effective in abating air pollution." [32] It found, for example, that the state of Indiana relied primarily on voluntary compliance by polluters.

> In establishing compliance schedules, Indiana sent approximately 2,400 letters to industries in 1969 advising them of the state's emission regulations and emphasizing that, if their emissions violated the regulations, they had to submit timetables for compliance before the end of the year. The director of the state agency estimated that, as of November 1972, only 94 of the 2,400 industries had replied. The director said that no followup had been performed on these letters and even though some additional replies may have been received, he could not confirm the number because they had not been recorded in a compliance schedule ledger.[33]

Massachusetts relied primarily on field investigators to locate, at random, construction of potential new sources of air pollution. Even if a potential new source was located and construction plans were received and approved, the State did not have followup procedures to insure that the facilities were constructed in compliance with the plans.[34] It is unlikely that more than three or four states know who their industrial air and water polluters are or how much progress has been made in actually achieving abatement by major pollution sources.

The ultimate sanction of the pollution control agency is court action. For this sanction to be credible and to have the necessary warning effect on actual or potential polluters, the cooperation of the courts is necessary. If the polluters actually taken to court are let off with admonishments or inconsequential fines, then the control agency is left without any final sanction to enforce its rulings. The action of the courts has been a major handicap to pollution control in many cities and states. Major firms have been fined $25 for violating air pollution codes or have been given no penalty at all. In some cases court interpretation of pollution statutes has been extremely narrow and limiting. However, in the past few years the courts have also proved to be a major weapon in the arsenal of citizen environmental groups (see Chapter 6).

The use of publicity to force polluters to comply with regulations can often be an effective technique. The major limitation here is the inability of the public to understand the complicated negotiations which may take place between the control agency and the polluter, and the reluctance or inability of the agency to publicize such negotiations. The public sees and comprehends the broad statements of policy issued by the agency, but the actual decisions made by the agency on individual polluters tend to be technical and little publicized. Such decisions are, however, the key to the success of any pollution control program.[35]

INTERGOVERNMENTAL RELATIONS

Air pollution and water pollution are both classic examples of problems which defy political boundaries.[36] Water pollution is a river basin problem, and almost all the major rivers in the United States cross state boundaries. Air pollution is an "airshed" problem. Nobody has been able to give a satisfactory definition of the extent of an airshed, but it is clear that air pollution is concentrated in the nation's metropolitan areas and more than a third of the metropolitan area population lives in areas which straddle state lines.[37] Thus, one of the major problems in controlling pollution is the difficulty of striking a balance between the regional scope of the problem and the state-centered sources of power capable of taking action.

The states suffer from the same problems of rivalry and lack of cooperation as the localities. State governments do not like to surrender power. The reluctance to impose stringent pollution controls for fear of hindering economic development is as much a factor in state thinking as in local calculations. The difficulty of the states getting together has resulted in limited, and on the whole, disappointing experience with interstate cooperation for pollution control.

The major mechanism for formal state cooperation has been the interstate compact. However, such compacts have been of only limited utility in the pollution field. In air pollution control there are no important interstate agencies, and the Congress, which must give its approval to interstate compacts, has generally discouraged interstate air pollution control compacts.

There are several interstate compact agencies devoted to controlling water pollution. The two most significant are the Ohio River Valley Water Sanitation Commission (ORSANCO) and the Delaware River Basin Commission.

ORSANCO has frequently been cited as one of the examples of a successful interstate commission.[38] ORSANCO began operating in 1948. It consists of three representatives from the federal government and three representatives from each of the eight member states—Ohio, West Virginia, Illinois, Indiana, Kentucky, New York, Virginia, and Pennsylvania. The commission has authority to issue enforcement orders and bring polluters to court, but it has exercised its enforcement power only rarely, and has never actually taken a polluter to court. Defenders of ORSANCO attribute this to the success which the commission has had in voluntarily persuading municipalities and industries to clean up their pollution. However, the limited use of ORSANCO's legal power may also be due to the fact that enforcement action can be taken only if a majority of the commissioners from a majority of the member states agree, and then only if a majority of the commissioners from the state from which the pollution originates assent. This requirement makes it politically almost impossible for the commission to use its enforcement authority. In recognition of this limitation, OR-SANCO has taken on the role of coordinating and supplementing the state programs rather than trying to exercise complete control over pollution in the Ohio River Basin.[39]

The Delaware River Basin Commission (DRBC) is among the newest of the interstate commissions, and it is unique in the scope of its powers. It was formed in 1961 by agreement of the federal government and the states of New York, New Jersey, Pennsylvania, and Delaware.[40] Each state is represented on the commission by its governor, and there is one federal representative.

The DRBC is responsible for all aspects of water resource development in the basin, not just for pollution control. The commission has adopted a basin-wide comprehensive plan, which includes provisions for water supply, pollution control, flood protection, and recreation; and it has a wide range of powers to implement programs in these areas, including authority to construct treatment works and other water development projects and to enforce pollution control regulations. It has not yet done much enforcement, having spent several years establishing water pollution control standards for the basin.

One of the major unsettled questions concerning interstate agencies is the form which federal representation should take. In the absence of federal representation, the compact commissions tend to compromise decisions to the lowest common denominator in order to get agreement among the member states, and the strength of the commission is thus reduced to that of the weakest partner. On the other hand, if there is a federal voting member on the commission, later review of the commission's decisions by the federal government will be difficult because the federal representative will have already taken a stand. Experience with interstate compacts has really been too meager to determine which is the most desirable approach.[41]

Federal representation on interstate commissions is only one of the many forms of interaction among the different levels of government involved in pollution control. Like all other governmental activities in America, control of air and water pollution does not break down into a neat and sharply defined division of labor between state, local, and federal government.[42] Functions are shared and tasks carried out by cooperative interaction between the different levels.

Responsibility for pollution control has followed a progression to higher levels of government. We have seen how both air and water pollution were originally the responsibilities of local government. Water pollution became increasingly a state responsibility in the late nineteenth and early twentieth century, and then, following World War II, the federal government assumed increasing authority. Control of air pollution has been progressing from the local to the state and regional level with the federal government playing an even larger role. It is not difficult to foresee, within the coming years, the growth of international cooperation and perhaps international authority in the vital task of preserving the environment.

The expanding role of higher levels of government has been due to the increasing geographical spread and the growing acuteness of the pollution problem, combined with the inadequate efforts of lower levels of government to enforce controls. It has been fostered by the general growth of ever larger public and private networks of power and by the development of administrative techniques to control large organizations and to deal with complex problems. Pollution control has thus been a part of the general twentieth-century trend toward increasing the scope of government in general and the higher levels of government in particular.

Although the Nixon Administration had in general attempted to turn programs back to the states and to resist efforts to increase the power of the federal government, the administration's environmental proposals were a notable exception. The tendency to centralize pollution control authority in federal hands has, if anything, been accelerated since 1969. The reason for this lies in the general factors cited above and, in particular, the recent preference for federal control among the large industries which were a major part of Nixon's constituency. Another factor is probably that the major growth in the air and water pollution control agency's manpower occurred during the Nixon reign, and thus EPA escaped the suspicion which attached to most domestic federal agencies of being dominated by Democratic holdovers.

It should not be assumed that the increasing role of the federal government has been totally at the expense of state or local power. The states have undoubtedly lost some power to the federal government in recent years, but the increasing authority of Washington is offset by two factors. First, each state never possessed the power of control pollution coming from outside its borders, and thus the federal responsibility for truly interstate pollution does not come at any government's expense. This is even clearer if we look at the state's assumption of local responsibility for water pollution control. During the nineteenth century the localities may theoretically have held the responsibility for controlling pollution, but they never had the power or ability to fulfill that responsibility. Thus the takeover by the state was not really a loss of power for the localities. Second, the increased federal role may actually result in greater power and authority at the state level. This is certainly the case for air pollution, where the Air Quality Act has stimulated states to take on authority and responsibility which they never had before.

Cooperation is the dominant mode in intergovernmental relations. The daily work of controlling pollution is in the hands of professional personnel who share a common dedication to getting the job done. This dedication is constantly reinforced by professional conferences, training programs, and informal contacts. The overlap of responsibilities results in frequent interaction among the different levels and it is not uncommon for engineers, chemists, and other professionals to have had experience working for local, state, and federal agencies. A former commissioner of the Federal Water Pollution Control Administration had previously been the chief of the Texas water pollution control agency, and a chief of New York City's Department of Air Pollution Control was formerly in charge of one of the federal government's regional offices. Many similar examples could be cited. Money and technical assistance from the higher levels to the lower help to keep the system operating reasonably smoothly.

While cooperation is the norm in federal-state-local interaction, conflict is not uncommon, as we have seen. Different constituencies, traditions, styles, and perspectives make some friction inevitable. Conflict between political officials at different levels is more common than between professionals, but the professionals have their share of problems and resentments. For example, Frank Graham quotes a federal official talking about enforcement actions who says that it is obvious that state officials assume federal intervention to be an attack on their professional reputations. "It looks like a reflection on the job they're doing, and, frankly, it is." [43]

What Morton Grodzins has called the "multiple crack" aspect of American federalism, whereby if an interest loses on one level it can fight on another, plays a significant part in pollution control. Thus the coal and oil industry, having lost a fight over federal regulations on sulfur dioxide air pollution, carried the battle to the state and local level. But it is not only the polluters who get multiple cracks. State and local groups urging stronger controls against pollution have often urged federal action if, in the view of such groups, the states and localities have not shown vigor in prosecuting polluters.

The ability of groups to pursue their interest at different levels does not negate the fact that particular interests consistently receive a more sympathetic hearing at certain levels. However, this factor may not be the dominant one in a group's political calculations. Up until the 1970s, the greater influence of industrial groups at the state and local level led them to lobby against greater federal power and in favor of devices such as interstate compacts which would keep power decentralized. With the growth of public support for pollution control the states and localities began to pass more numerous and meaningful pollution control regulations. Simultaneously, the concentration of business enterprises into large national and international firms continued unabated. The result was that the large corporations faced a choice between complying with numerous state and local regulations or a single federal regulation. For many of the firms with national markets corporate economics as well as a desire to simplify their political environment led to a preference for federal regulation—even though the federal standards were likely to be more stringent.

We have described the complex of factors and attitudes which play a part in the politics of pollution. The interaction between the many different groups becomes clearer if we examine their roles in the major aspects of pollution control. Thus we turn next to the major problems which concern those who have an interest in controlling pollution—research, standard-setting, and compliance.

Part III

THE POLICY PROCESS

CHAPTER 8

Research and
Standard-setting

RESEARCH

It HAS FREQUENTLY been stated that pollution can be brought under control with existing technology, that what is needed to obtain clean air and water is not research but money and political muscle. There is much truth in such statements—the major part of pollution in the United States can be eliminated by applying existing scientific knowledge. But there is also much about the effects of pollution and how to control them which is not known and which needs to be known. This is partially evidenced by the fact that almost half the EPA budget (excluding waste treatment grants) is devoted to research of one kind or another.

There are two basic areas of research in the pollution field. The first is concerned with discovering the effects of pollution. Although man has been making major changes in the natural order for at least a hundred years, we are still remarkably ignorant about the effects of such changes on natural processes or on human beings. We do not know whether many of the chemicals that we dump into the air, water, and soil are harmful to health nor, for those chemicals which are harmful, do we know what amounts will cause injury. We do not know whether the burning of fossil fuels is producing irreversible changes in the composition of the earth's atmosphere and, if it is, what the ramifications of such changes are. When we build dams, drain swamps, or irrigate large areas of land we do not know the full effects of such projects on water, soil, fish, or wildlife.

It is necessary to know the effects of pollution if one is to formulate a rational program of control. Until we know the effects of a pollutant it is difficult to determine whether it should be controlled and, if so, how stringent the controls should be. If, in fact, emissions from the burning of fuel are permanently changing the amount of carbon dioxide in the atmosphere, and if such a change will result in an increase in world temperature, the melting of the polar ice-caps, and consequent flooding on a massive scale, then clearly extraordinary efforts are warranted in controlling such emissions. If, on the other hand, such a chain of events is not likely then control of carbon dioxide emissions becomes a low-priority matter.

The second area of pollution research is concerned with methods of controlling particular kinds or sources of pollutants. In water pollution we still do not know practical ways of preventing the eutrophication of lakes or the runoff of sediment and chemicals into rivers. In air pollution adequate and economical control techniques are lacking for many pollutants. In several areas of both air and water pollution, methods of control are available but financial or political costs or other constraints on applying them make searches for alternative methods necessary. All of the combined sewers in the country could be ripped out and replaced with separate storm and sanitary sewers, but the cost of doing so would be very great and much effort has been expended in the search for less expensive alternatives. Sulfur dioxide air pollution can be controlled by burning low-sulfur fuel, but there is not enough low-sulfur fuel to meet the demand, and thus research is necessary to develop other ways of solving the sulfur dioxide problem.

The factors which determine the allocation of research funds and the setting of priorities among research projects are complex. To some extent the priorities are set by the working scientists. Their evaluation of what problems or approaches are interesting or important will go far in determining the work done in the laboratories. However, the politicians and the program administrators not only decide on the total amount of funds available for research but also have an important say in establishing priorities.

Some areas of research are promoted primarily because of political considerations. For example, the key positions on the relevant congressional committees held by representatives from Eastern coal-mining states has led to a series of major research projects on the control of air pollution from burning piles of coal mine wastes. Some areas of research are initiated and defended primarily by the scientists working on them. Much research has been done on the development of advanced methods of waste treatment, methods which will remove more impurities than the techniques currently in use. While the projects on advanced waste treatment have received congressional and executive branch support, their primary backers have been the scientists within EPA.

Probably the most common pattern is for the influence of scientists, administrators, or politicians to be almost inextricably intertwined in the determination of research activities. One of the current research priorities of EPA is the development of control methods for sulfur dioxide pollution. The ranking of sulfur dioxide as a major health hazard was a decision of the air pollution scientists. But the political repercussions of curbing the use of high-sulfur coal and oil led Congress and the executive branch to push for research on control technology.[1] Once the emphasis on control technology was established, however, initiative returned to the scientists as to which control techniques would be most fruitful. Yet even in deciding among alternative techniques, the judgment of the scientists was modified by factors of interagency rivalry, with the Department of the Interior advocating certain approaches and EPA others. Thus the pattern of actual research projects was a result of complex interaction involving interest group pressure, scientific findings, congressional and executive political sensitivities, and interagency conflicts.

The degree to which research projects are controlled and supervised by government personnel is determined primarily by whether the projects are undertaken "in-house," as it is termed, or through grants or contracts. In-house research is research done by government scientists in government laboratories. Research grants are given to individuals or institutions for projects chosen and developed by the applicants for such grants. Research contracts are awarded to educational institutions or private firms for carrying out projects selected by the government.

The major advantage of in-house research is that it enables the officials of an agency to exercise a high degree of supervision and thus to ensure that the research will be relevant to the problems the agency wants solved. Once an agency has built up a capability for doing its own research, it also acquires a certain degree of flexibility in pursuing research topics. It can investigate ideas which are simply hunches or which are still in a formative stage. On the other hand, the existence of such a capability creates an obvious pressure to make use of it, and thus the agency loses flexibility as to how much research it wants to undertake and whether it wants it done within the agency or in the private sector.

Obtaining competent personnel is one of the major limitations on in-house research. Government salaries for almost all types of scientists are significantly below those offered by educational institutions and private industry. While security, fringe benefits, or draft exemption may lure some scientists, government recruitment efforts are forced to rely primarily on the scientist's dedication to the public welfare. A less well recognized problem, but one which is becoming acute with the undertaking of large-scale, complex research projects, is the skill required to plan directed research. Modern, sophisticated administrative techniques are necessary for the successful planning and conduct of multi-million-dollar projects directed at producing specific outcomes; but, outside of the Defense Department, administrators who can apply such techniques are extremely scarce within the federal government. Finally, in-house research is at the mercy of political factors. Funds may be reduced with little warning, supervisors may suddenly be shifted to some other post, new laboratories may be created, thus scattering competent research personnel. Such problems also occur in the private sector, but they seem to happen with greater frequency in government.

Research grants often are designed as much to promote interest in some topic and thereby recruit scientific personnel as they are to produce worthwhile research findings. The grants are usually small, whereas the problems to be solved usually require a major effort. Although most agencies make some effort to award grants on the basis of the agency's own ranking of research priorities, coordination between agency objectives and the topics of research grants is often tenuous. Supervision of the research done under grants is almost nonexistent and it is not unusual for the grant project to follow a path quite different from that outlined in the grant application. Research grants are most useful in areas which are scientifically "underdeveloped," as air pollution was up to a few years ago. However, as a way of obtaining scientific findings, the value of research grants diminishes as the parameters of a problem become better known.

Partly as a result of the shortcomings of in-house research and research grants, the use of research contracts has increased significantly in recent years throughout the government and in the area of pollution control. Contracts enable a government agency to choose the institution best capable of undertaking a particular project. The agency does not have to create a competence in a particular area but can simply utilize the manpower and equipment already acquired in the private sector. The contract can spell out in detail precisely what the research should produce. As pollution research has moved increasingly toward seeking specific control techniques for specific problems, the contract approach has become more and more useful.

Many of the contracts in pollution control are made with private industry, and fears have often been raised that the outcome of some research may be biased by the interests of a particular industry. Many members of Congress and the executive branch exhibit a rather schizophrenic attitude, on the one hand urging that industry become more involved in pollution research and on the other recoiling in horror when government research monies are entrusted to private hands. Up to this point it is hard to find any examples of government contracts in the pollution area being abused or subverted because of private bias. The advantages obtained from involving industry have probably far exceeded the dangers of such involvement. But the stake which industry has in government research and its ability to influence the nature and direction of such research should not be underestimated.

The federal government's consideration of whether to undertake a study of an electric or battery-powered automobile provides an excellent example of the stake industry can have in government research. The possibility of a major government research effort directed at replacing gasoline-powered vehicles represented a direct threat to both the automobile and the oil industries. They, and their ally within the executive branch, the Department of the Interior, argued vigorously against such a research effort. The electric industry and its ally, the Federal Power Commission, argued with equal vigor in favor of the possibilities of electric vehicles. The White House, anxious to avoid both a major political controversy and an expensive research undertaking in a tight budget year, headed off the congressional proposals by setting up a study by outside experts under the aegis of the Commerce Department. The oil and auto industries were well represented on the panel of outside experts. The panel recommended against any federal support for research on electric or other nonpolluting vehicles.[2]

Most of the research on pollution control technologies is not done by the government but by private industry. In recent years Congress and the executive branch have developed a variety of methods for prodding or forcing industry to develop needed technologies.

The best example again is provided by the automobile. In the 1970 Air Quality Act Congress established a stringent set of emission standards for new automobiles and required the industry to meet these standards by 1975 or 1976. At least, according to the industry, the technology to meet the standards was not available at the time the law was passed, and three years later the industry was still claiming that the 1975 standards could not be met within the bounds of economic feasibility. The energy crisis has postponed a test of whether the standards can be met, but the success or failure of this approach to technology development could go far to determine whether other such regulatory attempts will be made.

A flat requirement is not the only legal approach which has

been used to encourage the development of a technology. Economic incentives and disincentives can also be used to prod the private sector. The current air and water pollution control laws both contain requirements for the use of "the best available technology." Thus a firm which develops an improved method of controlling a particular type of pollution is given a ready market because of the requirements of the federal law, assuming that the law is adequately enforced. However, this type of provision also may be a disincentive to a firm to install improved control techniques, because installation may then be required on all similar plants, some of which may be owned by the same firm. Economic disincentives to encourage new technology have not yet been enacted, but the tax on sulfur oxides proposed in 1971 by the Nixon Administration was intended in part to stimulate the development and installation of sulfur oxides controls by penalizing firms which did not control their sulfur emissions.

Legally requiring the development of new technology poses difficult problems because if the technology is not developed the government is left in the untenable position of requiring people to do something which cannot be done. The use of economic incentives or disincentives is likely to be more effective. For example, an emissions tax imposed on automobile manufacturers would probably accelerate the development of control technology more than the not very credible threat of closing down the automobile industry.

Research on the effects of pollution provides a necessary scientific basis for the setting of pollution control standards. But research by itself will not produce standards. This becomes evident as we examine the process of standard-setting.

STANDARD-SETTING

The establishment of standards is a crucial step in any pollution control program. Standards not only state the goals of the program, they also provide a measuring stick to determine the program's progress and a basis for determining what actions should be taken by the program. In a very real sense, standards are the "marching orders" for a pollution control agency.

Together with compliance, they are the core of the pollution control process.

To understand the standard-setting process it is necessary to distinguish among four kinds of standards, all of which are necessary for pollution control. First, there are the community goals, which state the objectives of the program in qualitative, nonnumerical terms. "Water suitable for swimming" or "Air which will not produce disease in healthy members of the population" are examples of goals. Second, there are *criteria* which are descriptions of the effects of different levels of pollutants. Criteria consist of statements such as "Water containing more than X parts per million of suspended solids is not suitable for swimming" or "X parts per million of sulfur dioxide will produce lung irritation in human beings."

Neither goals nor criteria are legally binding. The third and fourth types of standards are the ones generally found in pollution control laws. *Water quality or ambient air standards* combine goals and criteria into specific numerical levels of quality to be applied to a body of water or to the air circulating in a community. Thus, "No more than X parts of suspended solids in River Y," or "No more than X parts per million of sulfur dioxide for any 8-hour period in city Y," are water quality or ambient air standards. *Emission* or *effluent standards* prescribe how much of what kind of pollution is to be allowed from any given source, for example, "No industrial plant can discharge effluent containing more than X parts of suspended solids into River Y," or "No power plant can use fuel containing more than X per cent of sulfur in city Y."

The establishment of goals is basically a political question, as we pointed out in Chapter 1. The balance which must be struck in the political arena has been well described by the federal body responsible for setting radiation protection standards. "The use of radiation results in numerous benefits to man in medicine, industry, commerce, and research," states the Federal Radiation Council. "If those beneficial uses were fully exploited without regard to radiation protection, the resulting biological risk might well be considered too great. Reducing the risk to zero would virtually eliminate any radiation use, and result in the loss of all possible benefits. It is therefore necessary to strike some balance between maximum use and zero risk. In establishing radiation protection standards, the balancing of risk and benefit is a decision involving medical, social, economic, political, and other factors. Such a balance cannot be made on the basis of a precise mathematical formula but must be a matter of informed judgment." [3]

A community's designation of goals implies some kind of cost-benefit calculation, even though the calculation in most cases is intuitive or even unconscious. A community which decides that it wants to eliminate pollution in a given river to the extent that people can swim there is implicitly deciding that the benefits of being able to swim in the river are greater than the costs of eliminating the pollution. However, techniques are not now available, and probably never will be, to reduce the cost-benefit calculation to any kind of mathematical precision. The value which one community attaches to being able to swim may very well be different from that placed on swimming by the next community.

If there were complete knowledge of the effects of all pollutants, the transition from goals to quality standards would be almost automatic. Once it had been determined that River Y should be suitable for swimming, the scientists would be able to provide criteria for what level of control for each kind of pollutant was necessary to permit safe swimming. However, as we indicated above, such knowledge of effects is far from complete. In air pollution it is so incomplete that the distinction between goals and quality standards tends to become lost, and controversy often rages over numerical quality standards without any consideration of what the quality standards represent in terms of substantive goals. Without knowledge of the effects of particular pollutants, communities do not know what they are "buying" for the costs of establishing particular quality standards.

In some cases quality standards have been like Latin American constitutions, an expression of aspirations rather than intent; but in most cases quality standards have been established for the purpose of carrying out enforcement. Before any enforcement can take place the community must also establish emission standards. Cease-and-desist orders cannot be issued to a river and enforcement conferences cannot be held with the ambient air in a city. Enforcement must be directed against polluters, not against pollution, and it is only emission standards which prescribe the action to be taken by polluters.

The development of emission standards, despite the fact that they represent the "teeth" in any control program, has generally been considered the domain of the technicians. Community controversy usually takes place over goals and quality standards but only rarely over emission standards. It is presumed that once the quality standards have been established the emission standards can be mathematically calculated, although in fact the transition from quality to emission standards involves a number of assumptions which are by no means mathematical or automatic.

In many cases emission standards are not directly tied to quality standards, but rather are based on some standard of "good practice." Thus, a community may simply determine that all industries within its jurisdiction shall install the best control devices currently available. The 1972 Amendments to the Water Pollution Control Act require municipalities to provide secondary treatment for wastes. These kinds of emission standards are arbitrary in that they are not related to the achievement of goals or quality standards. The application of secondary treatment of all municipal wastes flowing into a particular river may make the river cleaner than it has to be or may leave it in a condition completely inadequate for the desired use, depending on the proportion of pollution contributed by municipalities, the size of the municipalities along the river, the amount of water flowing in the river, and a number of other factors.

In cases where emission standards are based on quality standards, the process of deriving the former from the latter is usually complex. There are two basic methods of deriving the emission standards. The first method is to calculate the percentage reduction necessary to get from existing levels to the quality standards and then to apply this same percentage reduction to existing emissions. The second method involves the use of mathematical simulation models to actually predict what quality level will result from any given reduction in emissions.

To take an actual example of the first method, New York

City's standard for sulfur was derived as follows: The desirable level of quality for ambient air was set at an annual mean concentration of sulfur dioxide no greater than 0.02 parts per million. This was the lowest level associated with increased respiratory disease death rates in man, with significant corrosion of metals, and with injury to perennial vegetation. It was determined that in New York the existing concentration of sulfur dioxide in the air needed to be reduced by 83 per cent to achieve the desired level. The total amount of sulfur dioxide emitted annually into the New York atmosphere was then divided by the total heat content of all coal and oil burned annually in the city expressed in British thermal units [BTU], resulting in the figure of 2 pounds of sulfur dioxide per 1 million BTU. If an 83 per cent reduction was to be achieved, then only 17 per cent of the existing emissions could be allowed to continue. Seventeen per cent of 2 pounds of sulfur dioxide per 1 million BTU is 0.34 pounds of sulfur dioxide per 1 million BTU which, with slight rounding, was the emission standard announced for the New York area.[4]

The kind of straightforward approach to calculating emission standards which calls simply for an equal percentage reduction from all pollution sources involves a number of assumptions which are open to question. It ignores the question of costs, although in many cases it would probably be much less expensive to have certain polluters reduce their emissions by 95 per cent and others reduce their emissions by only 75 per cent, rather than both sources reducing emissions by 85 per cent. A simulation study by HEW revealed that for certain types of air pollution control objectives, the uniform reduction approach may cost seven times as much as an approach which utilizes variations in emission standards.[5] Thus the across-the-board standard may be the most equitable or the simplest to administer, but it is often not the least-cost solution.

The uniform reduction approach also does not take into account the location of the emission sources, meteorological conditions (in the case of air pollution), and other factors which influence the dispersion of the pollution. It does not consider changes in the amount of pollution which will occur in future years because of industrial expansion, plant relocation, or other factors. Alternatives to emission reduction, such as stream reaeration in the case of water pollution or relocation of power plants in the case of air pollution, are usually not taken into account. In short, a number of simplifying assumptions are made, and if any of these assumptions were changed a different standard would probably result.

Some of these types of assumptions can also be illustrated by one account of how the automobile emission standards which Congress wrote into the 1970 Clean Air Act were set. To estimate existing pollution levels, the worst case cities were used—Los Angeles for hydrocarbons and nitrogen oxides, Chicago for carbon monoxide. Then a private study was used to estimate the expected growth in auto emissions. The private study projected a much more rapid rate of growth than comparable studies done by the Department of Transportation. To determine the desirable levels for protection of health, primary reliance was placed on individual studies: for CO a study of audio impairment; for NO_x a study of Chattanooga school children exposed to emissions from a dynamite plant; and for hydrocarbons a study of the performance of high-school cross-country runners in Los Angeles. After applying the proportional reduction method, the Muskie committee then rounded the results to an even 90 per cent for all three pollutants.[6] The least that can be said is that the calculations leading to the very important auto emission standards were crude. They illustrate the vital connection between research and standards, because it is inexcusable that such a critical set of decisions should rest on just a handful of health effects studies. The Chattanooga study was not even done for the purpose of setting standards. If we are to have reliable standards we must have adequate research.

The use of hydrological or air diffusion models is a much more sophisticated and rational method of deriving emission standards. However, the validity of the air pollution models has not been adequately proven, and the water pollution models usually have to be carefully tailored to each individual body of water. Also, the use of such models requires technically trained personnel who are in scarce supply at the state and local levels. Although EPA provided a standard diffusion model to the states to use in the development of their air quality control plans under the 1970 Act, only ten states actually used the model. All of the others used some variant of the proportional reduction method.

The difficulty of relating emission or effluent standards to ambient air or water quality standards has led Congress to a simple solution, namely to ignore the relationship. Thus the 1972 Water Pollution Control Act Amendments require effluent standards based on available technology rather than on the quality of the receiving water, although it also contains some escape clauses to avoid the most illogical outcomes of the technology-based standards (see below). Although such standards avoid the difficulty of defining how a particular pollution source affects the environment, they also thereby eliminate the logic for setting the effluent standard at the level set, and they raise a host of new problems. These new problems include how to adjust for the economic cost of the new technology, how to require the best technology without changing the requirements on a particular source every few years, and the high degree of inefficiency which may result from requiring the same techniques of control for a wide variety of sources.

Under the 1972 Water Pollution Control Act Amendments and the 1970 Clean Air Amendments standard-setting has been put on a roughly parallel basis for air and water pollution. However, there are a number of significant differences in the two areas and an examination of each will help to clarify further the standard-setting process.

AIR POLLUTION STANDARDS

The 1967 Air Quality Act established a time-consuming and somewhat cumbersome process for setting air pollution control standards. The process was initiated by the federal government designating "air quality control regions" containing communities in one or more states and by publishing "air quality criteria" and data on control techniques for particular pollutants. The states were then given up to nine months to adopt appropriate standards and controls for the pollutant covered by the criteria and an additional year to adopt a plan on how to achieve compliance with the standards. The standards became effective when approved by the EPA Administrator (previously the secretary of HEW), and if a state failed to adopt standards or its standards were not approved by the federal government, then the federal government could promulgate its own standards for the region.[7]

The Clean Air Amendments of 1970 changed this process in a number of significant ways. The idea of air quality control regions as areas requiring high-priority attention was changed by the simple expedient of declaring the area of each state not designated a control region prior to passage of the 1970 law to itself be a control region. Thus all areas of the United States were included within some air quality control region.

The requirements for publication of criteria and control technology documents remained generally the same. The criteria documents, however, played a less crucial role in the 1970 law than they had previously. It is necessary to examine the criteria concept to understand why this is so.

The federal government was first called on to publish criteria by the 1963 Clean Air Act. Under this act the criteria had no binding force but were designed simply to assist state and local governments in setting their own standards. But the act's description of criteria contained a basic ambiguity which was to be the source of considerable controversy. One section stated that "the Secretary shall compile and publish criteria reflecting accurately the latest scientific knowledge useful in indicating the kind and extent of such effects which may be expected from the presence of such air pollution agent (or combination of agents) in the air in varying quantities."[8] The next section read, "The Secretary may recommend to such air pollution control agencies . . . such criteria of air quality as in his judgment may be necessary to protect the public health and welfare."[9] Here were two quite different conceptions of what the criteria should be. The first definition implied that the document should be a descriptive compilation of scientific findings. The second that the criteria were to be a standard, a prescriptive recommendation as to what the proper level of air quality should be. The confusion between descriptive criteria and prescriptive standards was reinforced in the 1965 Water Quality Act, which stated that if the secretary "determines that . . . state criteria and plans are consistent with [the requirements of the act], such state criteria and plans shall thereafter be the water quality standards applicable to . . . interstate water." [10]

The blurring of the distinction between criteria and standards violates the basic logic of the standard-setting process. If the criteria are a descriptive compilation of scientific findings, then it is only by combining criteria with goals that one can arrive at a standard, because science only describes, it does not tell us what should be done. Insofar as the criteria are scientific they cannot prescribe standards, and insofar as the criteria attempt to lay down standards they are "unscientific." The political advantages of wrapping the cloak of scientific objectivity around the standard-setting process are obvious, but it is an abuse of logic to do so.

The 1967 Act required that the state air quality standards must be "consistent with the air quality criteria." [11] Many experts and state officials interpreted "consistent with" to mean "the same as," an interpretation which amounted to making the criteria equivalent to national, federally established, air quality standards.

The 1970 Act took the next logical step and formally and officially made the establishment and promulgation of national air quality standards an explicit federal responsibility. EPA is required to set two kinds of national standards—primary ambient air quality standards and secondary ambient air quality standards. The primary standards are those "the attainment and maintenance of which in the judgment of the Administrator, based on such criteria and allowing an adequate margin of safety, are requisite to protect the public health." [12] Secondary standards are those required "to protect the public welfare." [13]

The EPA has established primary and secondary standards for six pollutants: particulates, sulfur dioxide, carbon monoxide, hydrocarbons, nitrogen oxides, and photochemical oxidants. In the case of four of the six, the primary standard is the same as the secondary standard because the level of the pollutant required to protect health is also considered sufficiently low to protect welfare. Welfare, in the context of the Act, is equivalent to prevention of damage to materials, vegetation, and non-human animals. It would make no sense to establish a secondary standard more lenient than the primary standard, because the

Act requires the primary standards to be met by 1975 whereas the secondary standards only must be met within "a reasonable time." [14]

After EPA has promulgated a primary ambient standard, the states must set emission standards adequate to achieve the ambient standard. The emission standards are contained in the state implementation plans, and the standards and plans must be approved by EPA. If a state fails to submit a plan, or it is not approved by the EPA administrator, the administrator must promulgate his own implementation plan, including emission standards for the area and pollutants in question. The 1970 Act establishes very tight timetables for the submission and approval of the implementation plans, and therefore EPA has in a number of cases promulgated its own plans for all or parts of particular states.

In addition to giving EPA authority to establish national ambient standards and to promulgate implementation plans if the states do not, the 1970 Act also gave it authority to set emission standards in three very important areas—new stationary sources, hazardous air pollutants, and moving sources, notably automobiles.

The authority to set emission limits on new sources can potentially apply to "any building, structure, facility, or installation which emits or may emit any air pollutant," [15] and on which construction is started after passage of the Act. However, the EPA administrator must first publish regulations which list the kinds of sources to which the emission standards will apply. 120 days after a category of sources is covered, the administrator must issue the emission standards applicable to that category. The standards need not be limited to the pollutants covered by the national ambient standards. The EPA has been developing standards applicable to various categories of industry. By the end of 1973, standards applicable to more than twenty types of industries had been announced, including such major sources of air pollution as cement plants, power plants, and sulfuric acid plants. However, only five of these standards have received final approval.

New stationary sources thus are covered by the federal emission standards and existing sources are covered by the emission standards in the state plans to meet the national primary and secondary ambient standards. Because the federal emission standards applicable to new sources may set limits on pollutants other than those covered by the national ambient standards, the law also requires that a procedure be established for states to establish emission standards for such pollutants applicable to existing sources which are in the same categories covered by the federal new source standards. For example, if EPA sets standards for new phosphate fertilizer plants, one of the major pollutants emitted by such plants are fluorides. Because national ambient standards have not been established for fluorides, if the new source performance standards set limits on fluorides the states will be required to set fluoride limits for existing fertilizer plants.

The second type of federally established emission standards are those dealing with "hazardous air pollutants." The Act defines these as pollutants "to which no ambient air quality standard is applicable and which in the judgment of the Administrator may cause, or contribute to, an increase in mortality or an increase in serious irreversible, or incapacitating reversible, illness." [16] The standards are applicable to all new or existing stationary sources. The EPA has so far established standards for three such pollutants: asbestos, mercury, and beryllium.

The third type of emission standards, those applicable to moving pollution sources, have been the most controversial and are also the most important. The 1970 Act continued the previous authority of the administrator to establish emission standards for new cars, trucks, and buses. It gave him authority to regulate the content of fuels used in motor vehicles so that fuel additives (such as lead) could be prohibited or limited in amount. And it gave the administrator new authority to establish air pollution emission limits for all airplanes. But the most striking departure of the Act was that, rather than leaving the actual standards up to the discretion of the administrator as the previous laws had done, the Congress took it upon itself to name what the automobile emissions standards should be. As a requirement of the law, carbon monoxide and hydrocarbons emissions are to be reduced 90 per cent from the levels applicable to 1970 model cars and oxides of nitrogen are to be reduced 90 per cent from the levels applicable to the 1971 models. The carbon monoxide and hydrocarbon standards were to be met by 1975 and the oxides of nitrogen standard by 1976, but the law allows the EPA administrator to grant a one year extension and he has given the auto manufacturers such an extension. The 1974 legislation further extended the deadlines at least through 1977, but the administrator is required to set interim standards which the auto manufacturers must meet.

The process for setting standards contained in the 1970 Clean Air Amendments is detailed, complex, and stringent. The Act bristles with 90 and 120-day deadlines. The law describes who will set the standards and it also contains some significant criteria for what factors should be considered in choosing a standard. For example, the primary ambient air standards are to be based solely on considerations of public health, but in setting the new source emission standards the administrator must take into account the cost to the polluter of achieving the standard.

The language of the Act thus establishes the "rules of the game" by which standards will be set. But the rules allow much discretion in what the actual standards will be. Before finally promulgating the federal standards, the EPA administrator must consider the views of the technical experts, the state and local officials, other federal agencies, environmental interest groups, and affected polluters. Extended bargaining may take place between EPA and these groups. Even where the standards have been established by the law, as in the case of the automobile standards, there is considerable leeway in interpretation. The test methods and the enforcement procedure may be just as important as the specific numbers established as the standard.

The rules themselves may get changed in the course of bargaining over the standards. Thus the Sierra Club, wanting more stringent standards, succeeded in getting the courts to interpret the Act as not allowing any degradation of air quality. The EPA opposed this interpretation, claiming that not allowing air quality to be lowered anywhere, regardless of how clean the air was to start with, would result in stopping economic growth. The EPA lost the case and is now trying to establish regulations which will comply with the court ruling while still allowing for industrial development.[17]

After the federal ambient standards have been established, there are negotiations with the states over the emission standards necessary to achieve the ambient standards. As we described above, emissions standards are critical in air pollution control, and the translation from ambient to emission standards is often more a political than a technical process. Once the emission standards are set, they may still be significantly changed in the bargaining which takes place over their application to individual polluters. In short, there is a big difference between the rules of the game, as spelled out in the Act, and the game's final outcome. As Murray Edelman has stated, "To draft a law is not to reflect a public 'will'; it is only through subsequent bargaining and administrative decision-making that values find some sort of realization in policy. To formulate a law is essentially a job of constructing a setting in the sense of building background assumptions and limits that will persist over time and influence the quality of political acts but not their content or direction." [18]

WATER POLLUTION STANDARDS

As we have already discussed (see Chapter 2), the 1972 Amendments to the Federal Water Pollution Control Act is without question the most complex and extensive environmental legislation ever passed. This is particularly true of the standard-setting provisions of the new law. The provisions roughly parallel those of the 1970 Clean Air Act with the major exception that the federal government, not the states, is to set effluent standards for existing pollution sources. However, the interrelationships among goals, water quality standards, and effluent limits is far more complicated than the parallel provisions in the Clean Air Act, and the legislation is further complicated by numerous additional provisions, such as those relating to permits.

The 1972 Act begins by declaring two goals: by 1983 water quality should be good enough to provide for the protection and propagation of fish, shellfish, and wildlife and for recreation; and by 1985 the discharge of pollutants into all navigable waters should be eliminated. The 1983 goal is woven into the operative provisions of the Act through the effluent limits and water quality standards requirements. However, the total costs and benefits of achieving it are to be reviewed by a National Study Commission which will report to the Congress in 1975, thus raising the possibility that the goal might be revised. The 1985 goal is left as simply a goal—and not one that is likely to be achieved except if "pollutant" is given a rather restrictive meaning.

The heart of the 1972 Act is in its restrictions on effluents. Two types of effluent standards are to be set by the federal government and are to be applied to all existing point sources of water pollution (those sources which put effluent into the water at an identifiable point). By 1977 all publicly owned treatment plants are to have secondary treatment and all other point sources of pollution are to have the "best practicable control technology." In setting these effluent standards for industrial and other sources except municipal treatment plants the EPA administrator is required to take into account "the total cost of application of technology in relation to the effluent reduction benefits to be achieved from such application" as well as "the age of equipment and facilities involved, the process employed, the engineering aspects of the application of various types of control techniques, process changes, non-water quality environmental impact (including energy requirements) and such other factors as the Administrator deems appropriate." [19] In effect, he theoretically will have to set different standards for each individual plant and know as much about each plant as the plant manager. It has been estimated that there are more than 200 thousand industrial water users in the U.S., although only a small fraction probably will be subject to the best available requirement.[20]

The second type of effluent standard for existing sources is to take effect in 1983 and requires application of the "best available technology," regardless of cost, to all point sources other than municipal treatment plants. Municipal treatment plants are to install best practicable technology by 1983. The "best available technology" standards are to apply to categories or classes of pollution sources. The law provides for at least two avenues of modification of the best available requirement. On the side of leniency toward the polluter, the administrator can modify the application of a standard if the owner or operator of a plant can show that a less stringent standard "will represent the maximum use of technology within the economic capability of the owner or operator" and "will result in reasonable further progress toward the elimination of the discharge of pollutants." [21] On the side of stringency, if the administrator finds that the effluent standards are not sufficient to achieve water quality good enough for recreation, drinking water, and all other major uses he can impose more stringent requirements. More stringent requirements would presumably mean closing down the plant (because the existing requirement would be for installation of the best available technology), but such requirements cannot be imposed if the company affected can show that there is "no reasonable relationship" between the economic and social costs of the standard and the benefits to be obtained.[22]

The primary instrument for applying the national emission standards to individual pollution sources is the new permit program established by the 1972 Act. All significant point sources, including industrial plants, municipalities, animal feedlots, and irrigation return flows, will be required to obtain a permit specifying the amount of effluent that can be put into the water, schedules for further remedial measures that must be taken, and requirements for monitoring and reporting actual amounts discharged. The permits will specify the steps which each pollution source must take to reach the "best practicable" requirement and they will also set effluent limitations applicable in the interim, thus in effect establishing the standards which will be in effect until 1977 when the "best practicable" requirement is to be reached.

The Act establishes a mechanism for allowing the states to administer the permit program. As of November 1973, four states—California, Connecticut, Oregon, and Michigan—have been authorized by EPA to issue wastewater discharge permits. Other states are gradually coming in with requests for permit authority. For the states which have not been granted authority,

EPA will issue the permits, building on the groundwork laid by the applications for permits under the 1899 Refuse Act. Twenty-three thousand such applications were submitted to EPA, but the agency has been concentrating on approximately 2,700 major dischargers who are believed to account for the vast majority of all industrial water pollution.[23] Even after a state takes over the permit system EPA retains the authority to set guidelines for the system, to establish what categories of pollution sources will be covered, to disapprove the system and take over its administration, and to veto approval of any individual permit.

Several other types of effluent standards are contained in the 1972 Act. New pollution sources are to be covered by standards requiring the best available technology. This provision parallels the new source requirement in the 1970 Clean Air Act, although the water act specifies 27 industrial categories to which, at a minimum, the new source standards will apply. Also similar to the Clean Air Act, the 1972 water legislation requires the administrator to set effluent standards for toxic pollutants, although the definition of a toxic pollutant is less stringent in the water act than in the air act. The administrator also can set standards for pre-treatment of industrial pollution if such pollution is to be sent to a municipal waste treatment plant for final treatment. Several other effluent limitations are implicitly embodied in requirements for permits. These include permits for ocean dumping, authorized under the Marine Protection, Research, and Sanctuaries Act of 1972;[24] for disposal of sewage sludge; and for disposal of dredge and fill material. The permits for dredge and fill are issued by the U.S. Corps of Engineers under the authority of the 1899 Rivers and Harbors Act but are subject to EPA guidelines. Finally, the Act flatly prohibits the discharge into navigable waters of any radiological, chemical, or biological warfare agents or any high-level radioactive waste.

As can be seen from this very brief description of the standards requirements, the 1972 Act is not only complicated, it is also very flexible, in the sense that a good deal of discretion is left to EPA. Ironically, this discretion arises in part from the complexities of the legislation. By trying to cover all possible situations, and thus having several provisions dealing with closely related situations and functions, it is frequently left to the administrator to determine which section of the law to apply to a particular polluter or state. In part, the flexibility also arises from the discretion left to EPA to define key terms in the bill. The real effect of the law will depend on the interpretation given to such phrases as "best practicable technology," "best available technology," and "maximum use of technology within the economic capability of the owner." As with most laws, the Congress has established a framework and a set of rules, but passage of the law is the beginning not the end of the political struggle.

The setting of standards is also a beginning. The establishment of specific quantitative standards is the basic step which sets the pattern for future actions in controlling pollution. But once the standards become official, the long struggle to make them a reality must begin. This struggle is the compliance process. And the successful outcome of compliance must be the ultimate goal of any pollution control program.

CHAPTER 9

Compliance

COMPLIANCE is the process whereby existing pollution is halted or reduced or potential pollution is prevented. The prevailing legal framework for compliance in the United States is what might be called "enforcement," the establishment of effluent standards and the legal prosecution of those who violate the standards. However, within this legal framework there are many strategies which a governmental agency can pursue in order to achieve compliance, and most agencies rely on techniques such as persuasion, negotiation, and education far more than on formal legal sanctions.

The establishment of effluent standards and the legal prosecution of those who violate the standards is a "common-sense" approach which follows the model of all criminal law enforcement. As in criminal law enforcement, a high degree of voluntary compliance is necessary. However, controlling pollution presents problems which are quite different from those of controlling burglary or fraud. The enforcement of standards against individual polluters may be quite inefficient in terms of time, money, and results, and bargaining with violators may often be necessary. Especially in controlling water pollution, where there are a wide variety of alternatives which can be utilized, methods which treat the stream as a whole, such as stream re-aeration or low-flow augmentation, sometimes may be much less expensive and accomplished much more rapidly than trying to get each individual source of pollution to treat its own wastes.

EFFLUENT FEES

The major alternative which has been proposed to the standards and prosecution approach is a system of economic penalties or effluent fees.[1] This involves the establishment of a schedule of fees for emitting given amounts of pollutants into a stream or into the air. Each polluter must then pay a certain amount to a control commission, according to how much of what kind of pollutant he has emitted. The schedule of fees can be adjusted upward or downward to reach any desired level of stream quality or ambient air, although in the ideal system the fees would be based on the amount of damages (or costs) caused by the pollution. The money collected from the fees is used to provide centralized pollution control facilities and also for monitoring and other activities of the control commission.

The effluent fee system has been promoted primarily by economists who see it as a way of achieving the optimal economic balance between the costs of pollution damage and the costs of pollution control.[2] The technical obstacles to determining such a balance, particularly the cost of obtaining the necessary data, are very great.[3] But the political obstacles may be even greater, because it is unlikely that economists and other technicians will be left free to set whatever fee schedules they consider desirable. Neither the local chapter of the Izaak Walton League nor the local pulp mill will feel bound by the economists' formulas, and the optimal economic balance will be adjusted by the political balance which prevails in the particular area.[4] If the fees are set on a national basis, they will obviously be affected by the political balance at the federal level.

The major advantages of effluent fees are that they allow each polluter to control his pollution in the most economical way and that they encourage the establishment of the least-cost control system for a river basin or an airshed considered as a whole. In effect, the system utilizes the workings of the free market economy, controlling pollution by internalizing the so-called "externalities" of firms or municipalities by making them pay for their use of air or water. The administration of an effluent fee system might be simpler than the standards and prosecution approach, since, at least in theory, the activities of the control commission would consist only of setting the air or water quality standards, establishing the fee schedule, monitoring effluents, and billing the polluters. The initiative for installing control systems would rest with each polluter rather than with a centralized public body.

Effluent fees have been criticized by' some as constituting a "license to pollute." Insofar as the concept of effluent fees is based on collecting damages equal to the marginal costs of pollution, it would permit some pollution to occur, specifically that amount of pollution which is economically "optimal." However, given the impossibility of assigning accurate dollar values to many of the costs of pollution, such as the cost of ugliness or of foregone recreational opportunities, any effluent fee system would probably be based on standards derived from the same considerations as the currently used enforcement standards. Also, since current enforcement efforts can hardly be considered to have worked perfectly, the real question is not which system is theoretically perfect but which is actually capable of achieving the highest degree of compliance most efficiently. The generally discouraging performance under the existing system would seem to provide a real incentive to adopt an alternative approach.

With all these advantages, why hasn't the effluent fee system been applied in the United States? Partially it is due to institutional roadblocks. At the federal level, the administration for the past three years has submitted to Congress legislation for a national tax or fee on emissions of sulfur oxides air pollution. There has been no Congressional action because the legislation must go through the House Ways and Means Committee. Wilbur Mills, the powerful chairman of the Committee, is convinced that the federal tax system should not be used for any purpose except to raise revenue, and thus he has consistently declined to take any positive action on the sulfur tax proposal. Mills' opinion is shared by the U.S. Treasury Department, and thus the Executive Branch also has been divided on the merits of the proposal. Mills' opinion is also shared by Senator Muskie, although for different reasons. Muskie has a large stake in the existing system, having been responsible for creating much of it; effluent fees are a threat to the jurisdiction of his subcommittee; and he is also convinced that an effluent fee system would not be effective.

At the sub-federal level, it has usually been proposed that a fee system be instituted in an entire river basin or airshed. This would require a control agency which encompassed such an area and which had sufficient authority to impose fees, and there are few, if any, such agencies in existence. There is also the question of which area should go first in trying the system. Because the consequences of the system are not known, and the degree of pollution control achieved would hopefully be greater than it is at present, industries in the area would oppose the system and government officials would be reluctant to pioneer it because of possible adverse effects on economic development. Thus, even if there were many control agencies equipped with the legal and political power to impose an effluent fee system, none of them would be eager to be the first to apply it.

The debate over the sulfur oxides tax proposal has produced an unusual reversal in the opinions of the relevant interest groups. Environmental groups had opposed effluent fees primarily on the grounds that they were a license to pollute. The environmentalists were convinced by the Council on Environmental Quality and others that this was not a very good argument, at least under current conditions, and the environmental groups became strong supporters of the sulfur oxides tax. Industry groups had not really committed themselves but had tended to favor effluent fees as being more in keeping with a market economy. However, they opposed the sulfur tax on a variety of grounds, perhaps including fear of its effectiveness.[5]

An accurate assessment of the actual accomplishments of an effluent fee system necessarily entails a prediction of the politics of the system. Political factors are a potential weakness in the system, because it might be more difficult to muster public support for a control commission which was using effluent fees than for one which was employing the traditional standards and prosecution procedure. While the public might approve of the general idea of an effluent fee system, the actual setting of the fees is the kind of technical decision which it finds difficult to follow or understand. Industry groups, on the other hand, would understand the fees (since they would have to pay) and would follow such decisions closely. There is thus the risk that the public would be apathetic and would permit the fees to be set at too low a level to achieve the desired water quality. Effluent fees would not be imposed in a political vacuum, and the pressures exerted by industries and some public officials for lenient pollution controls would still be present.

Two examples lend some indirect empirical evidence to the fear of political forces undermining the effectiveness of an effluent fee system. In the Ruhr Valley in Germany a type of effluent fee system has been established, although on a scale and in a manner which makes the example not very applicable to the United States. The control bodies which set the fees, the "Genossenschaften," are heavily weighted in favor of the industrial polluters, and the outcomes of the system have included devoting one entire river to waste disposal. Regardless of the merits of this outcome, it is unlikely that it would have much political appeal here.[6] The other example is the setting of sewer rental charges, a practice common in many American communities. Such charges are in many respects analogous to effluent fees, and in most communities they have been set at a level considerably lower than that necessary to cover the costs of treating the sewage.[7]

On the other side of this argument, the standards which are now set are not exactly easy to understand. Even more to the point, the real process of compliance takes place in closed sessions with the polluters, and this process is inaccessible to the public. Thus it might well be that the setting of effluent fees, especially if done at the national level, would be more open and more subject to pressure by citizens' groups than the current standards and enforcement method.

The use of effluent fees would involve a sudden or gradual scrapping of the existing body of pollution control law. Even if the change were gradual, it would be a dramatic switch in the way in which pollution control in this country has been conducted. The American political system has constructed many barriers against change which is not incremental, and thus the political prospects of an effluent fee scheme are probably not good.

One other major approach to achieving compliance is the use of economic incentives, such as tax credits for the installation of pollution control equipment. Economic incentives can at best serve only as a supplement to, and not as a substitute for, other major approaches. It has been proven by the sad experience of the localities which have instituted incentives but not penalties that industries require a stick as well as a carrot to make them take action. We have already discussed some of the disadvantages of providing tax credits, but economic incentives do encourage compliance by reducing the costs of such compliance to private industry.

Many states and localities provide economic incentives for pollution control. In the past such incentives have usually taken the form of reducing or eliminating state and local taxes on pollution abatement equipment. A newer form of incentive, which began in 1971, is for local governments to issue tax-exempt industrial revenue bonds to finance the construction of pollution abatement facilities. The facilities are then leased to private companies. The total volume of such bond issues from 1971 through mid-1973 was nearly $1.5 billion.[8]

The federal government allows companies to claim accelerated depreciation on pollution control equipment and facilities, which has the effect of reducing corporate profit taxes. This provision of the federal tax law obviously does no good for the marginal firms most in need of financial assistance because they have little or no profits on which they must pay taxes. However, the pollution incentive is not used even by profitable companies because if they do use it they are not allowed to use the investment tax credit, and the tax credit usually provides a significantly larger subsidy than the special pollution equipment depreciation option.[9]

FEDERAL ENFORCEMENT

Until 1970, the basic procedure for federal enforcement against polluters was the same for air and water pollution. First a conference was held under the aegis of the federal pollution control agency. The conference established a schedule for cleaning up the pollution which allowed at least six months for action to be taken. If at the end of the six months sufficient progress had not been made, the administrator could call a public hearing. There was a mandatory six-months delay after the public hearing and then, if compliance was still not satisfactory, the administrator could request the attorney general to bring suit against the polluters.

The initiation of enforcement action by the federal government was generally limited to pollution which originated in one state but endangered the health or welfare of persons in another. The consent or request of the governor of the state was necessary for a federal action dealing with purely intrastate pollution. There were two exceptions to the interstate-intrastate differentiation. In water pollution cases enforcement proceedings could be initiated when "substantial economic injury results from the inability to market shellfish or shellfish products in interstate commerce because of pollution . . ." [10] The other exception was that immediate federal court action could be taken in situations where air pollution "is presenting an imminent and substantial endangerment to the health of persons" and state or local authorities have not acted to abate it.[11] This rather drastic procedure was placed in the 1967 act as a response to criticisms that in the case of a severe air pollution episode the lengthy procedures of the normal enforcement process would be useless and the federal government would be forced to stand idly by while lives were lost.

The 1965 Water Quality Act authorized a greatly streamlined version of the enforcement procedure, permitting the elimination of both the conference and the public hearing in enforcing the standards established under the act. The administrator must notify a violator of the standards 180 days before legal action is taken, but after such notice has been given and the required time has elapsed, the administrator can ask the Justice Department to institute suit. Parallel provisions for enforcement of interstate air quality standards were included in the 1967 Air Quality Act.

The 1970 Clean Air Amendments and the 1972 Amendments to the Federal Water Pollution Control Act made a variety of major changes in enforcement provisions. The move to national standards has been accompanied by a move to more direct and has cumbersome federal enforcement provisions. The 1970 Air Act retained the old language relating to conferences and public hearings, but it removed it as the major enforcement mechanism by stating that, "A conference may not be called . . . with respect to an air pollutant for which (at the time the conference is called) a national primary or secondary ambient air quality standard is in effect . . ." [12] Because the standards cover the major air pollutants it is difficult to envision a situation where a conference would serve a useful purpose. The 1972 Water Act eliminated the conference procedure altogether for water pollution control.

The new basic enforcement method for air and water pollution is relatively simple and straightforward. If the EPA administrator has reason to believe that any of the pollution control standards are being violated he must give a notice to the violator. Thirty days after giving such a notice, he can either administratively issue a cease-and-desist order to the polluter or he can ask the Justice Department to initiate court action against the polluter.[13] Under the water act, an order by the administrator can allow no more than thirty days for the violator to achieve compliance and the administrator can impose a civil penalty of up to $10,000 per day for failure to comply with his order. The no more than thirty days for compliance is probably not very meaningful or realistic, but the civil penalty power is an important weapon. Under the Clean Air Act the administrator must get a court decision to impose penalties on a polluter. Also, the water act makes it mandatory for the administrator to take enforcement action in a variety of cases, whereas the Clean Air Act leaves him more discretion.

The above provisions are related to individual polluters. The EPA Administrator is also empowered to take overall enforcement responsibilities from a state. Whenever he finds that violations of relevant standards or of conditions contained in a permit are so widespread as to appear to be due to failure of the state to carry out its enforcement responsibilities, he can serve notice on the state and, after serving the notice, assume direct responsibility for all enforcement within the state.[14] Given the realities of the political system it is unlikely that this power would actually ever be exercised, but it constitutes a significant club which the federal government can use to influence state governments.

An important innovation contained in both the air and water statutes is a provision for citizen suits to enforce federal standards. Private citizens can institute court action against any polluter for violations of applicable standards or of orders issued by EPA. Citizens may also institute proceedings against the EPA administrator if he fails to perform an act required of him under the law.[15] The power to sue the administrator will be particularly important given the mandatory character of many of the enforcement duties he is given in the water act. The impact of the citizen suit provisions is discussed in Chapter 6.

There are a number of other enforcement provisions which are contained in both the Clean Air Amendments and the Water Pollution Control Act Amendments. Both acts authorize direct federal enforcement of new source performance standards and of the standards dealing with toxic or hazardous substances. Both also contain authority for the administrator to go directly to court to get injunctions against polluters if an emergency situation exists.

The primary enforcement mechanism under the Clean Air Act is the state implementation plan. The state plans contain the detailed requirements which must be met, and it is violation of the plan which triggers an enforcement action. The comparable mechanism under the Water Pollution Control Act is the permit system. The EPA has already placed heavy reliance for enforcement on the permit provisions of the 1899 Refuse Act, the predecessor to the permit system contained in the 1972 Amendments.

Attaining compliance with the automobile air pollution emission standards presents a variety of unique problems. At the present time, samples of each type of car are given by the manufacturer to EPA for testing. If these test models meet the standards then all such models are considered to be in compliance with the standards. However, tests conducted on vehicles actually in use have shown that emissions were higher than expected under the applicable standards for well over half the vehicles tested.[16] Changes in the testing procedures instituted by

EPA in 1972 may improve this situation somewhat, but there will probably still be widespread non-compliance until there can be mandatory inspection of all cars on the road. The 1970 Act contains provisions for such inspection if the technology and the institutional means of applying such technology exist.[17] They do not exist now, and, given that only a few states have adequate state safety inspection systems for cars, it is unlikely that inspection of all cars will become a reality in the foreseeable future.

Automobile air pollution compliance also presents the problem of unworkable penalties if a manufacturer cannot meet the standards. The only action the administrator can take if one or all of the manufacturers cannot meet the 1975–76 emission standards is to prevent the non-complying cars from being sold. This is so drastic a penalty that it is unlikely to be invoked. The lack of any intermediate step to achieve compliance has already prevented action in one important case. Former EPA Administrator Ruckelshaus, when he announced his decision on the 1975 auto standards, stated, "The issue of good faith as it relates to Chrysler Corporation has been particularly troublesome for me in these proceedings . . . . If Congress had provided me with some sanctions short of the nuclear deterrent of in effect closing down that major corporation, my finding on good faith may [sic] have been otherwise." [18] Solutions to this problem, such as a tax on emissions, are possible, but the industry is undoubtedly happier with an unrealistic "nuclear deterrent."

WATER POLLUTION—FEDERAL ENFORCEMENT EXPERIENCE

Fifty-nine water pollution enforcement conferences have been initiated since the conference-public hearing provision became law in 1956. They have affected almost every state and have varied widely in scope, ranging from situations involving only one or two polluters to an effort to reverse the deterioration of Lake Erie involving five states and hundreds of polluters. The choice of targets for such conferences has been determined by the seriousness of the problem in the area and by the possible political ramifications of initiating an enforcement conference.

Only one of the conferences has resulted in the filing of a suit in federal court, and the experience with this case clearly indicates why all of the other conferences have stopped short of the final stage of going to the courts. The conference involving pollution of the Missouri River by the city of St. Joseph, Missouri, was held in 1957 and was one of the first to be initiated by the federal government. After the citizens of St. Joseph refused to approve a bond issue to provide the funds necessary for the construction of a treatment plant and connecting sewers, a public hearing was held in 1959. In 1960 the citizens again voted, the bond issue was defeated even more decisively, and the federal government then filed suit in Federal District Court. A court order, calling for completion of the necessary treatment facilities by 1963, was issued in 1961. In 1967 the city had completed work on the treatment plant but had only half completed installation of the sewers. The District Court, which had retained jurisdiction in the case, ordered the city to expedite work on the projects. However, city officials replied that they could not complete all the projects necessary to provide primary treatment for the city's waste until 1973. As of this writing, 17 years after the enforcement conference was held, the City of St. Joseph has completed an elementary, and by now inadequate, sewage and waste treatment system. EPA has given the city an engineering grant to plan for the installation of secondary treatment.

The conference procedure has been used primarily as a method to prod state and local officials and as a means of giving adverse publicity to the polluters.[19] It has obviously not been a way to impose penalties on polluters or to force them directly to take action. For these purposes EPA has relied on two other authorities—The Refuse Act, which became law in 1899 as part of the Rivers and Harbors Act of that year,[20] and the 180-day notice provision which became part of the Federal Water Pollution Control Act in 1965.

The 1899 Refuse Act was passed originally to prevent impediments to navigation. It prohibited the discharge of refuse (except that flowing from streets and sewers in a liquid state) into navigable waters without a permit or in violation of the conditions of a permit. The Army Corps of Engineers was responsible for the issuance of the permits. Although court decisions had supported the Act's use in water pollution abatement cases,[21] for seventy-one years the Corps administered the Act as a minor provision in the navigation statutes.

In 1970 the Act was discovered to be a potentially potent weapon in the fight against water pollution. The president, under prodding from Representative Henry Reuss, the Council on Environmental Quality, and conservation groups, issued an executive order[22] in December 1970 which established the Refuse Act as a major federal enforcement tool. All discharges into navigable waters or their tributaries were to be made subject to the conditions of a permit. Although the Corps of Engineers was to issue the permits, EPA was made responsible for determining the conditions of the permit as they related to water quality. Failure to make timely application for a permit subjected the discharger to an enforcement action.

The Refuse Act program was in effect for little more than a year. However, during this period (approximately from July 1971 to December 1972), EPA referred 371 enforcement actions to the Department of Justice for action under the Refuse Act. One hundred and six of these were civil actions, 169 were criminal actions, and 96 were for failure to apply for a permit.[23] Criminal actions were brought against such large firms as Allied Chemical Corporation, FMC Corporation, Gulf Oil, Cities Service, Jones and Laughlin Steel, Minnesota Mining and Manufacturing Company, Mobil Oil, Republic Steel, Texaco, and U.S. Steel.[24] In many of the Refuse Act cases agreement was reached on remedial measures and fines were imposed on polluters, although the maximum penalty under the Act was only $2,500 for any single offense.

The Refuse Act permit program was brought to a halt by two court decisions. In December 1971 a federal court ruled that each permit had to be accompanied by an environmental impact statement in accordance with the National Environmental Policy Act. The court also declared that no permits could be issued for discharges into nonnavigable tributaries of navigable waters.[25] While EPA was still trying to decide how to cope with this decision, the Third Circuit Court of Appeals ruled that a company could not be held criminally responsible for discharges under the Refuse Act until the permit system was fully in operation, a task that would take several years.[26] These decisions brought the permit program under the Refuse Act to an end, but the provisions of the 1972 Amendments to the Water Pollution Control Act restore and build upon the authority and experience gained under the Refuse Act. Thus the halt can be viewed as temporary, and the permit system, as contained in the 1972 law, is a primary component of EPA's water pollution authority.

The other weapon which has been used by EPA is the provision contained in the 1965 Water Quality Act which allows court action against a discharger alleged to be in violation of water quality standards after expiration of a 180-day notice period. After serving notice, EPA holds an informal hearing with the discharger in an effort to reach agreement and avoid the necessity of a court case.[27] Between December 1970 and December 1972, EPA issued 143 notices of violation of water quality standards.[28] In about half of these cases, agreement was reached during the 180-day period. The other half are either still in progress or have been recommended for legal action. However, *no* court cases have been initiated using the provisions of the 1965 Act. In the situations where legal action is considered necessary, EPA has proceeded under the provisions of the Refuse Act, apparently despairing of making any progress by using the provisions of the Federal Water Pollution Control Act. This is a sad commentary on the uselessness of the Water Pollution Control Act for enforcement purposes. Whether the 1972 Amendments have changed this situation remains to be seen.

AIR POLLUTION—FEDERAL ENFORCEMENT EXPERIENCE

There has been much less federal enforcement experience under the air pollution statutes than under the water pollution laws. This is partially because the federal government assumed responsibility for air pollution at a later date. In part it is because there has been no air pollution equivalent of the Refuse Act which is apparently the only law under which the government has found it possible to take a polluter to court and win the case in a reasonable period of time.

There have been eleven air pollution abatement conferences,

all but one of which were initiated prior to EPA's creation.[29] Like the water pollution conferences, these have been rather informal sessions aimed at giving bad publicity to the polluters and strengthening the backbones of the local enforcement officials.

There is also an air pollution equivalent to the St. Joseph story. Since 1959 the Delaware State Air Pollution Authority and the state of Maryland had been engaged in futile efforts to get a chicken-rendering plant located in Bishop, Maryland, to stop emitting noxious fumes which drifted across the state line to Delaware. Finally, in 1965, Delaware requested the federal government to hold an abatement conference. The conference was held in 1965 and, when the Bishop plant failed to take any remedial action, a public hearing was held in 1967. The hearing board ordered the plant to eliminate the odors within six months, but the plant took no action. In 1968 the secretary of HEW requested the attorney general to bring suit. The Federal District Court in Baltimore heard the case on March 3 and 4, 1969, but the court adjourned the hearing because there were few documented instances of pollution from the plant reaching Delaware, and the court stated that it "would prefer to have more evidence in the case than we have now, before deciding the case . . ."[30] After more inspections by state and federal officials, the court ordered the plant to stop operations by February 1970. The plant appealed, but the decision was upheld by the appeals court and, in May, 1970, when the Supreme Court refused to review the case, the plant ceased operations. However, in April 1971 the state found that the company was processing oils instead of rendering chickens although the federal court order had prohibited any operations at the plant. In July 1971, a Federal District Court held the company in contempt of court and ordered it to implement an EPA-approved abatement program as soon as possible. In November 1972, an EPA official reported that the company had complied with the court order.[31]

Four actions have been taken by EPA under Section 113 of the Clean Air Act which authorizes the administrator to issue compliance orders for violation of federally approved state implementation plans. Two of these were minor cases involving open burning at municipal dumps in Rhode Island. The other two involved large firms in the state of Delaware. The Delmarva Power and Light Company and the Allied Chemical Corporation were both given notice by EPA for violating the sulfur limitations contained in the Delaware implementation plan, the first plan to be fully approved by EPA. In July 1972, Allied Chemical agreed to the provisions of the compliance order issued by EPA. The Delmarva case was taken to court, but the federal courts upheld the EPA order.[32] The Delaware cases held out some promise that federal enforcement of the state implementation plans is possible. However, it is still too early to tell how frequently or with what effect such enforcement actions will be used.

Perhaps the most dramatic enforcement action which has been taken by EPA was a temporary restraining order which the agency obtained in Birmingham, Alabama, under the authority of Section 303 of the Clean Air Act. Section 303 authorizes EPA to obtain rapid court action to temporarily abate pollution if an imminent and substantial endangerment to health exists. Birmingham was in the midst of a severe air pollution episode due to an inversion. On November 18, 1971, EPA requested and got a court order requiring 23 firms to significantly reduce their emissions until the air pollution episode ended. The following day the inversion lifted and the court dissolved the restraining order at EPA's request. Although the EPA move was dramatic, it did nothing to reduce air pollution in Birmingham over the long run except perhaps to illustrate the severity of the city's pollution problem.

The Limits of Federal Enforcement

Three factors have limited EPA's initiation and prosecution of legal enforcement actions to achieve compliance—limitations contained in the air and water pollution statutes; a reliance on voluntary compliance; and reliance on state and local enforcement efforts.

The limitations contained in the statutes may make it difficult or impossible for EPA to win a case against a polluter within a reasonable time. Whether this will be true in the future must await court interpretations of the numerous and complex provisions of the 1970 version of the Clean Air Act and the 1972 Amendments to the Water Pollution Control Act. Although both acts appear to be strongly worded and to provide ample legal authority to EPA, experience with the earlier versions of these laws dictates caution about how strong the federal legal powers are until they have been tested in the courts.

A second check on federal enforcement applies equally to state and local governments. No law of any kind can be enforced successfully if there is not a high degree of voluntary compliance. The reason for this is very elementary—there are simply not enough policemen, inspectors, or judges to make it feasible to deal with anything except a very small minority of the potential violators of the law. There is an added reason to depend on voluntary compliance in pollution control because in most cases successful abatement depends upon positive action being taken by the polluter. It is not realistic to talk about closing down a plant except in rare instances. Thus abatement ultimately depends upon the polluter buying equipment, maintaining it properly, and making changes in the plant's operations. Throwing a polluter in jail will not directly bring these changes about.

The need for voluntary compliance is an important limit on how far enforcement action can go. But, at least at the present time, it is largely a theoretical limit. Nothing could be more mistaken than the argument that because voluntary compliance is necessary no legal actions should be brought against polluters. If there is to be general voluntary compliance it will be achieved by showing that noncompliance will be punished. As the director of the Los Angeles County air pollution control agency has stated, "Reasonable discussion with polluters about remedial steps is important, but there has to be the knowledge that if they don't shape up they're going to land in court as sure as God made little apples." [33] There is almost no state or locality today where a polluter who defies the pollution laws is certain that he will wind up in court. He has every reason to believe that he will not be prosecuted or, that even if he is, the penalties which will be imposed will be insignificant. In short, the current situation is one of widespread noncompliance because of the lack of any system to insure that polluters are adequately penalized for their pollution.

The third limit on federal enforcement is probably the most important. The Clean Air Act states that, "the prevention and control of air pollution at its source is the primary responsibility of states and local governments." [34] A similar, although less strong, statement is contained in the Water Pollution Control Act.[35] These statements have been contained in the federal pollution laws since their original passage, and, although their true meaning has been steadily eroded by the grant of ever greater enforcement powers to the federal government, they are still meaningful. The EPA has relied and will continue to rely on the states and localities for the bulk of the enforcement work.

Although EPA has much more manpower than its predecessor pollution control agencies, it cannot hope to have enough time or manpower to exercise inspection, surveillance, and prosecution over most polluters. It would take literally tens of thousands of federal officials to undertake adequate direct federal enforcement throughout the United States. Thus EPA would have to place heavy reliance on state and local enforcement action even if the law were silent about the "primary responsibility" of the subnational levels.

The EPA has shown less deference to the states than HEW or Interior did when they were responsible for pollution control. But given the time and manpower necessary for enforcement action, the primary purpose of federal enforcement has been to prod the state and local control agencies into taking action. This has been done in three ways: the negotiations between federal and non-federal officials which precede and follow an enforcement action; federal technical aid in pinpointing the problems and their solution; and the mobilizing of public opinion to demand that the state and local agencies take action.

There is some conflict between the technique of negotiating with the relevant nonfederal officials and the attempt to mobilize public opinion. It is difficult to publicize the existence of pollution without also implicitly criticizing the efforts of state and local officials and thus provoking the resentment of such officials at the federal intervention. The executive director of ORSANCO expressed this when he noted that

The conference provision . . . was conceived [by the states] as offering a means through which the parties concerned could be brought together for resolving viewpoints prior to, and hopefully without the necessity of, formal proceedings to reach agreement on proposed federal compliance actions. Instead, the federal authorities elected to conduct the conferences virtually as public hearings, generally in the ballroom of a large hotel and with advance publicity geared to generate the attendance of hundreds of people. Furthermore, these conferences were shrouded with the atmosphere of an adversary proceeding, in which the federal representatives appeared to cast themselves as the savior of streams with the states in the role as opponents of such good intent.[36]

The role of the states and localities is reinforced by the political system. Enforcement is the most politically sensitive aspect of the federal pollution control programs. The decision to undertake a federal enforcement action represents the intrusion of the federal government into an ongoing political situation. The existence of pollution in any particular state or locality represents a certain balance of particular forces (conservationists, industries, government officials, etc.), some of whom benefit from the status quo and some of whom want to change it. When the federal forces enter the picture they inevitably change the balance to some extent and thus benefit certain interests and damage certain others. These interests usually include people such as governors, congressmen, or big-city mayors who can influence the federal government. Thus, as a matter of self-preservation the pollution control agency must consider the likely political ramifications of undertaking an enforcement action.

The political ramifications must also be considered because they are crucial to the success or failure of the federal effort to get the air or water cleaned up. The state and local political forces are usually in a position, if they so desire, to undermine attempts to stop the pollution. The state legislature can override the decisions of the state or local pollution control agencies, a local mayor can delay almost indefinitely the installation of a waste treatment plant for his community, an influential governor can use his power to accelerate or retard the pace at which industries install pollution control equipment. The political sensitivities of the state and local pollution control agencies must also be kept constantly in mind.

All of these limits should not be taken to imply that more federal enforcement action should not be taken. Although EPA must rely on the states and localities, it has discovered that one of the most effective ways of prodding them into action is to initiate enforcement actions itself. Furthermore, strong federal action against major industrial polluters will prod other industries into a greater degree of compliance. Thus, an effective federal program will increasingly have to rely on federal legal action taken against polluters. We have already indicated the major weaknesses of many of the state and local programs (see Chapter 7).

PREVENTIVE ACTION

Compliance must eventually take the form of preventing pollution before it occurs rather than stopping it once it has happened. Only through preventive action can there be any hope of achieving and maintaining the goal of clean air and water.

The establishment of standards is the most essential step in preventing pollution. If industries building new plants or municipalities building treatment facilities know in advance the level of treatment which must be given to wastes, then the design of the plant can take pollution control into account. Without standards it is a matter of chance whether or not a new plant or facility will pollute the air or water.

Many municipalities employ a system of permits to ensure that new construction will comply with pollution regulations. Permits are an effective tool, but they are only as good as the standards they are designed to implement.

Planning and zoning controls can also be used effectively to prevent both air and water pollution.[37] More research needs to be done on ways in which planning techniques can be utilized; in addition, there are currently severe political limitations on the use of planning and zoning. Control over the location of industries is one obvious way of ameliorating or preventing pollution. An HEW simulation study on sulfur oxides pollution concluded that "The abatement achieved by the relocation of the power plants is substantial and the annual costs of achieving abatement by this technique, under the assumptions set forth herein, indicate that it may be the least expensive technique for control of power plant emissions." [38] However, given the political weakness of local planning boards and the patchwork nature of local jurisdictions, a rational allocation of industrial sites in a metropolitan area is almost impossible. The struggle of many communities to obtain industry is also a severe constraint on planning efforts.

The Clean Air Act Amendments of 1970 contain a potentially far-reaching provision to utilize planning controls for air pollution prevention. It requires that the state implementation plans include emission limitations "and such other measures as may be necessary to insure attainment and maintenance of such primary or secondary standard, including, but not limited to, land use and transportation controls." [39] The regulations EPA has issued to implement this section of the law require that states or localities must have a system for considering the air pollution effects of potential new sources of pollution, including all new facilities that may attract large numbers of automobiles. The implementation of these requirements would make pollution control considerations one of the major determinants of urban land use planning.

The compliance effort is today in a crucial stage. The implementation of the 1970 and 1972 laws over the next few years will be a critical test of whether the standards and regulation approach can adequately control pollution. It is almost certain that the specific deadlines which are contained in these laws will not be met. The states will not meet the primary air pollution standards by 1975, all municipalities will not have secondary treatment of their wastewater by 1977, and all major industries will not be using the best practicable water pollution control technology by 1977. The EPA administrator has already conceded that the 1978 nationwide water quality goals called for in the Water Pollution Control Act cannot be met. In December, 1972, Ruckelshaus stated, "The 1978 goal can't be achieved by any means. It is physically impossible to do it." [40] However, if substantial progress has been made toward meeting these goals then there is still hope that the current thrust of the federal pollution control effort can succeed. If such progress has not been made, either because the current approach is too cumbersome or because other national goals have taken priority over pollution control, then there are two alternatives. Either a drastic new approach can be adopted, such as effluent charges, or the nation can relegate pollution control to the status of a continuing but not very important program to maintain the current level of environmental quality and to prevent outright disasters. A major and continuing effort by EPA, the states, and citizen groups will be necessary to prevent the latter outcome.

CHAPTER 10

The Future of the Pollution Control Issue

ON THE WHOLE, the politics of pollution are generally similar to the politics of other domestic issues in the United States. There is the same clash of interest groups, the same kind of bargaining between the executive and legislative branches and within each branch, the same type of action by the courts, the same kind of dilemmas and opportunities presented by the intricacies of the American federal system. The pollution issue is primarily regulatory rather than distributive, it is concerned with preventing "bads" rather than distributing "goods." This has influenced the way in which the issue has developed from a minor local concern to a major national one, but there have been many similar issues in American history.[1]

In our examination of pollution politics we have noted many of the ways in which such politics share the general characteristics of the American political system. A consideration of the problems of centralization and decentralization will further illuminate this point. We shall then turn to some other aspects of the policy-making process for pollution control and consider the pollution problem in the broader context of environmental issues.

CENTRALIZATION VS. DECENTRALIZATION

As we have seen, the major trend in pollution control has been toward an ever greater centralization of formal and informal authority in the federal government. The pace of pollution control in the United States is now governed by the actions of the federal government. Federal legislation sets the framework and the agenda for state and local action. Federal research and regulations determine what the priority problems are and what the standards should be. The availability of federal funds is a major influence on how fast the states and localities move to control pollution.

This centralization has been due to a variety of factors. There is the obvious problem that neither air nor water pollution can be confined within the boundaries of a single state, and interstate problems have traditionally been considered federal problems. The interstate nature of pollution has been made more obvious by the general lack of success of the states and localities in controlling pollution. There is no guarantee that Washington can do any better, but in the face of state and local failure the American public tends to turn to the national government. In fact, the public looks to the national government to solve any major problem, regardless of how successful the other levels of government have been. This view of the federal system is not what was envisioned by the founding fathers, but it is a major centralizing force in the American system.

The nature of the pollution problem and the attitude of the public have been reinforced by the nationalization of the American economy. Almost all the goods we buy are now produced by very large firms, with plants and offices located throughout the United States. The local manufacturer, like the small manufacturer, is becoming a thing of the past. The political ramifications of this trend are vast, and they have made their mark on pollution control policy.

From the viewpoint of the national firm it is both economically and administratively damaging, if not chaotic, to have to deal with a variety of state and local regulations. It is almost impossible to produce and package products in fifty or a hundred different ways to meet fifty or a hundred regulations.

Even the largest firms find it difficult to lobby in fifty state
legislatures or to pursue court suits in a multitude of jurisdictions. In short, the national firms find it to their advantage to
deal with the national government. But it is only to their
advantage if national action preempts state and local action, and
thus federal environmental legislation in recent years has
increasingly contained provisions which restrict the ability of the
sub-national levels to act on their own.

From the viewpoint of government, the question, crudely put,
is whether government or the industry has more power. It is
obvious that a small town has little chance of influencing the
activities of General Motors. As the disparity of power becomes
less, relative power becomes more difficult to judge, but as one
measure it is worth noting that the budget of General Motors is
much larger than the budget of any of the states. Each of the
twenty largest U.S. corporations has a budget larger than any
state except California and New York.[2] When the corporation
has better technicians and better lawyers than the state, and an
active lobbyist as well, the chances of the state getting the
corporation to abate its pollution may not be good.

The problem of national markets and the problem of relative
power lead to the same conclusion—give more responsibility to
the federal government. In the future the national government
may have to yield some authority to international organizations
because the same centralizing factors—boundaries too small,
markets too big, power insufficient—are beginning to be evident
at the national level.

The boundaries of nations are clearly too limited to deal with
problems such as ocean pollution or contamination of the world
atmosphere by carbon dioxide. Rivers do not respect national
boundaries any more than they respect state boundaries and this
has become a major problem with bodies of water such as the
Rhine, the Colorado, and the Great Lakes. Even when dealing
with particular chemicals, the network of imports and exports
may dictate international action for successful control. For
example, an agreement among all of the nations of the
Organization for Economic Cooperation and Development
(OECD) was required to deal with the problem of contamination
from polychlorinated biphenyls, a commonly used chemical.

The multi-national corporation is now commonplace, as are international markets. Indeed, it is hard to overestimate the extent to which the economy has been internationalized in recent years. We have become familiar with our dependence on Arab oil and on the balance-of-trade. But specific examples give even more insight into the international economy. The Dow Chemical Company owns half of a Swiss bank to facilitate its international transactions. The other half is owned by the Government of Japan. A Cleveland steel firm received a contract to build a tunnel in Pakistan and built a processing plant in Luxembourg to fill the order. Such examples could be multiplied many times over.

Relative power between the private and public sector at the international level has not yet become an active issue because of the obvious weakness of existing international organizations. But already the most obvious industry power play at the state-local level, the threat to move elsewhere, is being used at the national level. The multinational firms do have choices as to whether to build new plants in the U.S. or somewhere else, and they have on occasion made clear that if U.S. environmental regulations become too stringent they will take their business elsewhere.

A number of international organizations have begun to take steps to deal with pollution and other environmental problems. The World Health Organization, The Organization for Economic Cooperation and Development, and the Common Market have all begun to develop standards for pollutants. But the full interdependence of the world's nations has yet to make a deep enough impression on the United States or other countries to result in meaningful multilateral action.

We have been discussing centralizing factors, the forces that have led toward pollution control responsibilities being assumed by higher levels of government. But within the United States there exists a set of counter-forces. Although the centripetal forces have been dominant, the centrifugal or decentralizing forces have also left their mark on pollution politics.

The most obvious of these forces has been the Nixon administration's "New Federalism," the attempt by the Republican administration to return power to the states and to decentralize the federal bureaucracy. In the pollution area, it clearly has not succeeded in returning power directly to the states, but it has decentralized EPA by giving a considerable degree of autonomy to the regional offices. Because the states can usually exercise more influence over the regional offices than they can over Washington, this step has had a significant decentralizing influence.

As experience is gained with controlling pollution under strong federal leadership, the traditional virtues of state control are likely to reassert themselves. The uneven impact of uniform national standards on different regions will become more obvious, leading to demands for more flexibility in standard-setting. The red tape and bureaucratic confusion inherent in trying to exert federal control through the states will become worse. The utility of the states as agents of innovation may become more needed as the inadequacies of parts of the existing system become more clear. The greater familiarity of the state or local government with the polluters in their jurisdiction may come to seem more of a virtue as federally imposed solutions prove unworkable. In short, some of the old arguments for a decentralized system may carry more weight as the shortcomings of centralization become more clear.

Another set of centrifugal forces has been exerting influence over government for the past decade. This is the demand for more citizen participation, for an opening-up of the decision-making processes so that the public can have a greater voice in the final outcome. At the federal level the impact of this demand has been evidenced by the Freedom of Information Act and an executive order requiring public notice and allowing public attendance at all federal advisory committee meetings. The environmental area has provided the most daring experiment in citizen participation through its requirement for environmental impact statements. The courts through their interpretation of this requirement, as well as in other ways, have opened a major avenue for citizen participation. The impact statement process has made clear the strains put on Congress and the bureaucracy by greater public participation. The extent to which the legislative and executive branches will tolerate such strains is not yet clear.

What kind of future balance will be struck between the centralizing and decentralizing forces remains to be seen. The general trends toward bigness, concentration, and interdependence point toward greater centralization over the long run. But the strength of the federal government in general and the presidency in particular is likely to be eroded in the post-Watergate crisis of confidence.

ORGANIZATIONAL PROBLEMS

The current centralizing of powers at the federal level has focused attention on the Environmental Protection Agency in which most of these powers are vested. In its three years of existence, EPA has proved the virtues of creating a new single-purpose agency if one wants forceful action.

The forceful action has not been without a price. The EPA has failed to realize one of the purposes for which it was formed, the creation of a more comprehensive view of environmental problems. Its basic authorities precluded the agency from taking action on such fundamental aspects of the environment as land use and water resource development. But even within its authorities, EPA has continued to pursue each separate program as if it were an isolated entity. This may be due largely to the influence of Congress which has also failed to seriously look at the different forms of pollution as parts of an integrated whole. But EPA has done little to provide Congress with an alternative framework.

The energy crisis and implementation of the 1970 Clean Air Act Amendments has now forced EPA into a generally defensive posture. It is likely that the agency will face an even more difficult time in the future. The deadlines established in the air and water pollution statutes will not be met; the cost to society of meeting them at any time will become even more apparent; and the standards established by EPA will receive rough treatment at the hands of the courts. Meanwhile, the priority accorded to environmental clean-up will sink lower as the energy crisis continues and new kinds of crises arise.

To defend itself EPA will have to rely increasingly on its technical expertise. The less it can rely on political support, the more it will have to rely on superior knowledge. One is not a substitute for the other, but without adequate research on the effects of pollution and on technologies for pollution control the agency will surely be unable to make its regulatory decisions effective.

The scientific basis for pollution control standards is woefully inadequate. We do not know the effects of most pollutants on human health, on plants and animals, or on anything else. It is one of the major characteristics of pollution politics that decisions are made in the context of a serious lack of knowledge about the effects of existing pollution and about the costs and benefits of any improvement in the existing situation. This ignorance increases the importance of public opinion and interest group influence. Power, rhetoric, and instinct must substitute for knowledge.

The Council on Environmental Quality, the other major organizational innovation for the formulation of environmental policy, faces an uncertain future. The Council's strength rests on its ability to innovate and to review policies unhampered by jurisdictional limits or commitments to ongoing programs. In its first few years its mainstay was innovation—new legislation, implementation of the new impact statement process, the attempt to instill new environmental values into traditional decision-making. But at the present time, there is no market for environmental innovation. This is not to say that change will not occur, but the changes will arise out of the shortcomings of existing programs and commitments rather than from a desire to open new areas of policy. The Council is probably in a better position to review these shortcomings, delineate the problems, and propose remedies than any other government agency. However, this role is not designed to win popularity among the agencies, the public, or the White House. Without some degree of support from these quarters the Council will not be able to function. Thus, it will be forced to walk the same tightrope between political support and policy values that it has treaded since its creation, but the number of influential people waiting for, perhaps even encouraging, a slip will become even greater.

THE REGULATORY FRAMEWORK

The shortcomings of existing programs may well result in casting doubt on the whole standards and enforcement approach to pollution regulation. The EPA will become increasingly enmeshed in trying to force corporations and governments to do things for which they have no incentive, in establishing regulations without adequate knowledge, and in imposing solutions to problems which are far more costly than other, equally effective, alternatives. We have experienced disillusionment with our efforts to improve deteriorating urban areas and to combat poverty. A similar fate for our pollution control programs would not be surprising.

Previous government efforts in pollution control and in other policy areas have been frustrated by the government's inability to deal with the intricate interdependencies that exist in the real world and by the political forces which have worked to undermine the government's declared objectives. The interdependencies produce policy failure because the policy is usually based on a small number of factors and simple cause-effect relationships. But the number of factors which turn out to be relevant is usually very large and the cause-effect relationships, if they can be discerned at all, turn out to be very complex. In short, the policy is inadequate to deal with the intricacies of the real world.

It is deceptively simple to say that a pollution control standard will be established for a plant and the owner will be fined or thrown in jail if he fails to comply with the standard. The factors which enter into the success or failure of this policy will include the nature and economic position of the industry, the firm, and the plant; the manufacturing process employed in the plant; the age, size, and location of the plant; the relative political influence of the firm and the enforcement agencies; the technologies available for pollution control; and many other factors. It is most unlikely that a government agency will have the information or resources to take account of all these factors for one plant, much less forty or fifty thousand plants.

The legislative framework within which regulatory policies are implemented has lent itself to negotiations over technical matters about a particular plant or industry. It is in the quiet negotiations between the bureaucrats and the polluters over particular cases that the goals of pollution policy often are eroded. They are eroded because the polluters' information about the particular situation is almost always superior to the government's, and the polluters have a great incentive to delay or to obtain leniency from the government. The legislation forces the bureaucrats to try to prescribe very specific actions for the polluters, actions which depend upon information which only the polluters are likely to possess. The key role of information is indicated by the fate of EPA's standards when they have been tested in the courts (see Chapter 6).

The conclusion which can be drawn by those who support the ⅴ objective of controlling pollution is that policy must be changed to provide less discretion for government bureaucrats, so that the policy goals cannot be quietly negotiated away, and more flexibility for non-governmental actors, so that official omniscience is not a necessary precondition for successful action. The ∧ flexibility for the private sector should not be flexibility to ignore the law. Rather the law should be structured so that the operations of the market and the resources and information possessed by corporations can be harnessed to further the law's objectives instead of working against them.

The major alternative to the current regulatory approach is a system of effluent charges or fees. Such a system would give less discretion to bureaucratic officials and more flexibility to the private sector. We have previously described some of the advantages and disadvantages of the effluent fee system (see Chapter 9). Given the lack of experience with effluent fees in the United States, predictions about their impact are obviously dangerous. But most of what we know theoretically about controlling pollution and our actual experience with the existing system indicate that effluent fees would be far more efficient and effective than the standards and enforcement approach.

THE ENVIRONMENTAL ISSUE

ⅴ Regardless of what regulatory scheme is employed, much of the success of pollution control will depend on the priority and importance which the public and the government attach to the issue. Its priority and importance are hard to predict because in the past few years it has become apparent that the pollution problem is only one part of a constellation of issues which have come to be known collectively as the environmental issue. Some of the dimensions of the broader environmental issue can be seen if we look at the current energy crisis.

At the present time the energy shortage has usurped pollution as the number one national issue. But the primacy of the energy issue does not represent just a lower priority for pollution control, because there are numerous connections between the two issues. The demand for certain types of fuel has been influenced by pollution control requirements as has been the fuel supply. Most of the major air pollution problems are the result of fuel combustion.

Some of the steps which will be taken to meet the fuel shortage, such as allowing power plants to use coal instead of oil, will make pollution worse. Other steps, such as reducing the amount of gasoline consumed by automobiles, will help to clean the air. The net result is likely to be negative, especially if the regulatory structure of the Clean Air Act is seriously weakened and if a large number of environmentally damaging projects, such as refineries, off-shore drilling, and oil shale production are built without adequate environmental safeguards.

Aside from these direct interrelationships between energy and pollution, the two issues are interrelated because they both give rise to a set of further issues such as resource availability and the desirability of economic and population growth.

The most immediate worry arising from the fuel shortage is that we will run out of vital natural resources. To some degree this worry is due to a misunderstanding about the causes of the energy shortage because the shortage is more due to a lack of refinery capacity and poor government planning than it is to any lack of oil. However, men have worried for many decades about exhausting resources, and our problems over energy were preceded by a widely publicized prediction that our civilization would come to a catastrophic end early in the next century in part because vital resources would no longer be available.[3]

It is unlikely that in the next few years the fear of impending doom will have much real influence on the steps taken to improve environmental quality, except if the fear is accompanied by an overall crisis of confidence on the part of the American people. The shortage of fuel is due to a variety of comparatively short-run factors. If we still have an energy shortage twenty years from now it will probably be because of an extraordinary combination of incompetence and bad luck.

The overall resource problem does not seem to warrant the sweeping conclusions that some have drawn. Economists for many years have argued that resource exhaustion is an exaggerated problem, and it is hard to argue with either their premises or their conclusions. The price of a resource governs both its supply and the demand for it, and there seem to be almost no basic resources for which the market mechanism cannot bring about a reasonable balance between supply and demand. As our technology continues to expand, new methods for extracting resources become available and new substitutes for natural resources are developed, and thus the effectiveness of the pricing mechanisms becomes even greater.

On a still broader plane, energy problems have given renewed emphasis to questions as to whether economic and other types of growth can continue in the United States and other industrialized nations. Given the limited supply of land and other resources and the potential dangers of increased pollution it is argued that nations should limit their growth or, at a minimum, that the consumption-oriented habits of Americans will have to change to become more conservation-oriented.

The debate over growth has tended to be diffuse and more a debate over life-style than over the future of the environment. Although it is obvious that infinite growth cannot take place on a finite planet, the relevant questions are what actions follow from this fact and when should such actions be taken. There have been no very good answers to the first question and most of the evidence on the second points to the answer "not now." For example, if we look at pollution control over the next thirty years, the overwhelming factor is the effectiveness of regulatory actions, not economic or population growth.[4] There are good reasons to want an end to population growth or a slowing of certain kinds of economic growth, but these reasons relate to a desire for a saner, happier, more dignified life, not to the need to avert catastrophe.

Although the destruction of civilization may not come about in the ways which it is now fashionable to predict, there will be no shortage of problems, some of which may contain the seeds of such destruction. Population growth in the United States will make all of our current problems more difficult to solve, but it will not make them insolvable. The same probably cannot be said for the less developed countries where rapid population growth is a cancer destroying any hope of a viable economy. As a result the disparity between the two-thirds of the world that is poor and the one-third that is rich becomes even greater. The *increase* in the U.S. economy between 1970 and 1971 was greater than the *total* gross national product for all of Africa.[5] How long such inequality can continue is an open question, but the images of Watts, Detroit, and Newark are not irrelevant. It will not be possible for the underdeveloped countries to focus on environmental problems until some progress has been made in solving their economic development problems. Also, their development problems may pose a threat to world resource availability because the instability in the lesser developed nations may lead them to cut off the supply of certain critical resources.

The disparities between rich and poor are due to the exponential growth of both underdeveloped populations and developed economies. Exponential growth is growth that occurs geometrically, that increases by a certain percentage rather than a certain amount. The Meadows, in *The Limits to Growth*, have familiarized us with the dangers of exponential phenomena.[6] The most obvious danger is the rapidity with which such growth can occur. This aspect of exponential growth has been accentuated by the vast increase in the speed of communications. Not only do we face more problems than past generations but they must be dealt with more rapidly. Everyone becomes aware of the problems sooner and expects immediate action to be taken.

Exponential growth which is considered undesirable can be curbed in part by the application of new technology. The effect of new contraceptive methods on U.S. population growth is perhaps a good example. But the rapid (exponential?) increase in technological development in itself presents a host of problems demanding rapid answers. The impact of modern technology is so great that it no longer allows the luxury of trying something out and then evaluating the results. If we were to build and fly a fleet of supersonic transports, and if the more dire predictions about the effects of such a venture turned out to be correct, it would be too late to remedy the mistake once it had been made. If we develop and use a new chemical which then turns out to persist in the oceans and to have adverse effects on marine life it might be too late to take any remedial action.

If problems such as the above are to be coped with successfully it will require new policy tools and a high degree of courage and faith to apply such tools. We will need a vast increase in scientific knowledge about the environment so that we will be better able to predict the potential impact of new technologies. We will need improved regulatory measures to insure that the knowledge we do have is brought to bear before it is too late. And we will need better social science models so that we can deal more adequately with the social and economic complexities of a technological civilization.

Despite the difficulties which lie ahead, and despite the fluctuations in political support for environmental issues which will undoubtedly occur, the environment as an issue will not go away. We may find ways to ignore our rural and urban poor or to insulate ourselves from the less developed countries, but nature is less amenable to human manipulation.

If the current forms of pollution get worse or if some new development upsets the natural equilibrium of an area, the results may dramatically force themselves upon our attention. Regardless of the political status of the environmental issue, it will be hard to ignore another Donora or *Torrey Canyon* incident. The limited tolerance of nature to withstand human insults sets definite limits on the ability of the political system to ignore environmental problems.

The signs of environmental degradation will be doubly difficult to ignore now that an awareness of man's potential to degrade or destroy his habitat has been impressed on our consciousness. As the Council on Environmental Quality has said, "We are realizing our dependence on the intricate web of nature of which we are a part. We have discovered that man's continued existence depends on the functions of microscopic bacteria and fungi and on the grand natural cycles which govern the flow of the major elements through the environment."[7]

To say that the environment will continue to be an issue is not to say that the contents or shape of the issue will remain the same. As we noted above, the emphasis on pollution control may already be waning because of new perceptions, such as the importance of land use, and new events, such as the fuel shortage. The future form of the environmental issue will continue to be shaped by the interplay of perceptions and events.

There are some who now perceive that environmental problems will require a major change in the ethics and institutions of society. They maintain that we must substitute conservation for expansion, the "land ethic" for the growth ethic, and that we must come to value ourselves as a part of nature rather than its master or exploiter.[8] Others believe that the application of existing technology, the development of new technologies, and some incremental adjustments in the political and economic system should suffice to improve the quality of the environment. A third group maintains that the whole environmental problem has been exaggerated and that it should be accorded much lower priority than it is now given.

These perceptions or beliefs are not compatible, and the long-run future of the environmental issue depends on which of them is dominant. Each of the three can be proven wrong by events, and therefore the luxury of choice may be limited by the hard realities of environmental conditions.

The only thing that can be said with certainty about the future is that it will be different from the present. Any attempt at long-range prediction is bound to be wrong either in whole or in part.[9] But there is no escape from the fact that *Homo sapiens* is but one among many species sharing a limited and fragile planet. We cannot separate ourselves from the natural environment, and, if we choose to ignore the links which bind us to our natural habitat, sooner or later the chain will be drawn tight around us. Rather than fight these links we must recognize them, value them, and, in the words of Dylan Thomas, learn to "sing in our chains like the sea."[10]

Notes

CHAPTER 1

1. On the severe limitations of cost-benefit analysis in pollution control, see J. H. Dales, *Pollution, Property and Prices* (Toronto: University of Toronto Press, 1968), chapters 3 and 4.

2. U.S. Council on Environmental Quality, *Environmental Quality—1972* (Washington, D.C.: Government Printing Office, 1972), pp. 276–77.

3. See U.S. Department of the Interior, Federal Water Pollution Control Administration, "Manpower and Training Needs in Water Pollution Control," Document 49, U.S. Senate (90th Congress, 1st session); and Air Pollution Control Association, "Report of the Education and Training Committee," *Journal of the Air Pollution Control Association*, XVI:11 (1966), pp. 610–13.

4. For a somewhat similar view of the development of environmental quality issues, see U.S. House of Representatives, Committee on Science and Astronautics, Subcommittee on Science, Research, and Development, "Managing the Environment" (1968), pp. 9–12.

5. State of the Union Address, January 22, 1970, reprinted in U.S. Council on Environmental Quality, *Environmental Quality—1970* (Washington, D.C.: GPO, 1970), p. 250.

6. See Earl Finbar Murphy, *Water Purity* (Madison, Wis.: University of Wisconsin Press, 1961), p. 55, and *Governing Nature* (Chicago: Quadrangle Books, 1967), p. 121.

7. U.S. Department of the Interior, "The Federal Water Pollution Control Program," (Washington, D.C.: GPO, December 2, 1968), p. 4.

8. Death rates per 100,000 population from typhoid were as follows: 1900—31.3; 1910—22.5; 1920—7.6; 1930—4.8; 1940—1.1; 1956—0.0. U.S. Department of Commerce, Bureau of the Census, *Historical Statistics of the U.S.: Colonial Times to 1957* (Washington, D.C.: GPO, 1960), series B 114—128, p. 26.

9. Ralph C. Williams, *The United States Public Health Service 1798–1950* (Washington, D.C.: The Commissioned Officers Association of the U.S. Public Health Service, 1951), p. 312.

10. Ibid. The statute is the Public Health Service Act, P.L. 78–410.

11. Ibid., pp. 312–13.

12. See Leon Weinberger, et al., "Solving Our Water Problems—Water Renovation and Reuse," *Annals of the New York Academy of Sciences*, Vol. 136, art. 5 (July 8, 1966), p. 138.

13. S. R. Weibel, et al., "Waterborne Disease Outbreaks from 1946 to 1960" (Cincinnati, Ohio: U.S. Public Health Service, February 1964).

14. Information submitted to House Public Works Committee by Environmental Protection Agency, May, 1972. Given to author by Mr. Ralph Palange, EPA.

15. FWPCA, "The Cost of Clean Water and Its Economic Impact" (January 10, 1969), vol. 1, p. 134.

16. See FWPCA, "The Cost of Clean Water" (January 10, 1968), vol. 1, pp. 20–21.

17. See U.S. Council on Environmental Quality, "Toxic Substances" (Washington, D.C.: GPO, 1971).

18. The bills being considered by the conference committee are S.426 and HR 5356.

19. U.S. Senate, Committee on Public Works, Subcommittee on Air and Water Pollution, "Water Pollution—1967" (Washington, D.C.: GPO, 1967), part 1, p. 322.

20. Some of the states, notably Pennsylvania, have initiated control programs. For a general review of the problem and what is being done about it, see ibid., pp. 313–422.

21. U.S. Atomic Energy Commission, news release, January 26, 1973. As of December 31, 1972, 29 power generating reactors were in operation, 55 were being built, and 76 were on order.

22. Remarks by Max N. Edwards, Assistant Secretary of the Interior for Water Pollution Control, before the National Resources and Public Utilities Sections of the annual meeting of the American Bar Association, Philadelphia, Pa., August 6, 1968, p. 1.

23. FWPCA, "The Cost of Clean Water and Its Economic Impact," p. 158. See also Burt Schorr, "Generating Plants Pose a 'Thermal Pollution' Threat to Rivers, Lakes," *Wall Street Journal*, December 1, 1967, 1:6.

24. Secretary of the Interior and the Secretary of Transportation, "Oil Pollution—A Report to the President" (Washington, D.C.: GPO, February 1968), p. 10.

25. Ibid., p. 13.

26. Murphy, *Governing Nature*, pp. 60–64.

27. U.S. Senate, "Water Pollution—1967," part 1, p. 448.

28. See U.S. Council on Environmental Quality, *Environmental Quality—1973*.

29. Data on fertilizer use in the U.S. Department of Commerce, Bureau of the Census, *Statistical Abstract of the United States—1972* (Washington, D.C.: GPO, 1972), p. 594.

30. FWPCA, "The Cost of Clean Water" (January 10, 1968), vol. 1, p. 36.

31. P.L. 92–516, The Federal Environmental Pesticide Control Act of 1972.

32. U.S. Council on Environmental Quality, "Integrated Pest Management" (Washington: GPO, 1972).

33. Jack Bregman and Sergei Lenormond, *The Pollution Paradox* (New York: Spartan Books, 1966), p. 6.

34. Boston: Houghton Mifflin, 1962.

35. Federal Security Administration, Public Health Service, press release, October 14, 1949.

36. See *Environmental Quality—1973*, p. 271.

37. See U.S. Senate, Committee on Public Works, Subcommittee on Air and Water Pollution, "Air Pollution—1967" (Washington, D.C.: GPO, 1967), part 2, p. 821.

38. Ibid., p. 805.

39. See *Environmental Quality—1972*, p. 29.

CHAPTER 2

1. For more detailed analyses of legislative events through 1966, see M. Kent Jennings, "Legislative Politics and Water Pollution Control 1956–1961," in Frederic N. Cleaveland, and associates, *Congress and Urban Problems* (Washington, D.C.: The Brookings Institution, 1969); James L. Sundquist, *Politics and Policy: The Eisenhower, Kennedy, and Johnson Years* (Washington, D.C.: The Brookings Institution, 1968), pp. 322–81; and U.S. House of Representatives, Committee on Science and Astronautics, "Technical Information for Congress," April 25, 1969, pp. 337–56.

2. Rivers and Harbors Act, 30 Stat. 1152.

3. The Oil Pollution Act, 1924, 33 U.S.C. 431, et seq.

4. In 1934 Roosevelt appointed a special advisory committee of the U.S. National Resources Committee to report to him on the problem of water pollution. It reported in 1935 that pollution abatement was a local responsibility, but that the Federal government should provide loans or grants to public agencies and loans to non-public agencies for the construction of treatment works. See U.S. Senate, Select Committee on National Water Resources, "Reviews of National Water Resources During the Past Fifty Years" (Washington, D.C.: GPO, 1959), Committee Print No. 2.

5. For a discussion of the major issues involved, see Herman G. Baity, "Aspects of Governmental Policy on Stream Pollution Abatement," *American Journal of Public Health*, XXIX:12 (December 1939), pp. 1297–1307.

6. HR 12764, 74th Congress.

7. HR 2711, 75th Congress.

8. See *Congressional Record*, vol. 83, part 8 (75th Congress, 3rd session), p. 9710.

9. S.685, 76th Congress.

10. P.L. 82–579.

11. U.S. House of Representatives, Committee on Appropriations, Report 228 (84th Congress, 1st session), p. 11.

12. See "Report of the Joint Federal-State Action Committee to the President of the U.S. and the Chairman of the Governor's Conference" (Washington, D.C.: Progress Report 1, filed December 1957, publ. 1958).

13. HR 3610, 86th Congress.

14. For the compromises which produced these proposals see Sundquist, *Politics and Policy*, p. 350.

15. See Robert Engler, *The Politics of Oil* (Chicago: University of Chicago Press, 1961).

16. See *New York Times*, April 16, 1967, 41:1. Wright later denied that he had submitted the amendment.

17. See "Report on International Control of Oil Pollution," House Report 628 (90th Congress, 1st session), September 11, 1967; Edward Cowan, *Oil and Water* (Philadelphia: Lippincott, 1968); and Richard Petrow, *In the Wake of Torrey Canyon* (New York: McKay, 1968).

18. S.2525, 90th Congress, sec. 2.

19. *1968 Congressional Quarterly Almanac* (Washington, D.C.: Congressional Quarterly Service, 1969), p. 569.

20. The financing provisions were not included because the new administration was working on its own version of a financing bill. The new bill was submitted in July 1969, as HR 12913.

21. See Congressional Quarterly, *Congress and the Nation*, vol. III (Washington, D.C.: Congressional Quarterly Service, 1972), p. 766.

22. The authorization for the water pollution program under existing legislation expired June 30, 1971. On July 9, 1971, the President signed P.L. 92-50 which extended the authority through September 30. P.L. 92-137 then extended the program through October 31. From November 1971 to February 1972 there was technically no authorization for the program. In February 1972, P.L. 92-240 extended the program through April 30, 1972.

23. See U.S. Senate, Report of the Committee on Public Works to accompany S. 2770, Report No. 92-414 (October 28, 1971).

24. S.2770, sec. 101(a)(1) and (2).

25. *Congress and the Nation*, vol. III, pp. 795–96.

26. "Message from the President of the United States Returning Without Approval the Bill (S.2770) Entitled 'The Federal Water Pollution Control Act of 1972'," (October 17, 1972), p. 2. The text of the message is contained in Environmental Policy Division, Congressional Research Service, Library of Congress, "A Legislative History of the Water Pollution Control Act Amendments of 1972," Serial No. 93-1 (January 1973) printed for the U.S. Senate, Committee on Public Works, vol. 1, p. 137.

27. For a more detailed analysis of legislative events through 1966, see Randall B. Ripley, "Congress and Clean Air," in Cleaveland, and associates, *Congress and Urban Problems*; and Sundquist, *Politics and Policy*, pp. 322–81.

28. See Ripley, "Congress and Clean Air," pp. 229–30.

30. Memorandum from Alex Greene to William Carey, April 30, 1955, Bureau of the Budget files.

31. P.L.86-365.

32. *Public Papers of the Presidents of the U.S.: John F. Kennedy—1961* (Washington, D.C.: GPO, 1962), p. 117

33. P.L. 87-761.

34. *Public Papers of the Presidents of the U.S.: John F. Kennedy—1963* (Washington, D.C.: GPO, 1964), p. 145.

35. P.L.86-493.

36. This account relies heavily on Sundquist, *Politics and Policy*, pp. 369–71.

37. "Proceedings: The Third National Conference on Air Pollution" (Washington, D.C.: GPO, 1967), pp. 14–15.

38. Ibid., p. 597.

39. The best description of the passage of the 1970 Clean Air Amendments is contained in a manuscript by Charles Jones of the University of Pittsburgh entitled "Cleaning the Air in a Federal System: Policy Development and Implementation in Air Pollution Control."

40. Comptroller General of the United States, "Assessment of Federal and

State Enforcement Efforts to Control Air Pollution from Stationary Sources," (August 23, 1973), p. 23.

41. See Allen Kneese and Charles Schultze, "Incentives and Public Policy: The Case of Pollution" (in manuscript).

42. New York: Grossman, 1965.

43. John C. Esposito, *Vanishing Air* (New York: Grossman, 1970) p. 290–92.

CHAPTER 3

1. Rowland Evans and Robert Novak, *Lyndon B. Johnson: The Exercise of Power* (New York: New American Library, 1966), pp. 201–2.

2. See J. Clarence Davies, 3d, and Charles Lettow, "New Administrative Arrangements" in Fred Anderson, ed., *Environmental Law* (Minneapolis: West Publishing Co., 1974).

3. See Ripley, "Congress and Clean Air," in Cleaveland and associates, *Congress and Urban Problems*, p. 259.

4. Senator George McGovern has commented: "We now appear to accept the curious notion that the legislative initiative rests with the executive branch. Indeed, students of American government are themselves surprised at the startling fact that nearly 90 percent of the legislation the Congress considers originates with the Administration." *Washington Post*, p. B5, col. 1, (January 28, 1973).

5. For a further discussion of the task forces, see Norman C. Thomas and Harold Wolman, "Policy Formulation in the Institutionalized Presidency: The Johnson Task Forces," in Thomas Cronin and Sanford Greenberg, *The Presidential Advisory System* (New York: Harper and Row, 1969).

6. Much of the information collected is contained in U.S. Council on Environmental Quality, "Toxic Substances" (Washington, D.C.: GPO, 1971).

7. Amendment #338 to S.1478.

8. Senate Report 92-783.

9. HR 16245.

10. House Report 92-1477.

11. S.888 and HR 5087, 93d Congress.

12. Senate Report 93-524, Report of the Senate Committee on Commerce on S.426.

13. House Report 93-360, Report of the Committee on Interstate and Foreign Commerce on HR 5356.

14. U.S. House of Representatives, Committee on Appropriations, "Report on Agriculture, Environment, and Consumer Protection Appropriations for Fiscal Year 1974," p. 54.

15. See *Congressional Record*, October 8, 1969, pp. H9224-9295; and *New York Times*, August 17, 1969, 40:1; September 29, 1969, 30:2; October 7, 1969, 19:1; and October 10, 1969, 1:7.

16. *Congressional Record*, October 18, 1972, p. 10266.

17. 37 *Federal Register* 26282 (1972).

18. 41 U.S. L.W. 2602 (D.D.C. 1973).

19. Civil No. 18-73-R (E.D. Vir. 1973).

20. P.L. 93-344.

21. See *CQ Weekly Report*, September 7, 1974.

22. Press release, Office of Senator Edmund S. Muskie, November 17, 1971.

23. Comptroller General of the United States, "Examination into the Effectiveness of the Construction Grant Program for Abating, Controlling, and Preventing Water Pollution," (November 3, 1969).

24. Comptroller General of the United States, "Water Pollution Abatement Programs: Assessment of Federal and State Enforcement Efforts," (March 23, 1972) and "Assessment of Federal and State Enforcement Efforts to Control Air Pollution from Stationary Sources," (August 23, 1973).

CHAPTER 4

1. Ido de Groot, "Some Airy Platitudes About Attitudes—Trends in Public Attitudes Towards Air Pollution," Paper 67-71, 1967 Air Pollution Control Association Meeting, Cleveland, Ohio, p. 1.

2. See David Easton, *A Systems Analysis of Political Life* (New York: Wiley, 1965), chapters 3 and 5.

3. See Table 4.1. For other data see Hazel Erskine, "The Polls: Pollution and Its Costs," *Public Opinion Quarterly*, Spring, 1972, pp. 120–35.

4. See Table 4.2.

5. de Groot, "Airy Platitudes," p. 6.

6. J. Schusky, "Public Awareness and Concern with Air Pollution in the St. Louis Metropolitan Area" (Washington, D.C.: HEW, Public Health Service, May 1965), pp. 13–15.

7. de Groot, "Airy Platitudes," p. 7.

8. See Table 4.3.

9. See Matthew A. Crenson, *The Un-Politics of Air Pollution* (Baltimore: Johns Hopkins, 1971), pp. 102–6.

10. de Groot, "Airy Platitudes," pp. 8–9.

11. *New York Times*, February 8, 1968, 29:1.

12. *Washington Post*, April 3, 1967, 2:1.

13. *New York Times*, December 3, 1967, 28:1; *Newsweek*, October 6, 1969, p. 46.

14. See Robert E. Lane, *Political Life: Why and How People Get Involved in Politics* (New York: The Free Press, 1965); and Lester W. Milbrath, *Political Participation* (Chicago: Rand McNally, 1965).

15. The correlation coefficient for two rankings was $r' = .34$. The Spearman rank correlation coefficient was $K = 1.126$.

16. "Conservation Policies of the Izaak Walton League of America," as revised January 1, 1964, brochure, n.d., p. 9.

17. See Murphy, *Water Purity*, pp. 89–90.

18. "Major Conservation Issues, 1968," resolutions adopted at the 32nd annual convention of the National Wildlife Federation, Houston, Texas, March 8–10, 1968.

19. *Environmental Quality—1973*, p. 380.

20. See League of Women Voters Education Fund, *The Big Water Fight* (Brattleboro, Vt.: Stephen Greene Press, 1966).

21. Ripley, "Congress and Clean Air," in Cleaveland and associates, *Congress and Urban Problems*, pp. 237–41.

22. National Tuberculosis Association, brochure, n.d.

23. See Harold M. England, "APCA: A Mission and a Method Through Sixty Years of Service," *Journal of the Air Pollution Control Association* (June 1967), pp. 371–73.

24. *Environmental Quality—1973*, p. 404, footnote 8.

25. Ibid., p. 387.

26. Ibid., p. 391.

27. Ibid., p. 88.

28. Ibid., p. 93.

29. Ibid., p. 107.

30. See Kneese and Schultze, "Incentives and Public Policy."

31. Twenty-three states have exempted pollution control equipment from property or other types of taxes. See J. F. Zimmerman, "Political Boundaries and Air Pollution Control" (Albany, N.Y.: Graduate School of Public Affairs, State University of New York, n.d.), p. 3.

32. Charles L. Schultze, *The Politics and Economics of Public Spending* (Washington, D.C.: The Brookings Institution, 1969), p. 122.

33. See "Cost Sharing with Industry?" (Washington, D.C: Working Committee on Economic Incentives, Federal Coordinating Committee on the Economic Impact of Pollution Abatement, November 20, 1967); and ABT Associates, Inc., for FWPCA, "Incentives to Industry for Water Pollution Control: Policy Considerations" (Cambridge, Mass., December 1967).

34. For example, see E. J. Cleary, *The ORSANCO Story* (Baltimore: Johns Hopkins Press, 1967), pp. 96–97, where he discusses the role of General Electric; and the series of ads during 1968 and 1969 run in national magazines by the Standard Oil Co. of New Jersey.

35. See *New York Times,* January 11, 1969, 1:3; September 12, 1969, 1:2; and October 8, 1969, 30:3. The fact that the suit was initiated only ten days before the Johnson Administration left office probably indicates the reluctance of the administration to incur the wrath of the auto companies.

36. U.S. Senate, Committee on Public Works, Subcommittee on Air and Water Pollution, "Air Pollution—1968," part 1, p. 30 (statement of Fred E. Tucker).

37. I am indebted to Mr. Wendell Pigman for this information.

38. Merrill Lynch, Pierce, Fenner and Smith, Inc., Securities Research Division, "Five Emerging Industries" (April, 1968).

39. *Environmental Quality—1970*, p. xv.

40. *Washington Post*, December 22, 1973, 1:7.

CHAPTER 5

1. P.L. 91-190, 42 U.S.C. 4321-4347.

2. See Ripley, "Congress and Clean Air," in Cleaveland and associates, *Congress and Urban Problems,* p. 228.

3. Ibid.

4. Ralph C. Williams, *The United States Public Health Service 1798–1950* (Washington, D.C.: The Commissioned Officers Association of the U.S. Public Health Service, 1951), p. 312.

5. Murphy, *Water Purity*, p. 18.

6. Section 3(b) of the act did not specify the exact locations of the labs, but rather the general area of the country (Northeast, Middle Atlantic, etc.) for each of the seven. The seven locations later specified included one in the district of John Fogarty, chairman of the relevant House Appropriations Subcommittee; one in Oklahoma, the home state of Senator Kerr, chairman of the Senate Rivers

and Harbors Committee; and one in the district of John Blatnik, chairman of the House Rivers and Harbors Committee. Appropriations for construction of the labs were vehemently opposed by the Budget Bureau because of the injurious effect such decentralization would have on the water pollution research effort. The Bureau succeeded in preventing one lab from being built and delayed construction of the others.

7. See Wilbur Cohen, and J. Sonosky, "The Federal Water Pollution Control Act Amendments of 1961," *Public Health Reports* (February 1962).

8. See Sundquist, *Politics and Policy*, p. 330.

9. Reorganization Plan No. 2 of 1966.

10. The idea of transferring water pollution functions to Interior was not without congressional precedent. In 1963, Representative Dingell, a major proponent of water pollution control, introduced legislation calling for such a transfer. See U.S. House of Representatives, Committee on Government Operations, "Water Pollution Control and Abatement" (May–June, 1963; publ. 1964), part 1A, pp. 400–401.

11. EPA Order 1110.18C, April 5, 1974.

12. See Marver H. Bernstein, *Regulating Business by Independent Commission* (Princeton, N.J.: Princeton University Press, 1955).

13. P.L. 91-190, 42 U.S.C. 4321-4347.

14. P.L. 91-224, Title II, 42 U.S.C. 4371 et seq.

15. Exec. Order 11472, May 29, 1969. The Council was abolished by Executive Order 11541, July 1, 1970, pursuant to Reorganization Plan No. 2 of 1970, which established a Domestic Council in the Executive Office of the President.

16. HR 6750, 91st Cong., 1st session, and S.1075, 91st Cong., 1st session.

17. See *Committee for Nuclear Responsibility, Inc.* v. *Schlesinger*, 404 U.S. 917, 920 (1971) (Appendix to opinion of Douglas, J.).

18. See *Washington Post*, September 17, 1973, A23:1.

19. See, for example, Richard Fenno, *The President's Cabinet* (Cambridge, Mass.: Harvard University Press, 1959); and U.S. Senate, Committee on Government Operations, Subcommittee on National Policy Machinery, "Organizing for National Security" (1961), vol. 3.

20. *Environmental Quality—1973*, p. 242.

21. See Davies and Lettow, "New Administrative Arrangements" in Anderson, *Environmental Law*; and Richard Liroff, "The Council on Environmental Quality," *Environmental Law Reporter* 3:50051-50070 (August 1973).

CHAPTER 6

1. *William Aldred's Case*, 9 Co. Rep. 57, 77 Eng. Rep. 816 (1611), in James E. Krier, *Environmental Law and Policy* (Indianapolis: Bobbs-Merrill, 1971), pp. 51–53.

2. Ibid.

3. See Krier, *Environmental Law and Policy*, pp. 209–10.

4. 42 L.W. 4087 (December 17, 1973).

5. Ibid.

6. 354 F. 2d 608 (2d Cir. 1965), *cert. denied,* 384 U.S. 941 (1966).

7. Ibid.

8. 397 U.S. 150.

9. Ibid.

10. 40 U.S.L.W. 4397, 3 ERC 2039, 2 ELR 20192 (1972).

11. Ibid.

12. 5 ERC 1449 (S. Ct. 1973). Also see *Environmental Quality—1973*, pp. 239–41.

13. 5 ERC 1449.

14. Joseph L. Sax, *Defending the Environment* (1970) (New York: Vintage Books, 1972), p. 115.

15. As quoted in U.S. Council on Environmental Quality, *Environmental Quality—1971* (Washington, D.C.: GPO, 1971), p. 172. The statute is Mich. Stat. Ann. 14.528 (201), et seq., reprinted in 1 ELR 43001.

16. See *Environmental Quality—1972*.

17. See *New York Times*, March 24, 1973.

18. P.L. 91-190, 42 U.S.C. 4321-4347.

19. Ibid., sec. 102(2)(c).

20. *Environmental Quality—1973*, p. 236.

21. 336 F. Supp. 882, 888, 3 ERC 1586, 1590, 2 ELR 20068, 20070 (W.D. Wis. 1971).

22. Ibid., as quoted in *Environmental Quality—1972*, p. 253.

23. *Environmental Quality—1972*, p. 252.

24. 499 F. 2d 1109, 2 ERC 1779, 1 ELR 20346 (D.C. Cir. 1971).

25. Ibid.

26. Ibid.

27. Ibid.

28. Ibid.

29. Ibid.

30. Ibid.

31. Ibid.

32. See U.S. Council on Environmental Quality, "Statements on Proposed Federal Actions Affecting the Environment: Guidelines," 36 *Fed. Register*, 7724-7729, April 23, 1971, sec. 11.

33. 5 ERC 1418 (D.C. Cir. 1973).

34. Ibid.

35. ERC 1126, 1 ELR 20469 (D.C. Cir. 1971). See also 3 ERC 1210, 1256, 1 ELR 20529, 20532 (D.C. Cir. 1971); and 404 U.S. 917, 3 ERC 1276, 1 ELR 20534 (1971).

36. 3 ERC 1558, 2 ELR 20029 (D.C. Cir. 1972).

37. Ibid.

38. 449 F. 2d 1109, 1113-14, 2 ERC 1779, 1781-2, 1 ELR 20346, 20348 (D.C. Cir. 1971).

39. 3 ERC 1558, 1561, 2 ELR 20029, 20032 (D.C. Cir. 1972).

40. See *Environmental Quality—1973*, pp. 242–45.

41. William O. Doub, "Technological Regulation and Environmental Law," remarks before the American Bar Association Annual Convention, Administrative Law Section, Washington, D.C., August 6, 1973, reprinted in U.S. Atomic Energy Commission, News Releases, 4:32 (August 8, 1973), pp. 7–10.

42. 337 F. Supp. 287 (D.D.C. 1971).

43. Doub, "Technological Regulation and Environmental Law," p. 8.

44. See *Environmental Quality—1973*, pp. 246–47.

45. The Clean Air Act, as amended, 42 U.S.C. 1857 et seq., sec. 304.

46. The Federal Water Pollution Control Act, as amended, P.L. 92-500, sec. 505.

47. 486 F. 2d 375.

48. See also *Essex Chemical Corp.* v. *Ruckelshaus*, No. 72-1073 (D.C. Cir., filed January 21, 1972); and *Appalachian Power Co.* v. *EPA*, No. 72-1079 (D.C. Cir., filed January 21, 1972).

49. 462 F. 2d 846, 2 ELR 20116,——U.S. App. D.C.——.

50. 352 F. Supp. 697 (D. Colo. 1972), 3 ELR 20024.

51. 3 ELR 20719.

52. 3 ELR 20133.

53. See The Clean Air Act, as amended, sec. 202.

54. 3 ELR 20137.

55. 3 ELR 20148.

56. 3 ELR 20149.

57. Civ. Action No. 1031-72 (D.D.C. May 30, 1972), 3 ELR 20262.

58. Sec. 101(b)(1).

59. *New York Times*, January 3, 1973.

60. *Fri* v. *Sierra Club*,——U.S.——(June 11, 1973), 3 ELR 20684.

61. See *Natural Resources Defense Council Inc.* v. *EPA*, D.C. Cir. January 31, 1973, 3 ELR 20155.

62. See *Natural Resources Defense Council Inc.* v. *EPA*, 1st Cir., May 2, 1973, 3 ELR 20375.

63. *City of Riverside* v. *Ruckelshaus*, Civil No. 72-2122–IH (C.D. Cal. November 16, 1972), 3 ELR 20043.

64. *Wall Street Journal*, January 16, 1973.

65. See Sax, *Defending the Environment*, pp. 125–35.

66. *Calvert Cliffs Coordinating Committee* v. *Atomic Energy Commission*, 499 F 2d 1109, 2 ERC 1779, 1 ELR 20346 (D.C. Cir. 1971).

67. *International Harvester Co.* v. *Ruckelshaus*, 3 ELR 20149.

68. See Victor G. Rosenblum, "The Continuing Role of the Courts in Allocating Common Property Resources," paper prepared for the Resources for the Future Forum on Governance of Common Property Resources, Washington, D.C., January 21, 1974, pp. 40–43.

69. The phrase "separated institutions sharing power" was coined by Professor Richard Neustadt of Harvard University.

CHAPTER 7

1. See Constance McLaughlin Green, *The Rise of Urban America* (New York: Harper & Row, 1967), pp. 8, 25.

2. Murphy, *Water Purity*, pp. 65–66.

3. See *New York Times*, February 9, 1969, 77:1.

4. EPA, "Environmental Program Administrators" (May 15, 1973).

5. For a fuller discussion see Elizabeth Haskell and Victoria Price, *State Environmental Management* (New York: Praeger, 1973).

6. *Environmental Quality—1973*, p. 87.

7. U.S. House of Representatives, "Agriculture, Environmental and Consumer Protection Appropriations—1974, Conference Report," Report 93-520, September 20, 1973, p. 21.

8. Federal Water Pollution Control Act, as amended, sec. 204(a)(3).

9. See Comptroller General of the United States, "Examination into the Effectiveness of the Construction Grant Program for Abating, Controlling, and Preventing Water Pollution," November 3, 1969, pp. 22–40.

10. Quoted in U.S. Department of the Interior, Federal Water Pollution Control Administration, "The Economics of Clean Water" (March 1970), vol. 1, p. 116.

11. See Davies, *Politics of Pollution,* first edition, pp. 126–27.

12. Jeane Lowe, *Cities in a Race with Time* (New York: Random House, 1967), pp. 134–38.

13. U.S. House of Representatives, Committee on Interstate and Foreign Commerce, "Hearings on S.780" (1967), p. 331.

14. Ibid.

15. "Progress in the Prevention and Control of Air Pollution," first report of the Secretary of Health, Education and Welfare to the U.S. Congress, Senate Document 92 (90th Congress, 2nd session), June 28, 1968, p. 33.

16. An exception is Pete Nelson, "Dimensions of Air Pollution Policies Among the American States," paper delivered at the 1972 Annual Meeting of the American Political Science Association, Washington, D.C., September 5–9, 1972.

17. Crenson, *The Un-Politics of Air Pollution.*

18. Ibid., p. 16.

19. Ibid., pp. 77–78.

20. Ibid., p. 90.

21. Stanford Workshop on Air Pollution, "Air Pollution in the San Francisco Bay Area" (1970), in Krier, *Environmental Law and Policy,* p. 371.

22. Ibid., p. 373.

23. Ibid., p. 373; Crenson, *The Un-Politics of Air Pollution,* p. 183.

24. Esposito, *Vanishing Air,* pp. 190–233.

25. Ibid., p. 230.

26. Lewis G. Green, chairman of the Missouri Air Conservation Commission in U.S. Senate, Committee on Public Works, Subcommittee on Air and Water Pollution, "Air Pollution—1967" (Washington, D.C.: GPO, 1967), part 2, p. 997.

27. There are considerable economies of scale in the construction and operation of waste treatment plants. "Per capita investment for a sewage treatment plant to serve half a million people is 75% that of a facility serving 50,000. There are also considerable savings in per capita operating costs with large facilities. For example, it costs an average of $8.00 per million gallons to provide primary sewage treatment with a 100,000,000 gallon capacity treatment plant, for a 10,000,000 gallon capacity plant the comparable cost is $23.00. And costs are $58.00 for a 1,000,000 gallon capacity facility." Advisory Commission on Intergovernmental Relations, "Intergovernmental Responsibilities for Water Supply and Sewage Disposal in Metropolitan Areas" (Washington, D.C.: GPO, October 1962), p. 39.

28. Ibid., chapters 3 and 4.

29. Matthew Holden, Jr., "Pollution Control as a Bargaining Process: An Essay on Regulatory Decision-Making" (Ithaca, N.Y.: Cornell University Water Resources Center, October 1966), p. 11.

30. Ibid., pp. 42–43.

31. See Murphy, *Water Purity,* pp. 101–102.

32. Comptroller General of the U.S., "Assessment of Federal and State Enforcement Efforts to Control Air Pollution from Stationary Sources" (August 23, 1973), p. 7.

33. Ibid., p. 9.

34. Ibid., p. 14.

35. See Holden, *Pollution Control,* p. 37.

36. The Advisory Commission on Intergovernmental Relations (ACIR) has ranked fifteen governmental functions as to whether they can best be performed on a local or area-wide basis. Water supply and sewage disposal and air pollution control were rated as the "least local" functions. See ACIR, "Performance of Urban Functions: Local and Areawide" (Washington, D.C.: GPO, September 1963), pp. 8–23.

37. J. C. Bollens and H. J. Schmandt, *The Metropolis* (New York: Harper & Row, 1965), pp. 544–45.

38. For a bull description of ORSANCO see E. J. Cleary, *The ORSANCO Story* (Baltimore: Johns Hopkins Press, 1967).

39. Richard A. Leach, "ORSANCO: A Twenty-Year Record," *State Government* (Winter 1968), pp. 49–56. Cleary denies that the provisions of the compact have hampered enforcement, but he also concedes that control of industrial pollution has not been totally satisfactory. See Cleary, *The ORSANCO Story*, pp. 214–17.

40. For the background leading to the formation of the DRBC see R. C. Martin, et al., *River Basin Administration and the Delaware* (Syracuse, N.Y.: Syracuse University Press, 1960).

41. For a fuller description of interstate pollution compacts see Davies, *The Politics of Pollution*, first edition, pp. 134–41. Also see David Zwick with Marcy Benstock, *Water Wasteland* (New York: Bantam Books, 1972), pp. 181–86.

42. See Morton Gredzins, *The Federal System* (Chicago: Rand McNally, 1966).

43. Frank Graham, Jr., *Disaster by Default: Politics and Water Pollution* (New York: M. Evans, 1966), pp. 100–101.

CHAPTER 8

1. This is a good illustration of Weinberg's thesis that technological solutions are easier than political solutions. See Alvin Weinberg, "Can Technology Replace Social Engineering?", *Bulletin of the Atomic Scientists* XXII:10 (December 1966), pp. 4–8.

2. See U.S. Department of Commerce, Panel on Electrically Powered Vehicles, "The Automobile and Air Pollution: A Program for Progress" (Washington, D.C.: GPO, October 1967).

3. "Background Material for the Development of Radiation Protection Standards," staff report of the Federal Radiation Council, May 13, 1960, reprinted May 1965 by HEW, p. 24. For a cogent argument along the same lines see Barry Commoner, *Science and Survival* (New York: Viking, 1967), pp. 90–102.

4. To translate this emission standard into a limitation on the sulfur content of coal, it is only necessary to know that 1 pound of sulfur will produce 2 pounds of sulfur dioxide and that an average pound of coal contains 13,000 BTU. By multiplying the emission standard times 13,000 and then dividing by 2, one can translate the limit of 0.34 pounds of sulfur dioxide per million BTU into a limitation of 0.2 per cent on the sulfur content of coal.

5. HEW, Office of the Assistant Secretary for Planning and Evaluation, "An Economic Analysis of the Control of Sulphur Oxides Air Pollution" (December 1967), p. V–1.

6. Jude Wanniski, "How to Clean Air Rules Were Set," *The Wall Street Journal*, May 29, 1972.

7. See Davies, *The Politics of Pollution*, first edition, pp. 157–63. Also Esposito, *Vanishing Air*.

8. Clean Air Act of 1963, sec. 103(c)(2).

9. Ibid., sec. 102(c)(3).

10. Water Quality Act of 1965, sec. 10(c)(1). See also Murphy, *Governing Nature*, pp. 239–40, and Cleary, *The ORSANCO Story*, p. 151 and p. 266.

11. Sec. 108(c)(1).

12. Clean Air Act, as amended, sec. 190(b)(1).

13. Ibid., sec. 109(b)(2).

14. Ibid., sec. 110(a)(2)(A) and sec. 110(e)(1). The law requires that the primary standards be met within three years of passage of the Act (the Act became law December 31, 1970) but it allows for a two-year extension of this deadline, an extension which has been granted in most cases.

15. Ibid., sec. 111(a)(3).

16. Ibid., sec. 112(a)(1).

17. *Sierra Club et al.* v. *Administrator of EPA*, U.S. Court of Appeals for the District of Columbia Circuit, case No. 72-1528. *Federal Register* 38:135 (July 16, 1973), pp. 18986–19000.

18. Murray Edelman, *The Symbolic Uses of Politics* (Urbana: University of Illinois Press, 1967), pp. 103–4.

19. Federal Water Pollution Control Act, as amended, sec. 304(b)(1)(B).

20. EPA, "Environmental Facts—The National Water Permit System" (July 1973) states that there are 300,000 industrial water users and municipal sewage treatment plants. At least two-thirds of these are industrial users.

21. Federal Water Pollution Control Act, as amended, sec. 301(c).

22. Ibid., sec. 302.

23. John R. Quarles, Jr., "Water Pollution and the Rule of Law," presented at the American Bar Association National Institute, October 26, 1972, New York City.

24. P.L. 92-532.

CHAPTER 9

1. See Allen Kneese and Blair Bower, *Managing Water Quality: Economics, Technology, Institutions* (Baltimore: Johns Hopkins Press, 1968), chapters 6–8. For a variation of the effluent fee proposal, see Dales, *Pollution, Property and Prices*, chapter 6.

2. In the economist's language, effluent fees would achieve the "Pareto optimal solution" in a watershed. See Kneese and Bower, *Managing Water Quality*.

3. See Otto A. Davis and Morton I. Kamien, "Externalities, Information and Alternative Collective Action," in U.S. Congress, Joint Economic Committee, "The Analysis and Evaluation of Public Expenditures," (Washington, D.C.: GPO, 1969), vol. 1, pp. 67–86.

4. For a simplified model which incorporates both economic criteria and political influence, see Robert Dorfman and Henry Jacoby, "A Model of Public Decisions Illustrated by a Water Pollution Policy Problem," in "The Analysis and Evaluation of Public Expenditures," vol. 1, pp. 226–274.

5. See *The National Journal*, October 21, 1972, pp. 1643–1650.

6. For a favorable estimate of the Genossenschaften, see Kneese and Bower, *Managing Water Quality*, chapters 12 and 13.

7. For other criticisms of effluent fees from the viewpoint of an economist, see Harold Wolozin, "The Economics of Air Pollution: Central Problems," in *Law and Contemporary Problems*, XXXIII:2 (Spring 1968), pp. 227–38.

8. *Environmental Quality—1973*, p. 105.

9. Ibid., p. 105, and p. 119 footnote 26.

10. Water Quality Act of 1965, sec. 10(d)(1).

11. Air Quality Act of 1967, sec. 108(k).

12. Clean Air Act, as amended, sec. 115(b)(4).

13. Ibid., sec. 113(a)(1); Federal Water Pollution Control Act, as amended, sec. 309(a)(1).

14. Clean Air Act, as amended, sec. 113(a)(2); Federal Water Pollution Control Act, as amended, sec. 309(a)(2).

15. Clean Air Act, as amended, sec. 304; Federal Water Pollution Control Act, as amended, sec. 505.

16. See *Environmental Quality—1973*, p. 156.

17. Clean Air Act, as amended, sec. 207(b).

18. EPA press release, "Statement by William D. Ruckelshaus, Administrator USEPA, on 1975 Auto Emission Standards," April 11, 1973, p. 5.

19. See Davies, *The Politics of Pollution*, first edition, pp. 180–90.

20. 33 U.S.C. 407.

21. See EPA, "The First Two Years" (February 1973), p. 19.

22. E.O. 11574.

23. EPA, "The First Two Years," p. 8.

24. Ibid., pp. 68–91.

25. *Kalur* v. *Resor*, F. Supp. 1, 3 ERC 1458, 1 ELR 20637 (D.D.C. 1971).

26. *U.S.* v. *Pennsylvania Industrial Chemical Corp.*, 4 ERC 1241 (3 Cir. 1972).

27. EPA, "The First Two Years," p. 18.

28. Ibid., p. 8.

29. Ibid., pp. 246–49.

30. Letter from John E. Daniel, staff assistant for Standards and Compliance, NAPCA, to the author, July 15, 1969.

31. Comptroller General of the U.S., "Assessment of Federal and State Enforcement Efforts to Control Air Pollution from Stationary Sources" (August 23, 1973), p. 4.

32. *Getty Oil Co. (Eastern Operations)* v. *Ruckelshaus*, 342 F. Supp. 1006; 467 F. 2d. 349; cert. den.,——U.S.——, January 15, 1973.

33. *New York Times*, October 19, 1969, 61:1.

34. Sec. 101(a)(3).

35. Sec. 101(b).

36. Cleary, *The ORSANCO Story*, p. 261.

37. See Sigurd Grava, *Urban Planning Aspects of Water Pollution Control* (New York: Columbia University Press, 1969); and C. Peter Rydell and Gretchen Schwarz, "Air Pollution and Urban Form: A Review of Current Literature," *Journal of the American Institute of Planners*, XXXIV:2 (March 1968), pp. 115–20.

38. HEW, "An Economic Analysis of the Control of Sulphur Oxides Air Pollution," p. III-13.

39. Clean Air Act, as amended, sec. 110(a)(2)(B).

40. *Washington Evening Star*, December 4, 1972.

CHAPTER 10

1. This must be taken more as a hypothesis than an established fact. The author is now at work on a study of how issues get on the national agenda and how similar the rise of the environmental issue has been to that of other issues.

2. Data are from U.S. Department of Commerce, Bureau of the Census, *Statistical Abstract of the U.S., 1972* (Washington, D.C.: GPO, 1972), Table 666, p. 422; and *The World Almanac,* 1974 ed. (New York: News Enterprise Association, 1973), p. 94.

3. D. Meadows et al., *The Limits to Growth* (Washington, D.C.: Potomac Associates, 1972).

4. See U.S. Commission on Population Growth and the American Future, *Population, Resources and the Environment* (Washington, D.C.: GPO, 1972), pp. 35–57.

5. *Environmental Quality—1972*, p. 71.

6. Meadows, *The Limits to Growth.*

7. *Environmental Quality—1971*, p. 264.

8. On the land ethic see Aldo Leopold, *A Sand County Almanac* (New York: Ballantine Books, 1970).

9. For a discussion of future forecasting see *Environmental Quality—1972*, chapter 2.

10. Dylan Thomas, "Fern Hill" in *The Collected Poems of Dylan Thomas* (New York: New Directions, n.d.), p. 180.

Index